THE CULTURE OF CONSUMPTION

THE CULTURE OF CONSUMPTION: CRITICAL ESSAYS IN AMERICAN HISTORY, 1880—1980

EDITED BY
RICHARD WIGHTMAN FOX
AND
T. J. JACKSON LEARS

PANTHEON BOOKS  NEW YORK

Library of Congress Cataloging in Publication Data
Main entry under title:

The Culture of consumption.

   Includes bibliographical references.
   1. Consumption (Economics)—United States—History—
Addresses, essays, lectures.   2. Elite (Social
sciences)—United States—History—Addresses, essays,
lectures.   3. Social values—History—Addresses,
essays, lectures.   I. Fox, Richard Wightman, 1945–
II. Lears, T. J. Jackson, 1947–
HC110.C6C84   1983   339.4'7'0973   83-2391
ISBN 0-394-51131-X
0-394-71611-6 (paperback)

Manufactured in the United States of America

First Edition

CONTENTS

INTRODUCTION

INTRODUCTION

The faces are familiar. An old woman, a middle-aged man, and a young girl—white, respectable, and neighborly. Their upturned heads meet a shaft of providential sunlight, and in their arms they clutch neatly bound packages. Residents of Norman Rockwell's America, they appeared in a 1944 *Saturday Evening Post* advertisement for the Hoover Vacuum Cleaner Company. Hoover's ad men shrewdly built on Rockwell's cover art by transforming his mythic American villagers into ideal American consumers. Three years after Roosevelt's "Four Freedoms"—freedom of religion and speech, freedom from want and fear—the Hoover ad urged that "the Fifth Freedom is Freedom of Choice." Preserving democracy meant not just destroying fascism or abolishing poverty, but protecting the consumer marketplace. The slogan was apt. By the 1940s most Americans probably did call consumer goods to mind when they heard the phrase "freedom of choice." Hoover's beatific buyers embodied the potent ideal that underlay the consumer society of the 1950s: a world of goods produced in profusion, packaged and marketed by advertisers with subtle skills, avidly acquired on the installment plan by middle- and working-class Americans.

But the American culture of consumption did not emerge full-blown at mid-century. Not only were middle-class Americans using credit to buy a vast array of goods in the 1920s; legions of publicists promoted, celebrated, or condemned the centrality of consumption in Americans' lives beginning in the late nineteenth century. For some observers it meant fulfillment, for others enslavement. The most widely read critic of industrial capitalism in the 1890s, Edward Bellamy, saw in consumption the promise of deliverance from routinized toil and social anarchy. In *Looking Backward* (1888) he imagined twenty-first-century Boston as a cooperative society of total leisure for all adults over 45; the masses passed their maturity in pursuit of "the good things of the world which they have helped to create."[1] Thorstein Veblen had a less sanguine view of consumption. In his *Theory of the Leisure Class* (1899) he mocked "pecuniary emulation" and "conspicuous consumption" as socially functional but morally bankrupt. After the turn of the century the "engineers"—for whom the "instinct of workmanship" was more precious than the possession of goods—gave him hope. But it was an engineer of genius, Henry Ford, who subverted his dream and created the cornerstone of the leisure society: the affordable automobile.

By the mid-twentieth century the celebrants of consumption were not visionaries like Bellamy or even Ford, but defenders of the status quo. Richard Nixon's "Kitchen Debate" with Nikita Khrushchev in 1959 was a pure expression of the times: the American way of life equated with the American "standard of living." The American system worked, Nixon told the Russians, because "44 million families in America own 56 million cars, 50 million television sets, 143 million radio sets, and . . . 31 million of those families own their own homes."[2] Even many of the countercultural youths who provoked Nixon's expletives a decade later were distinctive products of the culture of consumption; they were alienated by the adult world of work and responsibility, not by the acquisition of packaged goods, including their own "life-style."

Yet protest persisted as well. Some among the counterculture rejected high-level consumption and cultivated Spartan self-sufficiency. In many ways, their dissent implicitly embodied the ideas of such mid-century radical critics as C. Wright Mills, Paul Baran and Paul Sweezy, and Herbert Marcuse. Building on Veblen, these thinkers viewed consumption as a seduction, a form of captivity. The possession of commodities was poor compensation, they noted, for powerlessness at the points of production or policymaking.

Social observers of all stripes have agreed on the importance of consumption in twentieth-century American culture. But they have expended so much energy praising or blaming it that they have generally begged the most basic questions. Exactly what is a consumer culture? It is not enough to point to the abundance of televisions and automobiles, to call it a culture of leisure instead of work, since people obviously still work—assuming they can find a job. It will not do to view it as an elite conspiracy in which advertisers defraud the "people" by drowning them in a sea of glittering goods. The people are not that passive; they have been active consumers, preferring some commodities to others. They have also been more than consumers; they have pursued other goals in their leisure besides consumption. When and how did a consumer culture arise in the United States? What were the processes by which a nineteenth-century "producer ethic"—a value system based on work, sacrifice, and saving—evolved into a dominant twentieth-century "consumer ethic"? These are exceedingly complex questions, and the six historical essays in this volume aim to make a start in framing and answering them.

The authors believe that the best way to proceed in investigating American consumer culture is not to focus on patterns of consumption themselves, nor to examine the lives of ordinary consumers. Those are necessary tasks. But to discover how consumption became a cultural ideal, a hegemonic "way of seeing" in twentieth-century America, requires looking at powerful individuals and institutions who conceived, formulated, and preached that ideal or way of seeing. Most recent social history has focused on the cultures of the common people, a previously neglected subject. But it is impossible to understand the cultures of ordinary Americans without appreciating the ways those cultures are influenced and delimited by the ideals, plans, and needs of the powerful. The study of dominant elites—white, male, educated, affluent—is a critically important part of social history.

The search for the origins of consumer culture should begin by concentrating on the activities of urban elites during the last two decades of the nineteenth century. Historians have for many years agreed about the significance of three developments in the late-nineteenth-century United States: the maturation of the national marketplace, including the establishment of national advertising; the emergence of a new stratum of professionals and managers, rooted in a web of complex new organizations (corporations, government, universities, professional associations, media, foundations, and others); and the rise of a new gospel of therapeutic release preached by a host of writers, publishers, ministers, social scientists, doctors, and the advertisers themselves. The essays that follow will suggest that from the 1880s on these trends were closely connected. Perhaps the key development was the rapid expansion of the professional-managerial stratum, which included (among others) both the technicians who staffed the new corporate bureaucracies and the corps of reformers who consciously undertook to "harmonize" the relations between labor and capital. Accredited experts set out to manage not only the economic arena, but the rest of the social order as well. For the masses of employees who in a corporate economy could no longer aspire to become their own bosses, new authorities in personal adjustment promised not power through work but, in the phrase of the popular therapist Annie Payson Call, "power through repose." For these ordinary Americans the prophets of adjustment, of therapeutic consumption, provided the promise of health and worldly contentment. But for a still powerful group—the northeastern, Protestant upper bourgeoisie—the new experts in social and psychological harmony provided more than the hope of health: They offered a new legitimation.

It might even be argued that the chief historic role of the professional-managerial "class"—often linked to the emerging "service" sector—was not to provide services to society in the abstract, but to "service," to revitalize, the upper bourgeoisie at a critical moment. In the 1880s and 1890s the leaders of the WASP bourgeoisie confronted labor struggle, financial uncertainty, and the even more insidious threat of severe self-doubt. They felt cramped, "over-civilized," cut off from real life—threatened from without by an ungrateful working class, and from within by their own sense of physical atrophy and spiritual decay. Lost frontier hardiness might be restored by embracing Theodore Roosevelt's "strenuous life." But lost faith was far more serious. The old religious sanctions for the moral life, a life of sacrifice and toil, had begun to disintegrate in the face of both Darwin and the liberalization of Protestantism itself. A crisis of purpose, a yearning for a solid, transcendent framework of meaning, was not just Henry Adams' worry, but that of a much wider group. In this time of cultural consternation, the new professional-managerial corps appeared with a timely dual message. On the one hand they proposed a new managerial efficiency, a new regime of administration by experts for business, government, and other spheres of life. On the other hand, they preached a new morality that subordinated the old goal of transcendance to new ideals of self-fulfillment and immediate gratification. This late-nineteenth-century link between individual hedonism and bureaucratic organization—a link that has been strengthened in the twentieth century—marks the point of departure for modern American consumer culture. The consumer culture is not only the value-system that underlies a society saturated by mass-produced and mass-marketed goods, but also a new set of sanctions for the elite control of that society. While nineteenth-century elites ruled through ethical precepts that they encouraged people to internalize, twentieth-century elites rule through subtler promises of personal fulfillment. The older idiom was individualistic and moralistic; the newer one is corporate and therapeutic.

Consumer culture is more than the "leisure ethic," or the "American standard of living." It is an ethic, a standard of living, and a power structure. Life for most middle-class and many working-class Americans in the twentieth century has been a ceaseless pursuit of the "good life" and a constant reminder of their powerlessness. Consumers are not only buyers of goods but recipients of professional advice, marketing strategies, government programs, electoral choices, and advertisers' images of happiness. Although the dominant institutions of our culture have purported to be offering the consumer a fulfilling participation in the life of the community, they have to a large extent presented the empty prospect of taking part in the marketplace of personal exchange. Individuals have been invited to seek commodities as keys to personal welfare, and even to conceive of their own selves as commodities. One sells not only one's labor and skills, but one's image and personality, too. While the few make decisions about managing society, the many are left to manage their appearance, aided by trained counselors in personal cosmetics. Leadership by experts and pervasive self-absorption have developed symbiotically in American consumer culture. No doubt the spread of mass consumption has lightened old burdens and brought genuine material improvements to the lives of many Americans. But the cost has been high. People deserve a more democratic as well as a more affluent way of life. That belief unites the authors of these six essays.

These essays of course do not come close to exhausting the issues of the origin and character of American consumer culture. Major institutions like films and television, fundamental ideological shifts like the liberation of women, vital comparisons with European consumer culture—none of these is addressed. But the purpose of the essays is not comprehensiveness. It is rather to begin to account for the rise of consumer culture and to suggest how to conceive it. By examining the ways a consumer culture penetrated our religion and journalism, our literature and social science, our politics and government, they suggest how firmly based that culture is. By conceiving consumption as an ideology and a way of seeing, they direct attention to the powerful social groups that over the last century have promoted the cultural and institutional framework of contemporary Americans' lives.

The first two essays, by Jackson Lears and by Christopher Wilson, examine the central institution of consumer culture, advertising, and one of the key advertising outlets of early-twentieth-century America, the mass magazine. They make clear that advertising is more than an institution among others; it is a pervasive language. Lears focuses on the connections between advertising strategies and an emerging therapeutic ethos of self-realization—an ethos rooted in Americans' feeling that their sense of selfhood had become fragmented, diffuse, and somehow "weightless" or "unreal." Feelings of unreality were rooted in the corrosive impact of the market on familiar values, the dislocating impact of technological advance on everyday experience—and above all in the secularization of Protestantism, which by the turn of the century had become for many Christians a flaccid creed without force or bite or moral weight. Yearnings to escape a weightless void, particularly common among the educated professionals who staffed the emerging corporate system, promoted a favorable emotional climate for the spread of national advertising. Advertisers spoke to many of the same needs addressed by early therapists: the fretful preoccupation with sustaining a secure sense of selfhood through careful health management; the longing to revitalize an "unreal" sense of selfhood through bodily vigor and emotional intensity. Lears does not try to chart a cause-and-effect relationship between advertising strategies and what people did or thought. Rather, he shows how advertising practices joined therapeutic ideologies in responding to and reinforcing some key shifts in dominant values—particularly the shift from Protestant salvation in the next world to therapeutic self-realization in this one. Lears stresses that advertisers were often as confused and ambivalent as the audience they addressed. But their efforts paralleled those of moviemakers, amusement park operators, and other purveyors of mass-marketed amusements. All seemed geared to reduce weightlessness but ended by exacerbating it; all helped to create a new symbolic universe where an image of intense "real life" was projected but always kept just out of reach. By placing this symbolic universe in the broader context of an emergent therapeutic ethos, Lears illuminates the moral and psychological foundations of American consumer culture.

The desire to break the cake of Victorian custom and experience "real life" in all its intensity lay at the heart of the emergent culture, and the new forms of mass entertainment, like advertising and therapy, attempted to meet this new emotional need. As Christopher Wilson's essay demonstrates, a new breed of magazine publisher emerged around the turn of the century, skillfully packaging the blend of expertise and titillation that characterized so many cultural forms just then appearing on the market. Historians have generally seen the new mass circulation magazines as part of a long overdue revolt against a stale and elitist genteel tradition, a refreshing turn toward "progressive" politics and "realistic" literature. The problem with this view, Wilson makes clear, is that in the name of democracy the new magazines further undermined the political and cultural autonomy of their audience. Rather than cultivating a critical readership (as their predecessors had sometimes done) the new publishers advised their audience simply to "keep informed" by attending to the scientifically managed "real life" the magazines served up in predigested portions. The magazines provided a forum for muckrakers masking opinion as the inside dope on political intrigue, therapeutic professionals offering expert advice on health and happiness, "realistic" authors producing a spuriously factual fiction, and advertisers promising "richer, fuller living" through high-level consumption. Invoking the talismans of "efficiency" and "personality," publishers legitimized the transformation of male ideals from self-made manhood to salaried employment and of female ideals from guardianship of virtue to family management. Like advertisements and therapies, the new magazines sought to generate needs that only they could fulfill. The result was the loss of a reality that was denser and more historical than the counterfeit that readers were urged to embrace.

The specter of unreality in consumer culture also lies behind Jean-Christophe Agnew's analysis of Henry James. According to Agnew, James wrote at the critical historical moment when serious fiction (like religion and popular journalism) was opening itself up to the possibilities of a "defamiliarized" world where values and perceptions seemed in constant flux. Though James is typically viewed as an aesthete disgusted by modern consumer culture, he was in fact a remarkably articulate exponent of certain features of that culture. His "consuming vision," his particular way of seeing, places him unmistakably within the ideological enterprise of the professional-managerial class. Agnew begins with a theoretical excursus. Following the political scientist William Leiss, he argues that under advanced capitalism the characteristics of commodities become reified into "bundles of attributes"—symbols that are disengaged from the particular and immediate needs of everyday life. This forest of disembodied symbols closely resembles the "weightless" realm analyzed by Lears. But unlike Lears, Agnew does not focus on the impact of secularization; rather he dissects "the defamiliarizing dynamic of the market medium." As advertising constantly reshuffles and "recontextualizes" the alleged attributes of commodities, consumers increasingly want to possess not only the commodities but the symbols surrounding them. A strategy of "acquisitive cognition" arises. Consumers "acquire" commodities not only through purchasing them but through a kind of all-pervasive knowingness, a thoroughgoing acquaintance with commodities' actual and imagined attributes. This strategy reproduces the dislocating dynamic it was intended to reduce, because the attributes are constantly changing. Knowledge is constantly being redefined. As the rest of Agnew's essay makes clear, some of the earliest and most striking examples of "acquisitive cognition" appeared in the fiction of Henry James. Judging by the reified world of James's late novels, it seems clear that James and his fellow members of the "leisure class" were far subtler progenitors of the consumer culture than either functionalist sociologists or formalist literary critics have understood. Agnew's textual analysis reveals that James embodied and described in evocative detail a nascent consumer mentality—the outlook of those who no longer accumulate "primitively." In Agnew's essay, as in Lears's, some of those who recoiled from the consumer culture are seen to be its secret accomplices, collaborating in the "weightlessness" they wanted to analyze or escape.

The same pattern of unintentional collaboration emerges in Richard Fox's study of Robert Lynd. In this case, though, the critic in question is not a fastidious aesthete but a committed social planner. A product of the liberal Protestant therapeutic milieu described by Lears, Lynd ultimately revealed some of the characteristic shortcomings of the therapeutic world view: an uncritical faith in expert planners, a belief that the ordinary citizen's psyche was infinitely malleable, a failure to recognize (as John Dewey did) that individual fulfillment was of necessity communal as well. Though Lynd became an idiosyncratic and isolated figure during the last two decades of his life, his intellectual career has a wide significance. Beginning as a pioneering critic and analyst of the changes described in this volume, Lynd soon shifted his focus from the irrationalities of consumer culture to the irrationalities of consumers themselves. That later emphasis accurately anticipated the elitism which has plagued many "disillusioned" radical critics of consumer culture, from the Frankfurt School of the forties and fifties to the New Left of the 1960s. Though Lynd was an acute critic of advertising, like others on the Left he shared the assumption of many advertisers that "the masses" were thoroughly manipulable. In the end, Lynd sought only to substitute one set of manipulators for another: disinterested administrators for corporate advertisers. The dream of a meritocratic elite has been a characteristic delusion of twentieth-century social planners, and it continues to block serious discussion of democratic alternatives to our dominant culture.

If Lynd backed into a technocratic corner, the subjects of Robert Westbrook's essay did not. They were there from the start. In Westbrook's study of the rise of political merchandising, one finds Lynd's therapeutic vision expressed more glibly by the advertising executives, social scientists, and political consultants who have made the packaging of candidates and voters another "profession" in the consumer culture. Westbrook begins by noting that the idea of voters as consumers displaced an earlier and equally undemocratic notion of voters as soldiers. As in magazine publishing, the coming of "progressive" reforms at the turn of the century meant that one form of elite control began to give way to a newer, sleeker version: The ward boss gave way to the "professional" political consultant. Like the publishers, the new political consultants helped to transform potentially active citizens into "inside dopesters"—voter-consumers laden with spurious information, shopping for candidates whose attributes are packaged by experts in the politics of display. During the 1920s and after, as an alliance emerged between positivist social scientists and advertising strategists, political consulting displayed the characteristic assumption of professional-managerial elites in consumer culture: that ordinary people were fundamentally irrational and manipulable. Political consultants believed they could "make voters" just as advertising men could "make customers." But since the 1960s, as Westbrook points out, consulting strategies have become subtler though no less manipulative. Consultants no longer assume that voter attitudes can be readily changed; instead they use market research to package an "audience-commodity" so that candidates in turn can be packaged to suit the audience. Political consultants now try to contextualize candidates the way ad men contextualize products—by surrounding them with a constellation of attributes that (they think) will appeal to a particular pre-packaged audience.

If politics has been increasingly reduced to spectacle in the consumer culture, the same can be said of much government-sponsored science, as Michael Smith observes in his analysis of the manned space program. At least since the early nineteenth century, scientific explorations and technological developments have had a promotional or display value. But during and after World War II, policy elites orchestrated the display value of science and technology on an unprecedented scale. The sky became the limit. Using the techniques of national advertising, policymakers sought to surround their programs and products with a cluster of manipulable images—images that would not only sell government science to wary taxpayers but would persuade geopolitical rivals that "we" were still Number One. As in so many other areas of the consumer culture, impressions made by commodities became more important than the commodities themselves. And as Smith makes clear, the manned space program was the most dramatic and sustained example of this "commodity scientism." Claiming to restore a sense of national purpose, the program's advocates provided no specific purpose or policy aim but only an efficient, exhilarating process of "exploration." This preoccupation with efficiency and exhilaration as ends in themselves was common to therapists, advertisers, and social engineers of all sorts—professionals who could apparently no longer conceive of social or ethical ends. Not only was the space program supposed to galvanize a flaccid, purposeless nation, but the astronauts themselves were alleged to embody resourcefulness, autonomy, and control— "masculine" qualities that were increasingly problematic for ordinary people under corporate capitalism. The astronauts were space-age "Marlboro men." The irony was that the astronauts usually had far less control over their space capsules than they did even over their automobiles; far from embodying any triumph of personal will, their careers represented the immersion of the individual in a bureaucratic collectivity. Here as elsewhere in twentieth-century cultural history, images of autonomy obscured its eclipse.

Richard Wightman Fox
T. J. Jackson Lears

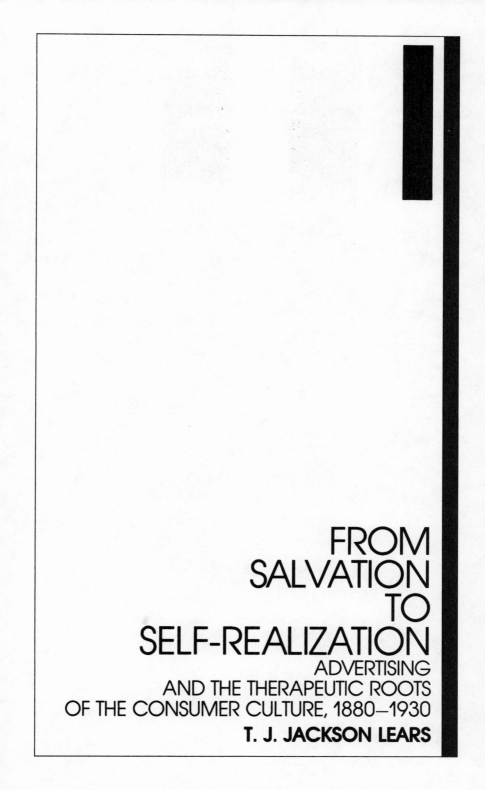

FROM
SALVATION
TO
SELF-REALIZATION
ADVERTISING
AND THE THERAPEUTIC ROOTS
OF THE CONSUMER CULTURE, 1880–1930
T. J. JACKSON LEARS

"On or about December 1910," Virginia Woolf once said, "human character changed." This hyperbole contains a kernel of truth. Around the turn of the century a fundamental cultural transformation occurred within the educated strata of Western capitalist nations. In the United States as elsewhere, the bourgeois ethos had enjoined perpetual work, compulsive saving, civic responsibility, and a rigid morality of self-denial. By the early twentieth century that outlook had begun to give way to a new set of values sanctioning periodic leisure, compulsive spending, apolitical passivity, and an apparently permissive (but subtly coercive) morality of individual fulfillment. The older culture was suited to a production-oriented society of small entrepreneurs; the newer culture epitomized a consumption-oriented society dominated by bureaucratic corporations.[1]

It is easy to exaggerate the suddenness or completeness of this transformation. Early on it occurred primarily within the official norms and expectations of the dominant social groups—and even there it was halting and only half conscious. Further, a producer orientation survived in the consumer culture, though it was cast in a secular mold. By the 1920s, among the American bourgeoisie, the newly dominant consumer culture was a muddle of calculated self-control and spontaneous gratification.

Focusing on the United States, this essay aims to explore the role of national advertising in this complex cultural transformation. Since the subject is too large for comprehensive treatment here, what follows will attempt to be suggestive rather than exhaustive—to indicate a new approach to the history of American advertising, which has long remained a barren field. Aside from in-house or administrative histories, there is little to choose from. The few historians who have addressed the subject in recent years tend to fall into two opposing camps, best represented by Daniel Boorstin and Stuart Ewen. Boorstin thoughtfully sketches some moral and emotional dilemmas in the culture of consumption, but he ignores power relations. To him advertising is an expression of impersonal technological, economic, and social forces. Ewen, on the other hand, can see nothing but power relations. To him the consumer is the product of a conspiracy hatched by corporate executives in the bowels of the Ministry of Truth, then imposed with diabolical cleverness on a passive population. Neither Ewen nor Boorstin grasps the complex relationship between power relations and changes in values—or between advertisers' changing strategies and the cultural confusion at the turn of the century.[2]

My point here is obvious but usually overlooked: Advertising cannot be considered in isolation. Its role in promoting a consumer culture can only be understood within a network of institutional, religious, and

3

psychological changes. The institutional changes have been much discussed elsewhere; the religious and psychological changes have not. To thrive and spread, a consumer culture required more than a national apparatus of marketing and distribution; it also needed a favorable moral climate. In this essay, I shall argue that the crucial moral change was the beginning of a shift from a Protestant ethos of salvation through self-denial toward a therapeutic ethos stressing self-realization in this world—an ethos characterized by an almost obsessive concern with psychic and physical health defined in sweeping terms.

Of course, one could argue that there is nothing specifically *historical* about this therapeutic ethos. People have always been preoccupied by their own emotional and physical well-being; all cultures, ancient and modern, have probably had some sort of therapeutic dimension. But my research in magazines, letters, and other cultural sources suggests that something was different about the late-nineteenth-century United States. In earlier times and other places, the quest for health had occurred within larger communal, ethical, or religious frameworks of meaning. By the late nineteenth century those frameworks were eroding. The quest for health was becoming an entirely secular and self-referential project, rooted in peculiarly modern emotional needs—above all the need to renew a sense of selfhood that had grown fragmented, diffuse, and somehow "unreal." The coming of the therapeutic ethos was a modern historical development, shaped by the turmoil of the turn of the century. And the longings behind that ethos—the fretful preoccupation with preserving secular well-being, the anxious concern with regenerating selfhood—these provided fertile ground for the growth of national advertising and for the spread of a new way of life.[3]

In the emerging consumer culture, advertisers began speaking to many of the same preoccupations addressed by liberal ministers, psychologists, and other therapeutic ideologues. A dialectic developed between Americans' new emotional needs and advertisers' strategies; each continually reshaped and intensified the other. Sometimes deliberately, sometimes unwittingly, advertisers and therapists responded to and reinforced the spreading culture of consumption. Their motives and intentions were various, but the overall effect of their efforts was to create a new and secular basis for capitalist cultural hegemony.

I use the term "hegemony" reluctantly but unavoidably, because it suggests an illuminating perspective on the consumer culture—a way to transcend the "one-dimensional" model developed by Herbert Marcuse without losing its grasp of power relations. The Italian Marxist Antonio Gramsci used the concept of cultural hegemony to suggest that ruling groups dominate a society not merely through brute force but also through intellectual and moral leadership. In other words, a ruling class needs more than businessmen, soldiers, and statesmen; it also requires publicists, professors, ministers, and literati who help to establish the society's conventional wisdom—the boundaries of permissible debate about human nature and the social order. Outside those boundaries opinions can be labeled "tasteless," "irresponsible," and in general unworthy of serious consideration. Even if ordinary people do not consciously embrace the conventional wisdom, it shapes their tacit assumptions in subtle ways. One thinks, for example, of Theodore Roosevelt's remark to a political foe that "we do not have 'classes' at all on this side of the water"—a conventionally wise belief that has shaped American opinion throughout the twentieth century. By helping to create a taken-for-granted "reality," the leaders of the dominant culture identify beliefs that are in the interest of a particular class with the "natural" common sense of society (and indeed of humanity) at large.[4]

Yet cultural hegemony is not maintained mechanically or conspiratorially. A dominant culture is not a static "superstructure" but a continual process. The boundaries of common-sense "reality" are constantly shifting as the social structure changes shape. As older values become less fashionable, they are widely discarded but persist in residual forms. Newer values, which sometimes seem potentially subversive at first, are frequently sanitized and incorporated into the mainstream of enlightened opinion. This cultural "progress" is a messy business, generating social and psychological conflicts that remain unresolved even among the affluent and educated. The changes in the dominant culture are not always deliberately engineered; at times they stem from attempts to resolve private dilemmas that seem to have little to do with the public realm of class domination. Without conspiring to do so, sometimes with wholly other ends in view, the ruling groups continually refashion the prevailing structure of feeling to express—more or less—their own changing social experience.[5]

This is a schematic and abstract way of stating my major theme. In what follows I plan first to sketch the emerging therapeutic ethos, which was promoted from the beginning as a liberation; then to show how it became diffused by advertisers and incorporated as a new mode of adjustment to the developing corporate system; and finally to turn to Bruce Barton, an advertising executive and therapeutic ideologue whose career not only illustrates the centrality of therapeutic attitudes in the new consumer culture but also demonstrates that a cultural transformation can never be reduced to a conspiracy or an impersonal conceptual scheme. Calculating, ambitious, and successful, Barton was also confused and ambivalent—a doubting high priest of prosperity whose work both celebrated and protested the emerging consumer culture. The domain of values remained a contested terrain, in Barton's divided mind as in the dominant classes generally.

THE EMERGENCE OF A THERAPEUTIC ETHOS

The origins of the therapeutic ethos are too complex to describe in detail here. In part, its genesis involved the professionalization and growing authority of medicine. That process had been under way at least since the early antebellum era, when health reformers sprouted like mushrooms, linking medical with moral standards of value. But during the late nineteenth century, medical prestige became far more firmly established. While urban ministers' authority waned, doctors of body and mind became professionalized into therapeutic elites. This meant a growth in influence not only for traditional M.D.s but also for neurologists, psychologists, social scientists with panaceas for a sick society, and even for mind curists on the penumbra of respectability. Ministers and other moralists began increasingly to conform to medical models in making judgments and dispensing advice.[6]

But besides the rise of medical authority, there was a subtler process at work as well. For the educated bourgeoisie in the late nineteenth century, reality itself began to seem problematic, something to be sought rather than merely lived. A dread of unreality, a yearning to experience intense "real life" in all its forms—these emotions were difficult to chart but nonetheless pervasive and important. They energized the spread of the therapeutic ethos, underlay the appeal of much national advertising, and mobilized a market for commodified mass amusements. They formed, in short, the psychological impetus for the rise of the consumer culture.

These feelings of unreality constitute a huge subject in their own right. In *No Place of Grace* I attempted to document these elusive emotions, to locate their origins in specific social and cultural changes during the late nineteenth century, and to connect the spreading sense of unreality with the emergence of a therapeutic world view. In the next few pages I must compress that argument without, I hope, losing sight of its full complexity. To begin: Feelings of unreality stemmed from urbanization and technological development; from the rise of an increasingly interdependent market economy; and from the secularization of liberal Protestantism among its educated and affluent devotees.

The first and simplest source of a sense of unreality was the urban-industrial transformation of the nineteenth century. Changes in material life bred changes in moral perception. As Americans fled the surveillance of the village, they encountered the anonymity of the city. Escape was liberating but also disturbing, as any reader of late-nineteenth-century literature knows. William Dean Howells, himself a refugee from village tedium, sensed the corrosive impact of urban life on personal identity. In Howells's *A Hazard of New Fortunes* (1890), his protagonist Basil March notes that the "solvent" of life in the metropolis seemed to bring out the "deeply underlying nobody" in everyone. Yet there was more to the change than urban malaise. During the second half of the nineteenth century, technological advance brought unprecedented comfort and convenience to the more privileged sectors of the urban bourgeoisie. To affluent Americans reared with the agrarian bias of republican moralism, urban "luxury" could be a symptom of "overcivilization" as well as a sign of progress. Freed from the drudgery of farm life, they were also increasingly cut off from the hard, resistant reality of things. Indoor plumbing, central heating, and canned foods were pleasant amenities but made life seem curiously insubstantial; they contributed to what Daniel Boorstin has perceptively called "the thinner life of things." Complaints about prepackaged artificiality may seem a recent and faddish development, but as early as 1909 cultural commentators were lamenting "the Era of Predigestion," which had rendered vigorous, firsthand experience obsolete. According to *The Atlantic Monthly*, "The world is by degrees getting ready to lie abed all day and transact its business." Yet this ease of life had not produced healthy people; on the contrary, the most comfortable people were also the most anxious, the most likely to fall victim to "our now universal disorder, nervous prostration."[7]

"Nervous prostration" or neurasthenia were shorthand terms for the immobilizing depressions that plagued many among the urban bourgeoisie during the late nineteenth century and after. While descriptions of neurasthenia varied, they were united by their emphases on the neurasthenic's paralysis of will, his sense that he was no longer able to plunge into "the vital currents of life," his feeling that life had become somehow unreal.[8]

Technological change alone could not account for such extreme symptoms. There was another and equally mundane source: the spread of an interdependent national market economy. Besides distributing the tinned meat, condensed milk, and other "modern conveniences" that insulated people from primary experience, the national market laid claim to venerable concepts of the self. As more and more people became enmeshed in the market's web of interdependence, liberal ideals of autonomous selfhood became ever more difficult to sustain. For entrepreneurs as well as wageworkers, financial rise or ruin came to depend on policies formulated far away, on situations beyond the individual's control. And by the 1890s, as Alfred D. Chandler and a host of economic historians have made clear, the large, bureaucratically organized corporation was becoming the dominant model for businessmen who sought to organize the national market. Jobs were becoming more specialized, more interdependent; personal autonomy

7

was becoming more problematic. It was not surprising that believers in self-made manhood grew uneasy. Even the privileged ones fretted over "Our Lost Individuality" as they pondered the coming of a mass society. "We *are* a mass," an *Atlantic* writer complained in 1909. "As a whole, we have lost the capacity for separate selfhood."[9]

As self-made manhood became ever more chimerical, the meaning of success began subtly to change. In a society increasingly dominated by bureaucratic corporations, one dealt with people rather than things; "personal magnetism" began to replace character as the key to advancement. In advice literature after 1900, as Warren Susman has observed, success seemed less often a matter of mastering one's physical environment or plodding diligently at one's trade, more often a matter of displaying one's poise among a crowd. The author of *Personality: How To Build It* (1916) advised his readers to "be original but retain the esteem of others" and to "love company, widen your connections." At work and at home, behavior became more finely attuned to the ubiquitous presence of "others."[10]

As success became more dependent on evanescent "impression management," selfhood lost coherence. The older ethic had required adherence to an internalized morality of self-control; repressive as this "inner-direction" had been, it helped to sustain a solid core of selfhood. The newer ethic of "other-direction" undermined that solidity by presenting the self as an empty vessel to be filled and refilled according to the expectations of others and the needs of the moment. After the turn of the century, success manuals increasingly prescribed what the sociologist David Riesman has called "modes of manipulating the self in order to manipulate others." The successful man or woman had "no clear core of self" (in Riesman's words), only a set of social masks.[11]

The notion of social masks had been abroad for centuries, but Americans had nearly always assumed the existence of a "simple, genuine self" beneath the layers of convention. By the turn of the century, for many Americans, that assumption was no longer tenable. From lowbrow success literature to the empyrean realm of theory (in the work of William James and George Herbert Mead), Americans began to imagine a self that was neither simple nor genuine, but fragmented and socially constructed. As Howells wrote in 1890, the human personality seemed like an onion which was "nothing but hulls, that you keep peeling off, one after another, till you think you have got down to the heart at last, and then you have got down to nothing."[12]

This feeling of inner emptiness was not confined to literati like Howells; it pervaded much of the educated bourgeoisie. One can sense it in many aspects of Victorian culture: in the immobilized depressions of neurasthenics, in youthful seekers' yearnings to "be a real person," in all the anxious earnestness which often seemed—by the late nineteenth century—to lack clear focus or direction. The autonomous self, long a linchpin of liberal culture, was being rendered unreal—not only by the growth of an interdependent market but also by a growing awareness of the constraints that unconscious or inherited drives placed on individual choice. As the educated public grew fascinated with "The Loss of Personality," multiple "selves," and other mysteries unearthed by psychiatrists, conventional definitions of "will power" began to seem oversimplified and familiar feelings of selfhood began to seem obsolete.[13]

The decline of autonomous selfhood lay at the heart of the modern sense of unreality. Without a solid sense of self to deny or control, standards blurred and Victorian moral boundaries grew indistinct. Yet the internalized injunction to "produce" remained. The result was anxious busyness. The magazines of the 1880s and after were full of complaints about "overpressure" in businessmen, housewives, and even schoolchildren. For some, repression seemed pointless but remained a psychic necessity. It was not surprising that the sufferers from "overpressure" often took to their beds with nervous prostration. Victorian imperatives persisted while their religious and even ethical sanctions faded.[14]

These difficulties were exaggerated by the sorry state of liberal theology. As Nietzsche had predicted, "with the decline of Christianity it will seem for a time as if all things had become weightless." Isolated and idiosyncratic as Nietzsche may seem, his observation aptly caught the platitudinous vagueness, the sheer banality of much late-Victorian Protestantism. And, as I tried to show in *No Place of Grace*, many late Victorians would have agreed with his characterization of their culture. Indeed, a feeling that one can call "weightlessness" reinforced the spreading sense of unreality among the educated bourgeoisie. As liberal Protestantism became assimilated to the secular creed of progress, as Satan became an Evil Principle and hell a metaphor, the preferred personal style shifted from shrill earnestness to formulized benevolence.[15]

Religious beliefs have historically played a key role in defining an individual's sense of reality. Without distinct frameworks of meaning, reality itself becomes problematic; the individual slides into normlessness, or anomie. It would be a gross exaggeration to assert that many educated late Victorians had reached that point. Most still celebrated liberal Protestantism as the best of all possible religions. Yet behind the paeans to spiritual progress there were many glimmerings of doubt. Numerous editorialists wondered whether the decline of orthodoxy had lessened intensity of conviction and endangered moral standards. The bicentennial of Jonathan Edwards' birth in 1903 stirred a *Century* writer to comment that while "the rigid atmosphere of old-fashioned orthodoxy" had produced "moral giants," the more relaxed religious beliefs of the twentieth century seemed unable to match that achievement. People seemed more tolerant of others' beliefs but less committed to their own. By the turn of the century such observations were common among the educated professionals who wrote for prominent magazines. It is possible to hazard some generalizations about religious experience among the late-Victorian bourgeoisie: As supernatural beliefs waned, ethical convictions grew more supple; experience lost gravity and began to seem "weightless."[16]

In all, the modern sense of unreality stemmed from extraordinarily various sources and generated complex effects. Technological change isolated the urban bourgeoisie from the hardness of life on the land; an interdependent and increasingly corporate economy circumscribed autonomous will and choice; a softening Protestant theology undermined commitments and blurred ethical distinctions. Yet a production ethos persisted: Self-control became merely a tool for secular achievement; success began to occur in a moral and spiritual void.

It was no wonder, then, that so many young Americans who came of age at the turn of the century found themselves gasping for air in their parents' Victorian homes, no wonder they yearned to fling open the doors and experience "real life" in all its dimensions. Among the educated bourgeoisie, this quest for "real life" was the characteristic psychic project of the age. It energized the settlement house movement, as legions of sheltered young people searched in the slums for the intense experience they felt they had been denied at home; it lay behind Van Wyck Brooks's attack on the anemia of American culture; it provoked Randolph Bourne's insistence that ossified school curricula be replaced by "education for living." This reverence for "life" as a value in itself was a new development in American cultural history. Never before had so many people felt that reality was throbbing with vitality, pulsating with unspeakable excitement, and always just out of reach. And, most important for my purposes, the feeling of unreality helped to generate longings for bodily vigor, emotional intensity, and a revitalized sense of selfhood.[17]

These new emotional needs underlay the shift in moral climate that began to occur during the late nineteenth century. At its most mundane, this change involved a loosening of the work ethic in response to "overpressure," a growing acceptance of what William James called "The Gospel of Relaxation" among educated business and professional people as well as factory and clerical workers. While avant-garde bohemians dramatized the appeal of life in extremis, captains of a nascent "leisure industry" played to the yearning for intense experience at all social levels. They commodified titillation at cabarets and in amusement parks; they catered to the anxious businessman as well as the bored shop girl; they assimilated immigrants and WASPs in a new mass audience. Roller coasters, exotic dancers, and hootchy-kootchy girls all promised temporary escapes to a realm of intense experience, far from the stuffy unreality of bourgeois culture. In more elevated tones, social theorists spoke to the same emotional needs: Attacking Victorian repression, men like Walter Lippmann and Simon Nelson Patten set about "the task of civilizing our impulses by creating fine opportunities for their expression" within the new corporate system. Intense experience was their philosopher's stone, anxious boredom their implacable enemy.[18]

But if the flight from unreality ranged widely, it was most clearly embodied in the therapeutic ethos. By looking more closely at therapeutic ideals, we can more clearly map out the territory claimed by therapists and advertisers alike. To a bourgeoisie suffering from identity diffusion and inner emptiness, the creators of the therapeutic ethos offered harmony, vitality, and the hope of self-realization. The paths to self-realization could vary. One might seek wholeness and security through careful management of personal resources; or one might pursue emotional fulfillment and endless "growth" through intense experience. These approaches were united by several assumptions: an implicit nostalgia for the vigorous health allegedly enjoyed by farmers, children, and others "close to nature"; a belief that expert advice could enable one to recover that vigor without fundamental social change; and a tacit conviction that self-realization was the largest aim of human existence. This last assumption was the most important: Whether one sought self-realization through controlled or spontaneous experience, commitments outside the self shrank to meet the seeker's immediate emotional requirements. Rooted in largely personal dilemmas, the therapeutic ethos nevertheless provided a secular world view that well suited the interests of corporate proprietors and managers in the emerging culture.

The older form of the therapeutic ethos had existed since early-Victorian times. It promoted a defensive, maintenance-oriented strategy toward psychic and physical health. This prudential attitude marked many early remedies for neurasthenia. The neurologist Silas Weir Mitchell designed a "rest cure" to "fatten" and "redden" his patients; others, like George Miller Beard and Mary Putnam Jacobi, simply counseled the careful hoarding of physical and emotional capital. Physicians and laymen alike resorted to money metaphors. In a *Good Housekeeping* story of 1885 a healthy lady remarked of her neurasthenic sister that "Louisa lived on her *principal* of strength, I on my *interest* . . . the secret of health, as of wealth, is to lay up a little each day." Similar analogies persisted well into the twentieth century. Dr. Harvey W. Wiley, president of *Good Housekeeping*'s "League for Longer Life," told readers in 1920 that "thousands have written for the League's questionnaire which will enable them to find out just where their health account stands—whether they may draw on it for many years or whether it is about to be closed out." The improvident faced bankruptcy if they failed to heed their investment counselors.[19]

This prudential attitude toward health rested on assumptions of physical and psychic scarcity. Children as well as adults were warned to conserve their energies; even babies faced psychic ruin if they became overexcited while at play. The older form of therapy, with its frequent money metaphors and its insistence on careful husbanding of resources, expressed the persistent production orientation within the dominant culture. The Victorian morality of self-control was surviving, but on a secular basis. Therapists counseled prudence because it promoted well-being in this world, not salvation in the next.

Yet by the 1890s there was a growing sense that health might not be exclusively a matter of moderation. Alongside the prudential "scarcity therapy" an exuberant "abundance therapy" began to appear. Charging that the prudent man was only half alive, abundance therapy promised to reach untapped reservoirs of energy and open the way to a richer, fuller life. More directly and aggressively than scarcity therapy, abundance therapy offered bracing relief from the stifling sense of unreality.

Assumptions of psychic abundance marked a wide variety of cultural figures. Annie Payson Call, a popular self-help writer, counseled neurasthenics to achieve *Power Through Repose* (1891): Instead of fighting fatigue, she advised, yield to it; instead of remaining constrained by "sham emotions" and "morbid self-consciousness," emulate the healthy baby who *"lets himself go"* with unconscious ease. "The most intense sufferers from nervous prostration," Call wrote, "are those who suppress any sign of their feeling." Contrary to the prudential view, Call believed that one could actually increase psychic energy through emotional release. She won a wide readership that included William James, who was fascinated by "The Energies of Men" and eager to explore doctrines of psychic abundance ranging from mind-cure to psychoanalysis.[20]

James's rival, the psychologist and educator G. Stanley Hall, was even more preoccupied by instinctual and emotional vitality. Like James, Hall drew on Bergson, Freud, and other European sources in formulating a vitalist critique of late-Victorian culture. His *Adolescence* (1904) was a paean to the spontaneity of the budding youth; his *Jesus, the Christ, in the Light of Psychology* (1917) presented his subject as an adolescent superman, strikingly handsome and brimming with enthusiasm—a model for bourgeois revitalization. World War I provoked Hall to his fullest statement of therapeutic ideals. In *Morale* (1920), Hall argued that the war had proven the bankruptcy of the old criteria of right and wrong. It was time to replace morality with morale, which he defined as "the cult of condition"—of feeling "alive, well, young, strong, buoyant, and exuberant, with animal spirits at the top notch." Morale "is found wherever the universal hunger for more life is getting its fill," Hall wrote. "The great religious, especially the Christian founders who strove to realize the Kingdom of God, that is, of man here and now, are perhaps the world's very best illustration of morale."[21]

Despite Hall's religious language, the tendency of his thought was fundamentally secular. He asserted that the Kingdom of God exalted "man here and now"; he believed that "more life" has its own reward. This was a typical pattern in the expression of therapeutic ideals: Clouds of religiosity obscured a growing preoccupation with worldly well-being. This pattern emerged most clearly among liberal Protestant ministers. Convinced that they were using psychology to renew spirituality, they unwittingly hastened the drift toward a more secular society. To be sure, religion has always had a therapeutic dimension; the "cure of souls" was an ancient Christian tradition. But in the Protestant pronouncements of the early twentieth century, psyche sometimes displaced soul; a larger supernatural purpose sometimes faded from view.

Among the most influential Protestant therapists were the Episcopal ministers Elwood Worcester and Samuel McComb, who joined with the psychiatrist Isador Coriat to found the Emmanuel Movement. In 1908, at their Boston church, they began to use hypnotism and autosuggestion in an attempt to heal disorders of body and mind among their parishioners. The Emmanuel Movement was founded at a propitious moment: Popular fascination with mysticism, mind cure, and depth psychology had reached unprecedented heights. News of the Emmanuel Movement's success spread quickly; soon other healing centers opened in New York, Chicago, Newark, Buffalo, Cleveland, and Northampton, Massachusetts. By stressing the therapeutic value of "unseen spiritual powers," the movement spoke directly to the bourgeois need for "more life." "We possess in our religion," its leaders claimed, "the greatest of all therapeutic agents, if only we deal with it sincerely." In their preoccupation with unlocking "the potentiality of human life" and their tendency to reduce religion to a "therapeutic agent," the Emmanuel founders anticipated the difficulties of much contemporary Christianity. Responding sympathetically to their troubled flocks, they unknowingly accelerated the secularizing process.[22]

The same difficulty can be seen at the apex of liberal Protestantism, in the thought of Harry Emerson Fosdick. By the 1920s Fosdick was probably the most influential Protestant moralist in the United States (at least among urban liberals). He was a brilliant preacher and a serious thinker; he certainly cannot be reduced to a bland apologist for therapeutic ideals. Yet Fosdick too was caught up in the moral confusion he sought to alleviate. And at times his pronouncements may have undermined the Christian faith he wanted to preserve. Faced with the challenge of positivism on one hand and fundamentalism on the other, Fosdick did as liberal theologians before him had done. He opted for accommodation with modernity. While he sometimes assaulted self-absorption, the overall thrust of his preaching (at least through the 1920s) was to provide religious sanctions for an emerging therapeutic ethos. Like Hall, Fosdick stressed Jesus's physical vitality and confidence in human potential. The starting point of Christianity, Fosdick claimed, was not an otherworldly faith but a faith in human personality. "Not an outward temple, but the inward shrine of man's personality, with all its possibilities and powers, is . . . infinitely sacred." By the 1920s that view had become a liberal commonplace.[23]

An emphasis on the sanctity of human potential led to a redefinition of religion. Flaying formalistic Christianity for its "endless unreality and hypocrisy," Fosdick charged that "religion and life have been drifting apart." As a result, "multitudes of people are living not bad but frittered lives—split, scattered, uncoordinated." To relieve this sense of fragmentation, Fosdick called for an *Adventurous Religion* (1926) that "will furnish an inward spiritual dynamic for radiant and triumphant living." According to Fosdick, every religious custom and doctrine must pass two tests: "First: is it intelligently defensible; Second: does it contribute to man's abundant life?" The problem, in other words, was not morality but morale. Like other religious leaders, Fosdick unwittingly transformed Protestant Christianity into a form of abundance therapy.[24]

Yet the advocates of psychic abundance could not entirely muffle the voice of prudence, even within themselves. Fosdick exalted character, will, and restraint as paths to abundant life; Hall warned that "those guilty of [sexual] self-indulgence have less reserve to draw on for any emergency"; Call insisted that her largest purposes were "efficiency" and "true self-control." The emerging therapeutic ethos was a muddle of spontaneity and calculation.[25]

This coexistence of abundance therapy with vestigial prudence surfaced clearly in the work of Luther S. Gulick—YMCA organizer, founder of the Campfire Girls, and apostle of *The Efficient Life* (1907). While Gulick frequently characterized health as the careful management of scarce resources, for him the efficient life was ultimately the exuberant life. He warned men that mere freedom from disease was inadequate; to be "men of power" they must cultivate "tremendous vitality." He warned women that "children inevitably grow away from mothers who do not keep themselves growing and their lives vivid."

Avoiding constipation, taking regular exercise, thinking "strong and happy thoughts" before bedtime—for Gulick these were not only defensive strategies but paths to "full living" and "continuous growth." There was no larger purpose in life.[26]

This fascination with "growth" as an end in itself linked Gulick not only with many other abundance therapists but also with a wide range of other cultural figures. Self-help advisers, social scientists, popular literati, and the avant-garde all began to elevate becoming over being, the process of experience over its goal or result. Some employed fashionable evolutionary analogies. "The true and living god," Hall wrote enthusiastically in 1920, "is the developmental urge." Others expressed conventional wisdom less self-consciously. The poet Ella Wheeler Wilcox, for example, warned in 1894 that "to love is to know happiness but not contentment, rapture but not peace, exhilaration but not satisfaction; for contentment means inertia, peace means stagnation, and satisfaction means satiety, and these three cannot exist where Love is." A dread of stasis affected many among the educated bourgeoisie.[27]

The worship of growth and process in the therapeutic ethos was closely allied with other transformations in American culture: a "revolt against formalism" among social scientists; a "revolution in manners and morals" among the middle and upper classes generally; the rise of a leisure ethic for those subject to a regimented workplace. At the most obvious level, the therapeutic injunction to "let go" eased adjustment to the rhythms of life under corporate capitalism. Hall, for example, assumed that modern work would be degrading and that workers therefore needed regular bouts of revitalizing leisure. "Everyone, especially those who lead the drab life of the modern toiler, needs and craves an occasional 'good time,' " he acknowledged. "Indeed we all need to glow, tingle, and feel life intensely now and then." According to therapists like Hall (and social theorists like Lippmann), liberation should occur in homeopathic doses. Even self-styled "philosophers of play" like Gulick argued that play impulses should be organized and channeled in "healthy" directions. Private spontaneity promoted public adjustment to bureaucratic authority.[28]

Even in the private realm, liberationist ideals concealed a coercive moral imperative. The therapeutic ethos implied not only that one ought to pursue health single-mindedly but also that one ought to be continuously exuding personal magnetism and the promise of ever more radiant, wholesome living. The coerciveness of the "ought" came less often from an internalized moral code and more often from the expectations of others; but the coerciveness was still there, wedded to ideals like "growth" and "spontaneity" that proved vague and elusive.

Indeed, there was something inherently self-defeating about a deliberate cultivation of spontaneity or a calculated shedding of inhibitions. For many, the therapeutic quest led ultimately in circles.[29]

There was a further problem as well. A loosening of repressive morality came at the price of increased banality. Defining the natural as the good, abundance therapists sought to liberate instinctual life by denying its darker side. Elwood Worcester expressed a common view when he said: "The subconscious mind is a normal part of our spiritual nature . . . [and] what we observe in hypnosis is an elevation of the moral faculties, greater refinement of feeling, a higher sense of truth and honor, often a delicacy of mind, which the waking subject does not possess. In my opinion the reason for this is that the subconscious mind, which I believe is the most active in suggestion, is purer and freer from evil than our waking consciousness." With assertions like these, abundance therapists waved aside the towering rages and the insatiable longings in the human unconscious. And they dismissed the painful conflict between instinct and civilization. Instinct liberated became instinct made banal; the reaction against weightlessness produced more weightlessness.[30]

Ultimately the most corrosive aspect of the therapeutic ethos was the worship of growth and process as ends in themselves. By devaluing ultimate purposes, abundance therapists (like "antiformalist" social scientists), tended to undermine possibilities for any bedrock of moral values. And by urging unending personal growth, abundance therapists encouraged the forgetting (one might say the repression) of the past. They embraced the creed of progress and transferred its effects to the most intimate areas of life. Devaluing the customs and traditions designed to preserve cultural memory, they devalued as well the personal memory enshrined in family continuity. Ancestral ties and familiar loyalties blocked personal as well as economic development.[31]

Yet the creed of growth remained unsatisfying. Even among therapists themselves, inchoate discontent persisted. Casting off the withered hand of the past, they slipped into nostalgia. That sentiment surfaced in Hall, Gulick, Call, and many others—in their distrust of the modern city, their admiration for the healthiness of rural life, their yearnings for a childlike state of nature. "Childhood," Hall wrote, "is the paradise of the race from which adult life is a fall." Gulick inveighed against the "mushiness" of modern urban life. Therapists wanted pastoral peace and technological advance, pre-oedipal innocence and bourgeois adulthood. The therapeutic ethos, in short, mirrored the contradictions of a class unsettled by the changes it was helping to promote.[32]

To sum up: The therapeutic ethos was rooted in reaction against the rationalization of culture—the growing effort, first described by

Max Weber, to exert systematic control over man's external environment and ultimately over his inner life as well.[33] By the turn of the century the iron cage of bureaucratic "rationality" had begun subtly to affect even the educated and affluent. Many began to sense that their familiar sense of autonomy was being undermined, and that they had been cut off from intense physical, emotional, or spiritual experience. The therapeutic ethos promised to heal the wounds inflicted by rationalization, to release the cramped energies of a fretful bourgeoisie.

Reacting against rationalization, the creators of the therapeutic ethos nevertheless reinforced that process by promoting a new and subtler set of controls on human behavior. The nature of control varied: Scarcity therapy addressed anxieties; abundance therapy addressed aspirations. But the main point is that longings for reintegrated selfhood and intense experience were assimilated by both therapeutic and business elites in the emerging consumer culture: not only by psychiatrists, social theorists, and captains of the nascent "leisure industry" but also by advertising executives. This was not a conspiracy but an unconscious collaboration. The elites' motives were diverse and contradictory; they were often as full of self-doubt as their clients and as enamored of the therapeutic promise.

This confusion was nowhere clearer than in the advertising profession. Responding to the therapeutic ethos, advertisers also reinforced it. Some were cynical manipulators; others were prophets of abundance deluded by their own ideologies; still others were uncertain seekers groping for secure identities in a rationalizing culture. Often their only intention was to sell a particular product, but their strategies accelerated their audience's endless quest for self-realization. As much as any other social group, national advertisers helped to popularize a pseudo-religion of health and an anxious self-absorption among the American population. But many would have been dismayed if they had known it.

ADVERTISING STRATEGIES AND THE THERAPEUTIC ETHOS

Between 1880 and 1930, the mushrooming institutional growth of national advertising was accompanied by a shift in advertisers' assumptions and strategies. With the spread of a national market and urban conditions of life, advertisers began to imagine a buying public that was increasingly remote and on the run. The trade journal *Printer's Ink* noted in 1890 that "the average [newspaper] reader skims lightly over the thousand facts massed in serried columns. To win his attention he

17

must be aroused, excited, terrified." While some advertising men deplored these habits of mind, others urged adjustment to them through the use of illustrations, brand names, trademarks, slogans, anything that might attract the attention of a busy, restless, and easily bored consumer. Amid a mounting din of product claims, many national advertisers shifted their focus from presenting information to attracting attention.[34]

The shift toward sensational tactics for attracting attention was accelerated by a broader movement from print to visual modes of expression. Technical advances in photography, film, and printing promoted a proliferation of images and made an exclusively verbal medium seem dull by comparison. "American civilization grows more hieroglyphic every day," Vachel Lindsay wrote in *The Art of the Motion Picture* (1915). "The cartoons of [Jay Norwood "Ding"] Darling; the advertisements in the back of the magazines on the billboards and in the street-cars, the acres of photographs in the Sunday newspapers, make us into a hieroglyphic civilization far nearer to Egypt than to England." Advertising was part of a new visual environment, where innumerable images jostled for the attention of a mass audience.[35]

But there was more to the change. By the early 1900s the most successful advertising agents were trying not only to attract attention but aggressively to shape consumers' desires. Albert Lasker of Lord & Thomas in Chicago typified this new approach by developing a new style of copy. Rejecting the dignified, low-key approach favored by professionals at that time, Lasker sought to arouse a strong demand through high-pressure "salesmanship in print." By 1904, six years after joining Lord & Thomas, Lasker owned a quarter interest in the company and an almost mythic stature within the advertising profession. Then he met Claude Hopkins, another phrasemaker who had sold astonishing amounts of beer, lard, and patent medicine by using what he called the "Reason Why" approach. The two men became an enormously successful team, and the term "Reason Why advertising" entered business school textbooks. Ironically it was not reasonable at all: Hopkins refused to appeal to a buyer's reason by listing a product's qualities; on the contrary he addressed nonrational yearnings by suggesting the ways his client's product would transform the buyer's life. Lord & Thomas writers applied such strategies to patent medicines, toothpastes, and automobiles. Other agencies followed suit.[36] Hopkins's "Reason Why" pointed advertising away from the product and toward its alleged effects, away from sober information and toward the therapeutic promise of a richer, fuller life.

Therapeutic strategies became institutionalized as some advertising firms hired psychological consultants. The most conspicuous was

John B. Watson, who joined the J. Walter Thompson Agency in 1920; but as early as the 1890s, *Printer's Ink* was discussing psychology in advertising, and Walter Dill Scott's text *The Psychology of Advertising* (first published in 1903) was in its third edition when Watson made his celebrated move. Whatever their theoretical perspective, early psychological consultants rejected the nineteenth-century view that the mind was a static collection of "faculties"; instead they followed the "new psychology" in viewing the psyche as a dynamic organism interacting in constant process with its environment. To some advertisers, the implication was clear that human minds were not only malleable but manipulable. And the most potent manipulation was therapeutic: the promise that the product would contribute to the buyer's physical, psychic, or social well-being; the threat that his well-being would be undermined if he failed to buy it.[37]

For many psychological consultants, therapeutic advertising became a method of social control—a way to arouse consumer demand by associating products with imaginary states of well-being. Scott, for example, challenged advertisers to speak more directly to consumers' desires for sensuous enjoyment. "How many advertisers," he asked, "describe a piano so vividly that the reader can *hear* it? How many food products are described so that the reader can *taste* the food? . . . How many describe an undergarment so the reader can *feel* the pleasant contact with his body?" Scott's approach was shaped by the concept of suggestion, which dominated academic psychology in the early twentieth century. Scott's version was that "every idea of a function tends to call that function into activity, and will do so, unless hindered by a competing idea or physical impediment." If an advertiser was persuasive enough, he could influence a consumer to act reflexively, without thought or hesitation.[38]

Simpleminded as it seemed, Scott's concept of suggestion embodied an important departure from familiar ideas of autonomy, will, and choice. It portended a view of human nature that has become common among advertisers and public relations men throughout the twentieth century. From this standpoint, human beings were fundamentally unthinking and impulsive. "Man has been called the reasoning animal but he could with greater truthfulness be called the creature of suggestion," Scott wrote. "He is reasonable, but he is to a greater extent suggestible." In 1912, William A. Shryer's *Analytical Advertising* altogether dismissed appeals to reason. Because "the ordinary conduct of life demands but little exercise of reason," Shryer asserted, "it is . . . unprofitable for the advertiser to center his appeal around copy that presumes the existence of a function so slightly developed in the average man." Lumping individuals en masse, manipulative strategies displayed a growing contempt for "the average man." It was left to Edward Bernays, nephew of Freud and "father" of public relations, to provide an epitaph for bourgeois ideals of individual autonomy and conscious choice. "The group mind," he wrote in *Propaganda* (1928), "does not *think* in the strict sense of the word. In place of thoughts it has impulses, habits, emotions." To ensure that consumption kept pace with production, Bernays advised, advertisers must learn how to "make customers" through an understanding of the "structure, the personality, the prejudices, of a potentially universal public."[39] The advertisers' job of "making customers" closely paralleled the new political consultants' aim of "making voters." From either view, the "public" was no longer composed of active citizens but rather of manipulable consumers.

In criticizing this shift I do not mean to endorse uncritically a liberal view of human nature as essentially rational and autonomous. On the contrary. Advertisers' growing recognition of human irrationality was a pale reflection of the most profound intellectual currents of the age: a recovery of the unconscious pioneered by Freud and Jung, a revolt against positivism led by James and Bergson, a broad questioning of the complacent liberal faith in human reason and progress.[40] The problem was that manipulative advertisers distorted this critique of bourgeois culture beyond recognition. Emphasizing human irrationality, they used that emphasis to limit rather than deepen understanding of the human condition—to reject human freedom, rather than acknowledge its precariousness. Instead of transcending bourgeois culture, manipulative advertisers (like early therapists) helped to revitalize and transform it, creating new modes of hegemony for new managerial elites in the coming era of corporate capitalism.

Even as psychological consulting helped to legitimize therapeutic strategies within the advertising profession, many advertisers continued to resist and deny the changes their business was accelerating. Striving for professional respectability, the editors of *Printers' Ink* assailed "the patent medicine evil," insisted on the informational dimension of advertising, and conducted innumerable "Truth in Advertising" campaigns. The National Association of Advertisers, meeting in Baltimore in 1913 under a huge electric sign that spelled TRUTH in ten-foot letters, adopted what became known as the "Baltimore Truth Declaration"—a code of ethics renouncing misleading copy. In part these actions represented cynical efforts to avoid federal regulation; in part they embodied advertisers' unease in a consumer culture where all values—including truth itself—seemed in constant flux. The same double significance can be assigned to the constant talk of "sincerity" in advertising trade journals during the early twentieth century. Many advertising men, like other carriers of the therapeutic ethos, were creating a culture they barely understood and only half desired.[41]

Yet in their creations—the advertisements themselves—the evidence was unmistakable. To be sure, informational approaches persisted; many products were simply not susceptible to a therapeutic appeal. But by the 1920s the symbolic universe of national advertising markedly resembled the therapeutic world described by Philip Rieff—a world in which all overarching structures of meaning had collapsed, and there was "nothing at stake beyond a manipulative sense of well-being."[42]

It is important to underscore the role of advertising in accelerating this collapse of meaning. The decline of symbolic structures outside the self has been a central process in the development of a consumer culture, joining advertising strategies and the therapeutic ethos. To get a glimpse of that process, we need first to take a hint from semiologists and acknowledge that national advertisements constituted a new and bewildering code, a set of verbal and visual signs for which the referents were unclear. Unlike therapeutic prescriptions, advertisements were not meant to be taken literally—or were they? That was the problem. The new attention-getting strategies, particularly the therapeutic emphasis on manipulating feeling rather than presenting information, led advertisers to a nether realm between truth and falsehood. Promising relief from feelings of unreality, advertising nevertheless exacerbated those feelings by hastening what the French sociologist Henri Lefebvre has called "the decline of the referentials"—the tendency, under corporate capitalism, for words to become severed from any meaningful referent. Think, for example, of the beating that words like "personality" and "revolutionary" have taken in the consumer culture. One does not need to assume a precapitalist unity between word and thing to concede Lefebvre's point. Under capitalism, visual and verbal signs become detached from all traditional associations and meaning in general is eroded. The world of advertisements gradually acquired an Alice-in-Wonderland quality.[43]

In part this devaluation of meaning involved the misuse of language. Apart from the bogus claims of patent medicine men, there were subtler strategies as well, such as the use of half-truths pioneered by Claude Hopkins. He played up Schlitz's steam-cleaned beer bottles as if the practice were unique, when in fact it was in common use among all brewing companies. The claim was hardly false, but neither was it completely true. There was also a common tendency to merge opposites: Factory-made furniture was associated with "traditional craftsmanship," canned foods with "old-fashioned home cooking." In the history of advertising, as at other points in our cultural history, the innovator presented himself as a traditionalist. And most generally, the devaluation of verbal meaning was accelerated by the advertisers' new therapeutic vocabulary, which emphasized diffuse states of feeling rather than precise information.[44]

The difficulty was even clearer in the use of illustrations as attention-getting devices. Early advertising "cuts" often had no relation to the product advertised; later illustrations were adopted primarily to associate pleasure with the buying of the product or fear with the failure to buy it. Information was rarely on the agenda. A 1928 *Good Housekeeping* advertisement for Drano posed the caption "Every waste-pipe faithfully free flowing . . . every day in the year" beneath a picture of a nude woman, towel draped over one shoulder, exposing back, shoulder, hip, and rump as she watched the water swirl down the drain, presumably due to Drano. At such times, the distinction between image and meaning was nearly complete.[45]

Advertising helped to create a culture in which there were few symbols rooted in specific customs (as in traditional cultures), nor even many signs with specific referents (as in Victorian print culture). There were only floating, detached images that (like the flickering faces in the movies) promised therapeutic feelings of emotional or sensuous excitement. But fulfillment seemed always just out of reach.

It seems sensible, then, to view advertising as the official art of twentieth-century capitalist culture, as the sociologist Michael Schudson has suggested. A counterpart to the poster art of Communist societies, advertising was garish rather than drab, titillating rather than didactic, and ceaselessly open to aesthetic novelty. It was no accident that by the 1920s and 1930s advertising had begun to assimilate the allegedly rebellious impulses of aesthetic "modernism." As the advertising executive Ernest Elmo Calkins recalled, "Modernism offered the opportunity of expressing the inexpressible, of suggesting not so much a motor car as speed, not so much a gown as style, not so much a compact as beauty." It offered, in other words, not information but feeling. Indeed one modernist strain specifically attacked the whole notion of content and meaning in art. From this view the advertisement (like the painting) was not a communication but a thing unto itself. Form was all.[46]

Only a handful of advertising men would have gone that far; most were convinced that they were communicating information about products. My point is not that we should ignore content in advertisements but that we should keep in mind their impact on all contents, all meanings outside the narrow sphere of personal well-being. The corrosion of meaning was gradual and largely unintended. National advertisers rarely attacked familiar values; instead they suggested a new set of values centering around the therapeutic promise of psychic security and fulfillment.

The earlier, prudential form of the therapeutic ethos was foreshadowed in the many Victorian advertisements that appropriated the prestige of science and played on intimate self-doubts while promising to restore or preserve the buyer's health and beauty. But after the turn of the century this approach became more intrusive as advertisers increasingly invaded that allegedly private sphere, the family, to promise the maintenance of domestic harmony through intelligent consumption. In 1900 Cook's flaked rice gave away a rag doll with every large package, warning that "Christmas is coming!" and "the children's pleasure must be planned for." Husbands and wives alike were constantly needled about their domestic roles. If husbands failed to provide a Laun-dry-ette or an Aetna Life Insurance policy, advertisements implied, their wives would soon degenerate into humpbacked slatterns. If wives overlooked the Puffed Rice or the Pro-Phy-Lac-Tic toothbrush, their children faced malnutrition and pyorrhea. The domestic ideal, long a focal point of Victorian morality, was being redefined to fit the new consumer culture.[47]

A characteristic therapeutic strategy linked domestic responsibilities with nostalgia for a pristine, "natural" state. "Mothers, do you not know that children crave natural food until you pervert their taste by the use of unnatural food?" a Shredded Wheat advertisement asked in 1903. "Unnatural food develops unnatural and therefore wrong propensities and desires in children." This marked an approach that has become even more common in our own time. The advertiser defined the "natural" as the good, implied that modern life was full of artificial imitations, and promised salvation through his product—which was ironically all the more natural in this case since it was *made in the most hygienic and scientific food laboratory in the world.*[48]

The appeal to nature addressed the half-conscious nostalgia of cosmopolitan elites. As the ties to their own past attenuated, the urban bourgeoisie became more susceptible to the commodified version of the past served up in national advertisements. Or so it seems when one surveys the advertisements in such middle- and upper-class periodicals as *Good Housekeeping, The American Magazine, Harper's Weekly,* or the *Saturday Evening Post.* These were aimed not only at old-style entrepreneurs but also at the mobile, metropolitan professionals and managers who staffed the developing corporate system. Housewives among this group were more likely to respond to the nostalgia peddled (for example) by the Mennen Company in "Aunt Belle's Comfort Letters," which began in *Good Housekeeping* in 1920. "Aunt Belle is a real person and that is her real name. She really understands babies. She would like to correspond with you about your baby." It is a little pathetic, this appeal to isolated young mothers who may have yearned for kin and community advice even as they sought vigorously to be "modern." As ancestral authority grew culturally or geographically remote, advertisements replaced it with a merger of corporate and therapeutic authority—but often in a pseudotraditional guise.[49]

More commonly the new forms of authority invoked by advertising were overtly medical. The white-coated doctor became a ubiquitous figure in advertising of the 1910s and 1920s. A 1920 advertisement typified the dark side of the new religion of health.

Is your child

Run down
Frail
Delicate
Underdeveloped
Pale
Always tired
Easily upset
Irritable
Backward in school
Not himself?

These are signs of malnutrition!

Citing two doctors, the advertisement warned that "one child in every three—rich and poor alike—is undernourished." The way out? Quaker Oats.[50]

By the 1920s appeals to anxiety had intensified and spread. Watson's Scott Tissue campaign warned that harsh toilet papers caused irritation that "is not only a source of discomfort but also a possible seat of infection." One advertisement showed a photograph of a woman lying despondent in a hospital bed, a concerned friend hovering at her side; another showed a team of surgeons preparing to operate on a hapless victim of harsh paper. Social fears, too, were more overtly addressed. Before about 1920, Listerine antiseptic presented itself as a wound dressing; after that time it became an antidote for "halitosis," cautioning any young man whose wife rejected his advances to "suspect yourself first!" Inventive maladies became the order of the day. In a 1928 advertisement, the purgative Pluto Water pictured a young man moping amidst an effervescent crowd: ". . . he used to be the life of the party . . . [but now he has] ASTHENIA"—a mysterious lassitude resulting from prolonged constipation. In advertising's symbolic universe, both invalidism and ostracism were omnipresent threats to a secure sense of selfhood.[51]

24

In the emerging other-directed society of managers and professionals, advertisements increasingly assumed the importance of creating a pleasant social self. After the turn of the century, men's toiletries
were no longer merely grooming aids; they became keys to success and
barriers against embarrassment. Women as well were reminded repeatedly about the possibilities of giving offense through bad breath, yellow
teeth, body odors, and shabby home furnishings. In advertising's symbolic universe, the allegedly sacrosanct home became a testing ground
for other-directed housewives. Guests were everywhere in *Good Housekeeping* during the 1920s—evaluating food, furniture, children's behavior, even the bathroom drains. From the advertisers' point of view, the
bathroom became "the *showroom* of your home." Epitomizing the older
therapeutic ideal of well-managed health, a spotless bathroom became
a focus for female achievement. The culmination of this tendency appeared in 1930, when Brunswick toilet seats printed the following caption beneath a photograph of women sipping coffee in an upper-class
living room:

"And . . . did you notice the bathroom?" At that moment the hostess reentered
the room. She just barely overheard. But it was more than enough. She began
talking about Junior, about bridge, anything—but like chain lightning her mind
reviewed the bathroom. She saw it suddenly as a guest must see it, saw the one
detail that positively clamored for criticism.[52]

That one offending detail was the obsolete wooden toilet seat; the appeal to other-directed anxieties could hardly be carried further. To
paraphrase Sartre: In the new consumer culture, hell was—truly—
other people.

Yet other-direction could embody aspiration as well as anxiety. By
the 1890s, while many advertisements still exploited fears of giving offense, others began to address longings for a more vibrant personality
and a fuller life. From this new perspective, toothpaste might do more
than prevent "acid mouth" and "pink toothbrush"; it might also provide
the consumer with a positively dazzling smile and (ultimately) intense
romantic experience.[53] While the same performance ethic underlay
both approaches, the newer one upped the emotional ante. Rooted in
doctrines of psychic abundance, it promised revitalization rather than
maintenance—a self not only made whole but made vigorous.

The newer abundance-oriented approach appeared earliest and
most clearly in health-related advertising. As early as 1873 an advertisement for Tarrant's Seltzer in *Harper's Weekly* noted that "thousands of
people who are not actually sick complain that they are—'never well.'"
This feeling of enervation promoted yearnings not merely for well-
regulated health but also for abundant vitality; during the 1890s

advertisers began addressing those yearnings directly. Paine's Celery Compound was promising to "increase the appetite" and "brighten the eye," Pabst Malt Extract to give "vim and bounce." By 1913 an advertisement for the White Cross Electric Vibrator was telling readers of *The American Magazine* that "nine out of ten people are only *half alive. How about yourself? Vibration is life.* It will chase away the years like magic . . . you will realize thoroughly the joy of living. Your self-respect, even, will be increased a hundred-fold." Like abundance therapy, this newer approach offered unprecedented possibilities for rejuvenated life at full throttle.[54]

That promise spread beyond the realm of health products; it became diffused among other varieties of advertising, though it was often expressed more obliquely. In 1916, for example, Home Billiards became the "year-round sport that banishes brain-fag, aids digestion, and *puts new blood into folks who work all day!*" and Lucky Strike appended the following jingle to a familiar winter scene:

> A glassy pond—
> A red-cheeked maid—
> And, mingling with the frosty air
> The rich relish of Lucky Strike
> In sweet-crusted pipe
> Or fragrant cigarette
> That's the sport to make
> The red blood leap and tingle!

No other tobacco gives you that old tasty yum-yum out-of-doors smack you get from Lucky Strike.[55]

Women as well as men proved an inviting audience for offers of revitalization. In 1924, Ellen J. Buckland, a "graduate nurse" writing for Kotex in *Good Housekeeping* noted that "the modern woman lives every day of her life" thanks to improved feminine hygiene. Here again there was the implicit assumption that without scientifically sanctioned consumer goods one missed out on full life. The same year, Cantilever Shoes pictured a fagged-out mother in a wicker chair: "Tired and listless, she sinks back in a chair to envy little children at play, to wish for their energy, their easy activity. Not so long ago she, too, was joyously active. Her feet were young. And they can be again. At this time of year there is gladness in the air and renewed life for those happy folks whose feet are young." In a culture increasingly enamored of youth, the promise of rejuvenation touched women with particular force.[56]

Women played a critical role in the spread of older and newer therapeutic strategies. They led in forming the "helping professions" that promoted therapeutic ideals; they dominated the clientele of mind cure and the Emmanuel Movement. Advertising trade journals constantly emphasized the importance of reaching women, who (it was assumed) managed household purchasing, read advertisements avidly, and proved especially vulnerable to emotional appeals. *Good Housekeeping* reinforced these conventional assumptions by acclaiming "The New Shopping" as a science that would be pioneered by female consumers who had received instruction from advertisers and other professionals.[57]

There is no doubt that many women were victimized in new ways by the leaders of the consumer culture. As dominant values were revitalized and transformed through incorporation of the therapeutic ethos, the chief beneficiaries were the upper-class male executives who managed the developing corporate system. There was no male conspiracy. Rather, tendencies inherent in the therapeutic ethos helped to defuse demands for female equality. Feminist political claims were deflected into quests for psychic satisfaction through high-style consumption. The emphasis on self-realization through emotional fulfillment, the devaluation of public life in favor of a leisure world of intense private experience, the need to construct a pleasing "self" by purchasing consumer goods—these therapeutic imperatives helped to domesticate the drive toward female emancipation. With great fanfare, advertisers offered women the freedom to smoke Lucky Strikes or buy "natural" corsets. They promised fake liberation through consumption, and many women accepted this new version of male hegemony.[58]

But it is easy to exaggerate the sexual dimensions of hegemony. Men, too, were being eased into conformity with all levels of the corporate system. As frequently as women, they were the target of therapeutic appeals. And even the relatively comfortable could be victimized in subtle ways. Promising wholeness or rejuvenation, advertisers addressed those immersed in routine work *or* domestic drudgery; they held out the hope that life could be perpetually fulfilling; and they implied that one ought to strive for that fulfillment through consumption.

By 1930 the therapeutic ethos was far more pervasive and intense than it had been in the 1880s. The older prudential style had spread; the newer abundance orientation had taken hold and had been applied even to products having little to do with health. The clearest illustration of this change appeared in automobile advertising. Pre–World War I advertisements were nearly all based on the straightforward presentation of technical details. By the twenties they were virtually devoid of information; instead they promised style, status, or escape to an exotic "real life" far from the reader's ordinary experience. The earlier ads assumed a knowledgeable, rational audience; the later ones offered therapeutic fulfillment of nonrational longings.[59]

It would be a mistake to read the changes in advertising as a direct indication of value changes in the advertisers' audience. Like the proliferating therapies, changes in advertising represented a shift in official norms and expectations, not a ground swell of popular sentiment. Unlike therapies, moreover, advertisements did not always contain direct prescriptions for behavior. And the advertisers' audience was neither as passive nor as gullible as critics sometimes assumed. Ever since the days of P. T. Barnum, at least a few advertisers had called attention to their own humbug for its entertainment value; exaggerated claims and publicity stunts were part of the confidence game pervading market society. As the historian Neil Harris has observed, Barnum's audiences expected humbug and admired his skill at it. There was a kind of inside joke between the humbug and the suckers. Twentieth-century advertising institutionalized this joke by mass-producing a fantasy world of wish fulfillment. No doubt many ordinary Americans refused to embrace this world literally, but they were drawn into it for its entertainment value—the sensual appeal of its illustrations, the seductiveness of basking (however briefly) in the promise of self-realization through consumption. Many advertisements took their place alongside other mass diversions—the amusement park, the slick-paper romance, the movies. None demanded to be taken literally or even all that seriously; yet all promised intense "real life" to their clientele, and all implicitly defined "real life" as something outside the individual's everyday experience.[60]

A web of connections joined national advertising, the therapeutic ethos, and the new forms of mass entertainment. One can see those connections, for example, in the cult of youthful vitality surrounding stars like Mary Pickford and Douglas Fairbanks, and in the star system itself. As the historian Lary May observes, "A star—unlike the nineteenth century character actor—was a young person who experimented with a number of roles, identities, and styles."[61] He was other-directed, creating and recreating a series of personalities according to the expectations of his producer and his audience. Further, movies and advertisements alike engaged in a therapeutic renovation of sensuality—cleansing sex of Victorian associations with poverty, disease, and dirt; locating eroticism in settings characterized by affluence, respectability, and, above all, health. Cecil B. De Mille's famous bath scenes closely paralleled advertisements for toiletries and bathroom fixtures: All presented half-nude females in scenes of cleanliness and opulence; all sanitized sex by associating it with health and high-level consumption.[62]

The clearest example of these connections was the career of Douglas Fairbanks—"Mr. Electricity," a tyro of abundant energy who was one of the first film stars to endorse products for pay. Therapeutic ideals, advertising, and mass amusement merged in Fairbanks's popular film *His Picture in the Papers* (1916). Fairbanks plays a young man who works in his father's office. The father is a dour vegetarian and temperance man; the son outwardly conforms to the paternal code but conceals a martini mix in his lunch bag. Rebelling against enervated refinement, the son learns to box, becomes attractive to several New Women, and ultimately acquires enough pep to rescue a big businessman from criminals. When reporters ask the secret of his strength, the young man answers "Pringle Products"—the cereal his father's company makes. Pringle Products sell merrily, now advertised as the creators of robust fun-lovers rather than boring vegetarians.[63] *His Picture in the Papers* typified the cultural packaging of Fairbanks. The film, like Fairbanks's whole career, suggested that in the new social world of the corporate system, the middle- or lower-level manager could tolerate dull work and bureaucratic paternalism, provided he had the chance to pursue intense experience in his leisure time. A quest for self-realization through consumption compensated for a loss of autonomy on the job. Therapeutic ideals converged with advertising and mass amusement to promote new forms of cultural hegemony.

Yet the human agents of that process often had other ends in view. Certainly many advertising executives would have been horrified to think of themselves as manipulators or mass entertainers; they remained committed to truth and convinced they were providing a public service. In part this was the self-serving myopia of the powerful. I do not mean to suggest that all advertising men were complex and troubled: Many were surely stupid and self-deceiving. Claude Hopkins's autobiography, for example, is a tale told by an egotist, full of heroic triumphs won through sheer force of will, signifying its author's moral obtuseness.[64] But some of even the most forward-looking executives were not merely confused; they were also troubled by nostalgia and doubt.

This complexity marked the career of Bruce Barton. His work is worth close examination because it illustrates nearly all my major arguments: that the therapeutic ethos often stemmed from personal quests for selfhood in an ambiguous moral universe; that therapeutic ideals linked diverse components of the new consumer culture; that the transformation of cultural hegemony was shaped by half-conscious psychic needs as well as by conscious class interests; and that even the most enthusiastic apostles of change could be troubled by persistent doubt. As a young man, Bruce Barton grew discontented with the "weightless" Christianity he had been offered in Sunday school. Since Barton's father was a liberal Congregational minister, the problem was intensely personal. Eager to please his father yet determined to establish a solid sense of independent selfhood, Barton sought to revitalize his religious faith by suffusing it with therapeutic ideals of "personal growth" and "abundant life." Most important for my purposes, those ideals tied together the many strands of his career. Barton was an influential popularizer of a therapeutic version of Christianity, a founder of a major advertising firm, and a phenomenally successful slick-paper journalist—an early expert at concocting the blend of titillation and uplift that constituted mass entertainment in the twentieth century. Animated by therapeutic ideals, Barton's work entwined and expressed the major preoccupations of the emerging consumer culture. Yet it also embodied fitful protest against that culture. Sometimes clinging to older bourgeois values, sometimes doubting the worth of his own vocation, Barton yearned for transcendent meaning even as his profession corroded it. His personal turmoil has a broader historical significance: It illuminates the moral and psychological conflicts at the heart of our consumer culture.

THERAPY, ADVERTISING, AND DOUBT: BRUCE BARTON

Barton was born in 1886, the first child of Esther Bushnell and William Eleazar Barton. His father soon became an eminent Congregational pastor in Oak Park, Illinois, as well as a popular biographer of Lincoln. In 1907, during his senior year at Amherst, Barton won a fellowship to study history at the University of Wisconsin. A restless, driven student, he had finished undergraduate work in three and a half years and had been selected to Phi Beta Kappa. But soon after graduation Barton's psychic and physical health collapsed; he gave up the fellowship and went to a railroad camp in Montana for revitalization through physical labor. After six months he left Montana to travel aimlessly. The whole postgraduate period of drift, Barton recalled, caused "great distress, both to myself and to my parents." He performed well enough in business but had no interest in it; he gave up attractive job offers "merely because I was tired and had no ambition." Finally he sought success in journalism but floundered; several magazines failed under his editorship. Then in 1913 his laudatory article on the evangelist Billy Sunday in *Collier's* caught the eye of John Siddall, editor of *The American Magazine*, who hired Barton as a major contributor. The following year Barton took over the editorship of *Every Week*, a syndicated Sunday supplement that typified the new mass-market journalism. In 1919 Barton turned to more lucrative pursuits. He and Roy S. Durstine founded the advertising agency that by the 1920s had become the fourth largest in the United States—Batten, Barton, Durstine, and Osborne. Yet Barton continued to pour out magazine articles and inspirational books, including *The Man Nobody Knows* (1925), an extraordinarily successful best-seller that presented Jesus as "the founder of modern business."[65]

Historians have usually dismissed Barton as an archetype of business vulgarity in the 1920s, but his writings even at their crudest are historically significant. They reveal the importance of therapeutic ideals in fusing a cohesive consumer culture. Melding therapeutic religiosity with an ideology of consumption, Barton retailored Protestant Christianity to fit the sleek new corporate system. Rejecting the "weightlessness" of liberal Protestant sentimentality, yearning for a more vigorous and manly religion, Barton produced a creed even more vacuous than its predecessor.[66]

In his earliest articles for the Chicago *Home Herald*, a nondenominational religious magazine, Barton began to merge religion with therapy and corporate business. His "Peers of the Pulpit" series (1908) celebrated eminent divines for their success in building up church membership through modern business methods, including advertising. One of these ministers was the Reverend A. C. Dixon, pastor of the church founded by Dwight L. Moody in Chicago, who sent men into the streets with "floats" advertising his lunch-hour meetings at the Great Northern Theater. He also wrote a weekly newspaper column where, in Dixon's words, "I put the gospel white hot before a million readers." Advertising, spectacle, and self-promotion were already being widely adopted by urban Protestants, and Barton applauded them for it. He also lauded ministers who belied their profession's weak-sister image. Billy Sunday, above all, seemed to Barton to embody energy and virility. Focusing on Sunday and others, Barton began to create a cult of ministerial personality rooted in nineteenth-century antecedents but well suited to a new and therapeutic version of Christianity.[67]

By his late twenties, Barton had found his voice as a therapeutic ideologue. Like Hall and Fosdick, he exalted Jesus as a healthy personality. *A Young Man's Jesus* (1914) presented Jesus as "a young man glowing with physical strength and the joy of living" who had "our bounding pulses, our hot desires," not to mention "perfect teeth." And this Jesus would enthusiastically attend the spectacles of the consumer culture. "If there were a world's championship series in town, we might look for Him there," Barton wrote. This refashioning of Jesus was only part of Barton's promotion of the therapeutic ethos. His *Every Week* editorials frequently stressed the importance of health in attaining "maximum efficiency" and told young men how "to grow instead of stagnate." His book titles suggested the willed optimism of the search for self-realization: *More Power to You* (1917), *It's a Good Old World* (1920), *On the Up and Up* (1929).[68]

During the 1920s, Barton slipped his promotional activities into high gear. Besides *The Man Nobody Knows*, he published *The Book*

Nobody Knows (1926) and *What Can a Man Believe?* (1927), two other books that also sought to trim faith down to fit the business creed. In the *American Magazine*, Barton interviewed other leading therapeutic ideologues. G. Stanley Hall told him "How You Can Do More and Be More." Harry Emerson Fosdick recommended the belief in immortality as a tonic, "lifting us at moments of crisis out of lassitude and onto a wave of great deeds." Fosdick also epitomized Barton's cult of ministerial personality. Vigorous, muscular, "Dr. Fosdick is 44 years old and looks as if he spent every morning in a gym," Barton marveled. Elsewhere, Barton warned against "the petty thoughts that fritter away power," urged faith as a cure for depression, and presented Jesus as a psychotherapist. In Palestine two thousand years ago, Barton told *Good Housekeeping* readers in 1928, "Whoever was mentally unbalanced, whoever had suffered a nervous breakdown, was said to have a devil. The devils which Jesus expelled from sick folk were the devils of shattered nerves and divided minds, what we term 'complexes.' " And, Barton implied, he can do the same for you. Like many of his contemporaries, both within and without the churches, Barton reduced Christianity to a therapeutic agent.[69]

During the same period, Barton linked therapeutic ideals of "enjoyment" and "growth" to the brave new consumer culture. Having interviewed Henry Ford for *The American Magazine*, Barton hailed the installment plan and the five-dollar day as signs that a repressive era was ending. Calling for training in "creative leisure," Barton rejected "the old fashioned notion that the chief end in life is a steadily growing savings account, and that one must eliminate all pleasures from his vigorous years in order to prepare for possible want in old age." He insisted that "life is meant to live and enjoy as you go along. . . . If self-denial is necessary I'll practice some of it when I'm old and not try to do all of it now. For who knows? I may never be old."[70] The unwillingness to postpone gratification became a hallmark of the dominant culture under corporate capitalism.

Barton, like other prophets of consumption, tied this multiplication of wants to a larger scheme of progress. Victorian moralists had long linked work and progress, had long assumed that civilizations (like individuals) must not stand still. But Barton's scheme was slightly different: One worked in order to satisfy wants for consumer goods, not because one had to survive or because one was committed to Victorian notions of character. In fact, Barton often seemed to dismiss character formation in favor of personal magnetism and social poise. Success, he said, is "eighty-five percent . . . personality." In 1922 he told *American Magazine* readers "What to Do If You Want to Sit at the Boss's Desk": Learn to express yourself clearly, put yourself in the boss's place, know his petty likes and dislikes, and shape your own habits and preferences accordingly—down to and including the choice of a necktie. Barton's views on success often seemed tailor-made for the other-directed world of the corporate bureaucracy. And if individuals required a pleasing "image," so did corporations. Echoing Bernays and other public relations consultants, Barton said in 1929 that the greatest question facing business was "How are great aggregates of capital going to make themselves not merely tolerated but actually liked?" Therapeutic ideals of personality and popularity were assimilated to corporate needs.[71]

Barton's advertising copy assisted that assimilation. Though he was preoccupied with managerial decisions and his own journalism, the advertisements he did write reflected the wider diffusion of therapeutic strategies. He specialized in snappy slogans, such as "A man may be down but he's never out" for the Salvation Army, but he also wrote institutional advertisements, such as the one for Bankers' Trust Company (1928) which emphasized the "radiant personality" of the bank's president, Henry Davison. Advertising the Oakland Motor Car in 1928, Barton resisted the manufacturer's plea for a technical description, dimissing it as a "product job" and urging instead an emphasis on style and "popular favor." In short, Barton's approach to copy was closely attuned to the transformation affecting the advertising profession at large.[72]

The Man Nobody Knows contained the clearest evidence of Barton's importance as a cultural weather vane. While the Y.M.C.A. and other liberal Protestant groups had long been urging Barton to republish *A Young Man's Jesus*, Barton's *The Man Nobody Knows* was more than a restatement of his earlier book. The new book joined advertising ideology to therapeutic ideals of abundant vitality and intense experience, suffusing the whole with an atmosphere of religiosity. Barton's Jesus personified personal magnetism and outdoor living. He was no weak-kneed Lamb of God; "no flabby priest or money changer cared to try conclusions with that arm." His personality was not fragmented or divided against itself; all responded to his "consuming sincerity" and "the steel-like hardness of his nerves." Women adored him. The most popular dinner guest in Jerusalem, this vibrant Jesus was also the most successful advertising man in history—a master self-promoter who created "big stories" by healing the sick and provoking controversy. His parables were models of advertising copy—simple, condensed, repetitive, sincere. Indeed, "sincerity glistened like sunshine through every sentence he uttered." Far from denying life, his creed enhanced it. "He did not come to establish a theology but to lead a life," Barton wrote. "Living more healthfully than any of his contemporaries, he spread health wherever he went." He offered righteousness as the path to "a happier, more satisfying way of living."[73]

This was not merely a businessman's Jesus, but a Jesus fashioned to meet widespread longings for "more abundant life" and a revitalized sense of selfhood. It comes as no surprise that *The Man Nobody Knows* was soon made into a motion picture, or that Cecil B. De Mille hired Barton as a consultant on *King of Kings* (1926), Hollywood's first Biblical spectacular. Barton's version of Jesus was a perfect emblem of the "real life" peddled by therapeutic ideologues, advertising men, and the makers of mass entertainment.[74]

For all that, Barton was neither a cynical huckster nor a one-dimensional man. Eager to believe in his own optimistic vision, he was nevertheless troubled by it. His writing often reflected the nostalgia implicit in the therapeutic ethos. Celebrating economic development and personal growth, he worried about their impact on stable communities and secure identities. Complaining about the pace of life in New York, he noted the anxious faces on Wall Street and observed in irritation that "before a building has acquired the decent drabness of age it is torn out by the roots and a gay new structure leaps to the sky." He yearned fitfully for the rural and the natural. As early as 1908, having just returned from his regenerative stint in Montana, he asserted that "the open life of the country still gives men better opportunities to live *natural* lives, which means *better* lives." Throughout his young manhood, Barton remained nervous, driven, and plagued by a worsening insomnia that finally drove him to a sanatorium for a brief period in 1928. An earlier generation might have called him "neurasthenic." Office work and modern life in general often seemed "artificial" to him; "true producers" remained on the land. Despite Barton's zeal for a therapeutic consumer culture, he sustained deep commitment to an imagined simpler past.[75]

There was more involved here than nostalgia. Barton was genuinely divided between consumer and producer values. In one breath he praised personality and teamwork as agents of success; in the next, character and individual initiative. His son could have any job he wanted, Barton said, as long as he had to start at the bottom so he could learn to scuffle and hustle. Even as Barton extolled the merits of the corporate system, he complained in 1922 that young WASP males of his own class no longer had "*the courage to dive off the dock*" into individual enterprise.

This courage used to be pretty common in America. . . . But what are the descendants of the Yankee traders doing now? They're wearing white collars and saying "Yes, sir" and "No, sir," and "Right away, sir" to the sons of men who came over in the steerage, or off the farms, and built businesses of their own out of nothing but nerve.[76]

This was a new concern, rooted in old republican fears of elite decay. In fact, Barton fretted like any republican about the effects of prosperity on moral fiber. "It is the men who 'stand like a beaten anvil' who have done the great things," Barton wrote in 1926. "But men can't stand like beaten anvils if they're made of French pastry, or are wrapped up always in the gentle softness of prosperity."[77] Apologist for a new economy of abundance, leisure, and high-level consumption, Barton was also at times its bitter critic.

In part, this inner conflict stemmed from Barton's own search for an identity that measured up to his father's. The father-son tension mirrored a broader clash of values: between the older Protestant supernaturalism and the newer therapeutic ethos, between producer and consumer cultures. Bruce Barton remained suspended between two worlds. Troubled by his inability to enter "his father's business" of preaching, Barton may also have sensed at times that his therapeutic ideals were hollow even by comparison to liberal Christianity. As a boy, young Bruce had worshiped his father and had dreamed of someday sharing a pulpit with him. But during his senior year at Amherst, Bruce turned away from the ministry—not, he claimed, because he had lost his faith or because the financial rewards were inadequate. "Rather, the thought of the ministry began to lose its appeal as I came to know myself, to realize that never under any possible conditions could I be as successful in it as my father had been." Now, Barton wrote in 1914, "I try to convince myself that I am doing as important a thing in my business as he did in his. . . . But . . . I fall somehow short of being assured." Even after he had scaled the heights of power and popularity, Barton may have felt himself a Barnum, a bit of a humbug in his father's long shadow.[78]

The problem was not that William E. Barton was a stern patriarch. Far from it: His liberal Protestantism anticipated and paved the way for his son's banalities. "I am prepared to expect that men will interpret Christ in the phraseology of another and later age," the elder Barton told his congregation in 1898. He collapsed nature and the supernatural, exalted electric lights and radios as evidence of Providential design in the universe, and celebrated Jesus for creating a religion of "more abundant life." As he grew older, William Barton grew more liberal theologically, embraced the Chamber of Commerce mentality of his suburban flock, and collaborated sympathetically in the planning, research, and writing of his son's books.[79]

If anything, the father was too helpful. By all accounts Bruce adored his father and wanted to please him, but continuing dependence on the father may have generated a quiet desperation in the son. Particularly in his two books on Jesus, Bruce Barton seemed determined to throw off the burden of a religious past that was associated with his father. "It is time," he wrote in A Young Man's Jesus, "for those of us who are this side of thirty-five to unite and take back our Jesus." It was

35

a conflict of generations, a question of youth versus age. The introduction to *The Man Nobody Knows* was an acerbic attack on the sickly-sweet image of Christ that Barton had been presented throughout his youth. One can assume that his clergyman father played a role in that presentation. Barton's critique of mainstream Christianity may have been in part a veiled and oblique outburst against paternal authority.[80]

Yet any hints of hostility were overshadowed by Barton's admiration for his father. Always an outwardly dutiful son, Bruce Barton even dedicated *A Young Man's Jesus* to his father, "a young man's preacher." Revering an idealized image of paternal authority, the son remained half convinced that he could never meet the ministerial standard. Doubting the worth of his own vocation, he tried to endow it with religious significance. Even more than success mythologists before him, Barton strained to find a religious vocabulary for business success. "Should an Industry have a Soul?" he asked. Yes! and businessmen should have faith—in the United States, in the business system, and above all in themselves. It was no accident, Barton claimed, that *credit*, the basis of modern business, was derived from *credo:* I believe.[81]

Even Barton's most ringing declarations of independence revealed his continuing insecurity about the identity he had chosen. Far from debasing Jesus into a businessman, Barton sought to transform businessmen into ministers of Christ. It was nonsense, he claimed, to distinguish between "work and *religious* work." Echoing traditional Protestant ideas, Barton was certain Jesus knew that "all business is his father's business. All work is worship. All useful service prayer." And most important, Jesus established Barton's own particular brand of service—advertising. The most dynamic young men on Madison Avenue were writing modern versions of Jesus's parables, Barton suggested, with the same high purpose. The most effective advertisements were "written by men who have an abiding respect for the intelligence of their readers, and a deep sincerity regarding the merits of the goods they have to sell.[82]

Barton protested too much. Insistently equating business with transcendent "service," he eased his personal transition from salvation to self-realization by denying that it had occurred. The new corporate system was not secular but divine; that was Barton's message. But the stridency with which he repeated it betrayed his continuing self-doubt, and the enthusiasm with which his audiences received it suggested that they shared his need for self-assurance. Given Barton's enormous popularity, it seems fair to say that his writings articulated widespread longings. In the Barton collection at the University of Wisconsin there are hundreds of letters responding warmly to his writings. Most are typed on business letterheads; but some are crudely handwritten, in pencil, on torn notepaper, from secretaries, stock boys, and barely literate marginal men. Whatever their source, their main message was gratitude—for recognizing the spiritual nature of business enterprise, for making Jesus seem human and "real," for giving hope in times of despair. Neither Barton nor his audience could remain at ease in the emerging consumer culture. Implicitly acknowledging that the older Protestant supernaturalism seemed bankrupt, they still longed for transcendent meaning and purpose in a secularizing society. For many, the only available ideals were therapeutic; and Bruce Barton supplied them. Spiritualizing the corporate system, he provided a theology for a secular age.[83]

In his later years, Barton wrote fewer articles and books, turning his attention to politics. He was elected to Congress from Manhattan's "silk-stocking district" in 1938; for a time he was considered a vice-presidential or even presidential possibility. Until his death in 1967, he kept a hand in at the B.B.D. & O. office, devising (for example) a therapeutic appeal that urged nervous Americans to "un-tense" with Lucky Strikes. In 1948–49, lighting Luckies at tense moments became "the way to keep younger and get some fun out of life." And in 1952 his advertising agency handled the packaging of Dwight D. Eisenhower. But during this later period Barton retreated into private life. His chief cultural importance lies in his early career as success mythologist, advertising executive, and therapeutic ideologue.[84]

Bruce Barton's early career suggests some larger speculations about the changing dominant culture in the early twentieth century. His enthusiasm for a therapeutic culture of consumption arose not only from his class interests but also from his half-conscious effort to realize a secure and independent sense of selfhood. The effort was never unambiguously successful; the enthusiasm was always clouded by uncertainty. Barton's career suggests that the convergence of national advertising and therapeutic ideals strongly reinforced the spreading culture of consumption; but it also suggests that the process was generated by unfocused anxieties as well as deliberate strategies.

The therapeutic ethos, which united so many facets of the consumer culture, originated in the thickets of the troubled self. Private needs had unintended public consequences. Advertising executives played a central role in promoting the consumer culture, but they sometimes resisted and often only unwittingly reinforced the changes that were under way. Raymond Williams, referring to contemporary Britain, has put the matter well: "The skilled magicians, the masters of the masses, must be seen as ultimately involved in the general weakness which they not only exploit but are exploited by. . . . Advertising is then no longer merely a way of selling goods, it is a true part of the culture of a confused society."[85] My evidence suggests that by the early twentieth century this was already the case in America; and that by the 1920s there was a larger Lost Generation, whose members haunted luncheon club and bedroom suburb as well as bistro and atelier.

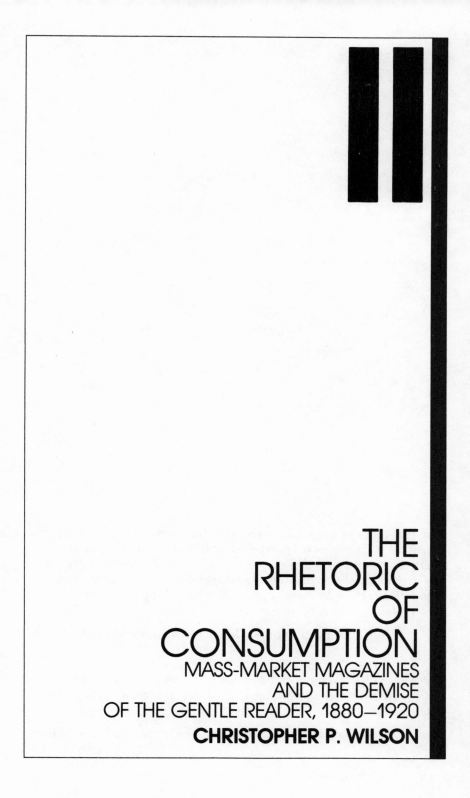

THE
RHETORIC
OF
CONSUMPTION
MASS-MARKET MAGAZINES
AND THE DEMISE
OF THE GENTLE READER, 1880–1920
CHRISTOPHER P. WILSON

Th' first thing ye know there won't be as many pages iv advertisin' as there are iv lithrachoor. Then people will stop readin' magazines. A man don't want to dodge around through almost impenethrable pomes an' reform articles to find a pair iv suspenders or a shavin' soap. Another thing, th' magazines ought to be compelled to mark all lithrachoor plainly so that th' reader can't be deceived.

       —Finley Peter Dunne, "Mr. Dooley on the Magazines" (1909)

Page with all his respect for literature . . . is disposed to look upon it chiefly for what it accomplishes and will see in the magazine an instrument rather than a vehicle.

       —Diary entry of Horace Scudder, editor, *Atlantic Monthly*,
          (August 18, 1896)

For Victorian Americans of the upper and middle classes, the activity of reading served as a haven of revered cultural values: tradition, restraint, cultivation. It was the archetypically private endeavor in an era when the public realm struck many as impersonal, chaotic, even debilitating. Spiral staircases, formal dining rooms, back entrances—all testified to the prescribed and intricate rituals of daily life; reading parlors and personal libraries, by contrast, were regarded as sanctuaries. As Burton Bledstein writes, the entire experience of reading was, by consensus, internal and contemplative. "Detached from any face-to-face confrontation, apart from any mass audience, oblivious to any restriction of time, the individual alone could read and reread the written work in the privacy of any room. . . . Isolated, the reader required no intermediary as interpreter, no set stage, no responsive listener."[1]

And yet, around the turn of the century, a few commentators detected the beginnings of a transformation in the reading process itself. In a 1900 issue of *The Atlantic*, for example, the one-time minister of Boston's Unitarian First Church, Samuel McChord Crothers, decried an impending demise in the traditionally conceived "gentle reader." In place of gentility, Crothers described a new reading style ascending to cultural supremacy. He noted the disappearance of literary conventions like the dedication and the narrative intrusion in favor of more realistic effects in fiction; he pointed to the passage of admitted prejudice and opinion, displaced by the era's obsession with news, information, and objectivity. He argued, furthermore, that contrary to the supposed personal touch provided by a new "frankness" in print, reading had actually lost some of its intimacy: Printed texts, he said, no longer offered the active yet gentlemanly exchange between reader and author. "I sometimes fear," he wrote, "that reading, in the old-fashioned sense, may become a lost art." Similarly, critic Gerald Stanley Lee described current literature in *The Lost Art of Reading* (1902) as a "headlong, helpless literary rush" which subdivided and fragmented modern readers into mere paragraph skimmers. *Harper's* editor Henry Mills Alden, actively resisting the era's trend toward "timely" articles, said magazines no longer adhered to the liberal arts spirit, but had embraced the specialization of the modern university. Bliss Perry, editor of *The Atlantic*, said "cheerful" magazine reading—which he compared to polite attention to after-dinner speeches—was fast becoming a thing of the past.[2]

In hearkening back to the ideal of companionate readership, these writers alluded to a literary convention with a long history. Its origins went as far back as the classical author's traditional invocation of the Muse or patron—guiding spirits bourgeois society had transformed into the sympathetic soul of the gentle reader. The notion of a reciprocal reading contract had achieved its most sophisticated expression in the eighteenth-century British novel. Authors like Fielding, Richardson, and Sterne had consciously allowed contemplative "space," and even "resting places" in their narratives, so that the reader could pause, reconsider, and even collaborate in the meaning of the text. Reflecting roots in letter writing, these novels worked in active yet restrained dialogue between writer and reader; the latter was not bowled over with details—with "realism"—which reduced his interpretive input.[3] In America this conception had been resuscitated primarily in the "family house" journals—*Harper's, Scribner's, The Atlantic, The Century*— where the "gentle reader," ostensibly sharing an "implicit understanding" with her editor, symbolized the guiding spirit of Victorianism itself.[4] Fears about her impending demise were a serious matter.

Of course, the turn-of-the-century decades witnessed a whole series of shock waves to the hallowed concept of gentle reading: the sensationalism of the metropolitan tabloid, the frenzy of the "best-seller" system in book publishing, the proliferation of commercial images and slogans, the rise of mass entertainments. Yet the medium most often singled out as responsible for reshaping reading was the "cheap" magazine, which rose to cultural prominence after 1885. The choice was practically unavoidable. During the span of the Progressive era, topical magazines achieved a centrality in American life never duplicated before or since. They were the original home of large-scale national advertising and market research; the primary popular medium within which the "helping professions" and other experts first reached a mass audience; the principal exponents of the ostensibly nonpartisan, "independent" political style promoted by the muckrakers; and, in general, supporters of the "realistic" trend in American letters. Topical magazines were a crucible of modern consumer culture. The furor over the "gentle reader" suggests that this strategic role involved more than the magazines' diffusion of new products, values, and ideas; it also depended on their zeal for the transformation of the reading process itself. They sought to acclimate readers to a new social environment, to "naturalize" that environment by managing the reading experience.[5] By focusing on the reading process I do not mean to discount other factors that contributed to the rise of the magazines: advertising revenues, favorable postage legislation, technological innovations in printing and papermaking, and the broader communications revolution.[6] These developments help account for the potential scope and terrain of the new periodicals. But historians have not yet gone beyond describing those admittedly vital trends to consider the innovations in style, format, and reader participation that contributed directly to the genesis of consumer culture.

This essay will try to illuminate that strategic role by examining the magazines from three vantage points: first, their roots in the personal backgrounds of a new managerial elite in magazine editing; second, the institution by that elite of a new "anticipatory" design in magazine production; finally, the implementation of this design in four pathbreaking magazines—*McClure's*, *The World's Work*, the *Saturday Evening Post*, and the *Ladies' Home Journal*.[7] My thesis is that the change in the reading process derived essentially, although not exclusively, from a "consumerist" reorientation implemented by a group of men well versed in the verbal, communicative, and organizational skills of a sales economy; that these skills changed magazines not only at the level of production, but in the very "voice" they conveyed; and finally, that these editors' penchant for "anticipatory" production resulted in design strategies and narrative devices that attempted to streamline and manage the reading process itself. In each magazine editors orchestrated a mode of "realism"—in different variations of authority, factuality, intimacy, and common sense—which created an aura of legitimacy around their offerings.[8] Under the banner of this "realism," the magazine became a primary American institution by which a consumer rhetoric, confined originally to the service or sales economy, penetrated other spheres of American life—politics, contemporary affairs, even family life.

I choose the word "rhetoric" rather than "ideology" or "structure of feeling" because I am primarily intent upon describing a mode of language (in its broadest sense), a way of discussing and seeing that embraces diction, tone of voice, and narrative design. Furthermore, my analysis is necessarily tethered to the editorial end of the communication process, and to an "immanent" critique of editors' goals and magazine formats. No analysis can entirely reconstruct the reading experience of Americans eight decades after the fact. We cannot account fully for readers' prior expectations or competing environments; nor can we assume that readers adopted editorial wisdom uncritically. But attention to the origins and intentions of the new magazines can begin to "flesh out" the particular historical relationship between ascending managerial elites and the shape and texture of consumer culture in one of its pivotal institutions.[9] By exploring the naturalizing process, we can begin to understand some of the contradictions of that emergent culture: how, in the magazines, the passivity of political spectatorship came to seem like active citizenship; how the hierarchies and power gaps of modern corporate life came to seem like a classless country town; how efficient buying became the chief calling of domestic responsibility.

The managerial incursion into editing had significant consequences for the production, voice, and format of modern magazines. But it is not my intent to portray the outcome of the naturalizing quest

43

as an unqualified success. Mushrooming circulations may have been attributable not only to the magazines' new agenda, but also to the way they fed upon the passivity, anxiety, and dependence for which they themselves were partly responsible. The new "pitch" cannot be taken at face value. The reader was coaxed to exchange idle fancy for a vigorous embrace of "real life"; to forgo his affection for the past in favor of staying informed on current events; to sacrifice his private thoughts and cooperate in a new program of "frank" exchanges with editors. Yet in many instances the magazines' version of real life bore little or no relation to the readers' own; their professed objectivity was often only a carefully managed credibility; their intimate confidences, at times, a patronizing facade. The "realism" the magazines offered was a particularly spurious variety—a world of illusory power and participation that masked delimited options and prefabricated responses. Such misleading packaging was unavoidable in a "naturalizing" that was founded in a rhetoric of illusion.

II

Although the leaps and bounds of magazine circulation during these years are now commonplace items in textbook histories, to date we still know very little about the new magazine audiences. Gilded Age journals carefully guarded their subscription figures and lists; Progressive era periodicals exaggerated theirs. The sparse data that do exist come mostly from the pioneering forays into market research done by Curtis Publishing, the firm responsible for the *Saturday Evening Post* and *Ladies' Home Journal*.[10] Existing fragments suggest that the new magazines continued to reach for the northeastern elites that had been the mainstay of Gilded Age audiences; they also targeted families of slightly lower income levels. The magazines remained firmly rooted in the middle class. Much of their circulation growth seems to have come from new regional elites, largely in cities with populations over 10,000. When the Lynds surveyed Muncie, Indiana, in 1924, aggregate circulation for the *Post* and the *Journal* was roughly sixty times that of older magazines like *Harper's* and *The Century*.[11]

In part, the newer magazines may have spoken to a Middletown audience because they were themselves the product of "outsiders" to the northeastern literary elite that had dominated periodical publishing for decades. With a few notable exceptions, since the Civil War the world of magazine editing had been centered in the established gentry of Boston and New York. The profession retained residual elements of amateurism and patronage, and though remunerative enough, echoed the temper of a gentleman's voluntary association. Editors adhered to an Arnoldian view of their craft—to offer culture as an alternative to anarchy. But after the mid-1880s, the editing profession seemed to follow a pattern established earlier in metropolitan journalism, and repeated later in the film industry: a period of relative accessibility to recent immigrants and outsiders, if still principally male, white, and Northern European. Edward Bok and S. S. McClure, for example, were first-generation immigrants (Dutch and Irish respectively); Walter Hines Page of *The World's Work* was a Southerner; George Horace Lorimer of the *Post* was a Midwesterner, and second-generation Scotch-Irish.[12] As with the immigrant entrepreneurs of nickelodeon houses, amusement halls, and filmmaking, the outsider status seemed particularly adaptable to cultural media that were intrinsically vicarious and voyeuristic in design—that worked, in short, in the mode of emulation. The new magazines typically reflected the viewpoint of men "outside looking in" on power and status—in gossip columns, in celebrity profiles, even in muckraking. The outsider status also contributed to the new editors' paradoxical mixture of rebellion and accommodation vis-à-vis bourgeois values. On the one hand, the critical distance of these new figures from Brahmin culture was reflected in their impatience with the ideal of "cultivation" and the "feminization" of literary taste. On the other hand, the fact that these new men were outsiders to literary culture also meant that their initial training had come more directly than their predecessors' from the commercial mainstream. The new editors felt greater affinities for the "masses," for realms beyond Boston and New York, for more mundane, nonintellectual activities— and for business itself. They rehabilitated genteel culture by infusing it with managerial skills and work values.

During the Gilded Age, when periodicals had been based mainly on subscription income rather than advertising revenue, and primarily directed at northeastern, well-to-do family circles, editing had been thought of as a task of mutual cooperation and cultivation among editors, contributors, and audiences. The working model was the professional-client relationship. Often writers of imaginative literature, editors thought of themselves mainly as literary men, whose job it was to sift, scrutinize, and select literary manuscripts, always watching over established boundaries of taste and propriety. To this paternalism most of the ills of these older magazines—prudishness, eccentricity, elitism —can be traced. But even the well-deserved notoriety of Gilder et al. for censoring manuscripts tells us much about their editorial role: It reveals that *editing*, in the literal sense, is what these men thought their job to be.[13]

This ideal of editing was based in an office system of relatively undifferentiated assignments or tasks, contributions that arrived unsolicited, and a pace set by the demands of careful reading. In cramped offices cherished for their distance from the "bustle" of downtown, with limited staffs and modest revenue, there was little room, opportunity, or desire for the internal division of labor. Editorial roles at *Scribner's* and *The Century*, for instance, were deliberately overlapped or left undefined so as to avoid specialization and needless hierarchy. Even forty years after the fact, L. Frank Tooker, who made a career at *The Century*, recalled his initial surprise in finding tasks shared on a random basis rather than having been parceled out in any systematic fashion. Both the moderate pace and shared tasks reflected, as well, the system of voluntary submissions rather than commissioned articles. Articles were not "drummed up" in elaborately planned promotional schemes with specific time lines; they came in irregularly. In fact, older editors had taken pride in the fact that they did not solicit content—in effect, that writers came to them. Editors generally hesitated about contracting for pieces yet unwritten, for fear that the final product might violate standard canons of taste and prudery. Horace Scudder of *The Atlantic* boasted about never having invited a submission; Robert Underwood Johnson of *The Century* compared commissioning to putting one's head in a noose.[14]

The editorial voice, in turn, reflected this relatively passive notion of editing. During these years, what Bliss Perry and others called the "tolerably short," carefully phrased, virtually anonymous editorial manner reflected a professional conception of editing that valued its restraint, its very avoidance of salesmanlike "pep." Looking for a word to describe this tone, Johnson chose "genuine." There was, he said, no "straining after effect," no "simulated robustness," none of the cocksureness of "made to pattern" writing; the primary mood was one of "grace and serenity." Writers commonly adhered to the older convention of leaving articles unsigned; regular columns were penned from the "Editor's Study" or the "Editor's Easy Chair." Recalling the analogy Perry made about the ideal reading mood, partisans and satirists alike termed the Gilded Age style a "toastmaster" voice or "the rule of the dinner table." These conventions seemed anachronistic and inefficient to the new editor-publishers. In a few decades they transformed the profession into what David Riesman terms an "other-directed," aggressive practice, marked by transatlantic searches for authors and ideas, office rationalization, and a change in the editorial voice. As *The Independent* observed, "The modern editor does not sit in his easy chair, writing essays and sorting over the manuscripts that are sent in by contributors. He goes hunting for things." Abandoning the genteel "we," McClure intoned: "I never got ideas sitting still."[15]

The biographical profiles of the new editors reveal some important common denominators. All of these men looked fondly back upon training in practical fields that emphasized communicative, managerial, and interpersonal skills. For instance, many of them—Bok, Lorimer, Page, and most of McClure's staff—had apprenticed in daily journalism. The new editors clearly imported to magazines an orientation toward the "news" commodity, which displaced literary content in favor of "timely," topical items of practical affairs; editors also transplanted office efficiency techniques, particularly the new "assignment system." Newspapers also provided models of format by which the reader's eye was attracted and held by headlines, subheads, and photographs. Journalism experience also bred a liking for brief, almost blunt colloquial prose.[16] The principal beneficiary of this training was Page, who liked to tell writers that the creation of the world had been told in a single paragraph; one of his subordinates called *The World's Work* a "glorified monthly newspaper." Later Page followed a traditional route for journalists: He became a diplomat, another job emphasizing verbal and interpersonal skills.[17]

Although other occupational training grounds varied considerably, these editors all exhibited a fascination for the efficient manipulation of space, words, and audience. Bok began as an autograph hunter who designed his own "authorized" collection of photographs with printed biographies on the reverse side of each portrait. Later, he worked in telegraphy, and even became a stenographer for Jay Gould. Then, while doing stenography, promotion, and part-time editing for *Scribner's*, he became a devoted fan of Henry Ward Beecher, from whom Bok said he learned the value of "shorter sermons" loaded with "practical facts." He then developed his fascination for celebrity-hunting into a profession by becoming one of this country's first literary syndicators. Meanwhile, he undertook writing advertisements and a syndicated column of literary gossip. Both enterprises eventually drew him to Cyrus Curtis. McClure solicited ads for a newspaper at Knox College, where he gave a graduation speech on "Enthusiasm" which, he proudly noted, lasted only five minutes. Later, he learned shorthand in business college, and apprenticed at *The Wheelman*, a Pope Bicycle Company publication that later merged with *The Outing*. In the 1880s he developed his magazine along syndicate lines after the idea had been rejected by *The Century*. But in his autobiography (1914), McClure said he developed his true editorial instincts during one summer of college, when he worked as a country peddler. Similarly, Lorimer (the son of an actor turned minister) apprenticed in telegraphy and stenography, worked in journalism, but spent his most important years as a traveling salesman for P. D. Armour, one of his father's parishioners. Armour and Company was a staging area of early impression management: P.D. himself emphasized the importance of public speaking, a lesson lost

47

neither on Lorimer nor on another employee, Dale Carnegie. In sum, all these men brought to magazines a fascination for skills of management, voice, and personal impressions—skills that emphasized the importance of sounding an audience's needs, creating a relaxed setting, and then delivering a product or idea.[18]

The trademark of this new elite was the rapprochement it effected between the business and editorial sides of magazine publishing. The essence of the change, as *The Independent* described it, was to apply "scientific management" to the magazine. Articles would be well planned, boiled down to readable formats, and consist of "what is most important to be known of what the world is doing and thinking."[19] The new editors' penchant for advance scouting itself necessitated new organizational techniques back at the office. The new elite soon began wholesale bidding for authors, article commissioning, and finally the formation of internal magazine writing staffs. This acceleration involved a basic restructuring of article publication. As the journalist Mark Sullivan remembered it, while "the older magazines . . . were still following the placid paths of the past, selecting from the daily batch of manuscripts voluntarily submitted," periodicals like *McClure's*—more efficient and armed with better finances from advertising revenue —were actually "originating ideas, sending out not one man but half a dozen to get the material." The initiation of Charles Hanson Towne, who began at John Brisben Walker's new *Cosmopolitan*, reversed that of Frank Tooker. Towne remembered expecting to sit quietly at desks sifting manuscripts. He soon learned that editing had become a matter of "extract[ing] ideas from authors," a "looking ahead profession if there ever was one; a constant feeling of the public's pulse." Lorimer put it more bluntly: Magazine publishing, he said, was "the business of buying and selling brains; of having ideas, and finding men to carry them out."[20]

Editors, of course, had not suddenly become prophets. Rather, it was a matter of making the production process more predictable at both ends. At one end, editors wrested inspiration away from unpredictable voluntary contributors and placed it within the magazine office system itself. At the other, editors covered their bets with readers by carefully designed promotion. Thus rather than actually forecasting, what the new editors relied upon was a form of controlled response. This restructuring of production enabled editors to implement many of their own ideas, and more to the point, to generate a "trademark" style.

This reorientation had several other effects. First, it compounded the turn to "timely" articles that became the dominant trend in magazines; careful planning and promotion were what *made* an issue or article timely.[21] Likewise anticipatory production contributed to an increased emphasis on celebrities, experts, and established writers, both by intent and by the fact that commissioning numerically reduced the chances of unknowns.[22] But the principal effect of the system was its reinforcement of a "robust," direct magazine voice. The reduction of magazine content to an "idea" that could be "farmed out" to a writer, and then "gotten across" to a reader, only enhanced these editors' bias against a sophisticated or allusive literary style. Page, Munsey, Bok, McClure, Lorimer, and several other key editors all agreed, as McClure put it, that the "decoration of phrase is a very secondary matter," that an author "can say the same thing in fifty different ways."[23]

These editors valued a style that did not obscure the assigned "idea"—a simple, direct, persuasive style akin to everyday speech. Arguing that "the message itself is of greater import than the manner in which it is said," Bok said a "readable, lucid style is far preferable to what is called a 'literary style'—a foolish phrase, since it often means nothing except a complicated method of expression." Page, the champion of what he termed a "homely realism," said that though "the somewhat leisurely style of a generation or two ago pleased the small circle of readers within its reach," modern conditions demanded writing with "more directness, more clearness, with greater nervous force." ("Women can't write editorials," he once explained to Horace Scudder; "neither can feminine men.") Thinking good writing "as common as clam shells," Frank Munsey said he wanted *stories*, "not washed out studies of effete human nature." The principal effect, he said, was that writing should get a grip on the reader.[24]

Written words, to put it another way, were valued in direct proportion to their clarity, "strength," and above all, their ability to persuade, to cut through the reader's barriers of resistance and "impose" an idea. The salesman slant made literary style into a "pitch" that attempted to encircle the reader with a mood that would lead him to relax his defenses.[25] In this respect, what editors sought was a modified form of "realistic" discourse that attempted to convey authority, authenticity, or expertise. The importation of a direct, forceful prose style was the first step in the managerial "naturalization" of content; it was done by conveying the glow of conviction.

It could also work by conveying personability and commonsensicality—what Dale Carnegie or Bruce Barton were wont to call, in a misnomer, "sincerity."[26] In this variation, editors attempted to personalize the voice of the editor, to erase the conventional tone of anonymity upon which Gilded Age editors had relied. Referring proudly to his own point of entry, Bok said, "The method of editorial expression in the magazines of 1889 was also distinctly vague and prohibitively impersonal. The public knew the name of scarcely a single editor of a magazine: there was no personality that stood out in the mind: the accepted editorial expression was the indefinite 'we'; no one ventured

to use the first person singular and talk intimately to the reader."
Clearly, "the time had come . . . for the editor of some magazine to
project his personality through the printed page and to convince the
public that he was not an oracle removed from the people, but a real
human being who could talk and not merely write on paper." Even
though Bok couched his memory in democratic and humane terms, he
really saw his personality as a "projection," a manipulated mask "convincing" the reader as if he or she were a buyer. Even Bok's autobiography used a third-person narrative, because he actually thought of
"Edward Bok" as a different person. In this light it is not surprising that
Bok also said that he had been more honestly attracted to the "science
of advertisement writing, which meant . . . the capacity to say much in
little space," than to his literary assignments.[27]

Nor is it shocking that *The Nation* ridiculed his despair of "attaining so high an ideal" as bringing his articles up to the level of his ads.
"We hasten to add," the editors wrote wryly, "that the editorial policy
of nearly all the magazines we know is happily approximating the advertising policy. In a superb miscellaneousness, in timeliness, in direct
and vociferous appeal to the reader, the editors are, after all, not lagging
so much behind."[28] To *The Nation*, or to Peter Finley Dunne, there
was little doubt that a prose style that tried to "get a grip on the reader,"
to cut through his or her resistances with a direct and personalized
voice, was a style bred in the commercial mainstream. *Bookman* analyst
Algernon Tassin pinpointed the mode when he termed it a kind of
"buttonholing," the very quality Roland Barthes singles out as a "naturalizing" dimension of modern consumer mythology. This was the
change in the reading experience that so troubled the likes of Crothers,
Perry, and Johnson: a "made to pattern" form of "realism" full of pep
and information, but which actually threatened to limit the intellectual
latitude the reader enjoyed. But the design of the editorial voice was
only part of a larger plan by the new elite: to create specialized reading
environments that began to anticipate, direct, and solicit readers' expectations in order to market controlled choices. As Tassin put it in
reference to Bok, the new editor did not go forth to the family circle:
He inscribed a circle around himself, and invited the reader in.[29]

III

That four such different periodicals—a newsmagazine, a muckraking
monthly, a businessman's weekly, and a woman's domestic journal—
united around this new plan is itself testimony to the pervasiveness of

the new consumer rhetoric. These magazines varied considerably in content, format, and political ideology. Neither *The World's Work* nor *McClure's*, for instance, ran much advertising; while in the Curtis publications, advertising ran over 25 percent of content. Moreover, not all the features of the new "cheap" magazines were clear departures from earlier Gilded Age guidelines. McClure had worked at *The Century*, Bok at *Scribner's*, Page at *The Forum* and *The Atlantic*. Page and McClure's sheets especially showed ties to the traditional form of the miscellany; *McClure's* even ran reproductions of art works in its early years, hearkening back to the traditional role of the magazine as a vehicle of culture.[30] But for all their differences, these magazines shared a fundamental desire: to make their content more "practical," worldly, and up-to-date. A magazine succeeded, Bok said in retrospect, when it ceased to be "an inanimate printed thing" and became "a vital need in the personal lives of its readers."[31]

Page once penned a summary of *The World's Work*'s goals that, with minor variations, outlined the major objective of the new topical magazines:

. . . the earnest purpose to interpret the important things that are done . . . to make an interesting magazine that should have a higher aim than to fill an idle hour, and a more original aim that to thresh over the old straw and call the chaff "Literature," or to publish the commonplaces that men in official positions dictate in their decline for cash. For the most important things and the most interesting things are the very tasks that men now have in hand—men who do something and love their work—Social Problems that directly affect human well-being; Education in its wider reach and more effective methods; Political Duties that are imminent and real; Literature that has substance as well as form and that takes hold on modern life; Invention and Industry in all their advances; Agriculture . . . whatever men do better than men have done before.[32]

Both the style and substance of Page's summary were revealing here. With an encyclopedic and fervent tone, Page listed the trends that inverted the priorities of the Gilded Age: a turning away from "literature" to timely topics; a tendency toward an "interpretive" rather than simply a selective editorial role; and a bias toward the romance of business, professions, technology, and politics. Like the Luce publications in later years, *The World's Work* (as its title suggested) was an international digest drenched in the romance of progress.[33]

The general trend toward the coverage of business, professions, and politics was an attempt to court more male readers (and voters). Page outlined his ideal as a "cultivated man in an industrial era," still well-bred, but now business-minded and democratic in sympathy, ready to adapt to the new conditions—trusts, unions, international trade—outlined by the magazine. *McClure's*, although it also ran fiction, announced it wanted to reach a greater mass of readers by providing the latest scientific advancements and "a moving, living transcript of the intelligent, interesting, human endeavor of the time." *McClure's* felt that the very "vitality of democracy" lay upon the "popular knowledge of complex questions."[34]

This fascination for the "romance of real life" carried over into many features. In *McClure's*, its presence was felt in the regularly appearing celebrity profiles, popular science features, and even muckraking articles. In each case a common motif recurred—what Neil Harris terms the "Operational Aesthetic," long a basic element of nineteenth-century popular culture and entertainment. McClure, no doubt drawing upon his peddler days, always exuded a whiff of Barnum: Commonly working in concealment and display, his magazine often endowed the mundane with thrills and chills ("Adventures with the Leaping Tuna: The Skill and Endurance Required to Catch the Tiger of the Sea"). But also like Barnum, the magazine recognized the curiosity value of showing the audience *how something was done*—whether it was training dangerous animals, switching trains in a railyard, or bribing a legislature. The motif was not restricted to spectacular activities. In fact, the magazine just as often showed the reader that seemingly complex activities involved operations similar to those within his own experience. This reversible strategy carried over even into biographical pieces. Lives could either be exposed as common clay or endowed with the "romance of industrial achievement"—valued for success, or because "side by side with the stirring story . . . there runs . . . the accompaniment of a sunny, personal life, of devotion to friends and family." This was a motif that appeared again and again in the new magazines: a convertible strategy of exposure that allowed editors to glamorize the mundane world of work and yet also humanize the celebrity.[35]

Of all the magazines that expressed this fascination for the "ins and outs" of practical life and business, Lorimer's *Post* was in a class by itself. Merging "seriousness" with a middle-class notion of "sanity," it aimed at the clean-living, law-abiding, safe breadwinner—the office worker, the small businessman, and the limited investor. In line with this pitch, the *Post* allowed no liquor advertising, no real estate ads, and no financial ads. Lorimer the editor—who had lost his place with Armour due to an ill-advised venture—spoke out against speculation and financiers. "Men who stay rich and grow old gracefully," he warned, "are not the gamblers of the stock markets and the grain pits"; "successful money-getting calls for soberness of living and evenness of mentality." In these years, a *Post* series entitled "Your Savings" was the magazine's longest-running feature. Lorimer never swayed from his feeling that there was "no finer product of modern civilization than the American businessman." When told in 1926 that his magazine was starting to attract "thoughtful" readers, Lorimer quipped that he would try to correct the error. He even set out on a talent search to find writers who would write business fiction appropriate to the values of achievement in American life. The most famous feature in this mode was his own best-seller, "Letters from a Self-Made Merchant to His Son," which ran originally in the *Post*.[36]

If Page and McClure were in the business of "interpretation," Lorimer's forte was gossip and advice. Practically blind to what Max Weber saw as the "iron cage" of modern bureaucracy, the upbeat *Post* insisted that "given moderate ability and fair health—the endowment of the average man—and any youth with good staying powers may still work through to the fore." The magazine would run series like "The Making of a Railroad Man," an account written by employees on every step of the corporate ladder. In a column called "Poor Richard Junior's Philosophy," Lorimer crafted his own aphorisms of successful office politics. Promotional material for Curtis also pointed with pride to the trademark *Post* biographies, which took lessons from "an actual record of life" far superior to "deliberate and deadly" advice of the past. Practical advice for the reader was couched in realistic narrative.[37]

The *Post* also capitalized on the reader's interest by longing looks at celebrities in regular features like "Men and Women of the Hour," "Publick Occurrences," and its most prominent section, "Who's Who and Why—Serious and Frivolous Facts about the Great and Near Great." As this final title indicates, the *Post*, like *McClure's*, realized the endless possibilities of interchangeably glamorizing and humanizing. The overall intention was to bring the well-known figure off either the pedestal of adulation or the cross of infamy. "Even in politics it [the *Post*] opened up a rich field, hitherto unsuspected," Curtis Publishing claimed. "Everybody with an 'honorable' prefixed to his name had been regarded either as a saint or sinner. The *Post* argued that he was a human being, made of the same sort of dust as the doctor or village blacksmith." The small-town faith in the common denominator of "humanity" gave the *Post* a homogenized feel for which it became famous.[38]

Despite the general trend toward "male" readership, the new emphasis on practicality and work was nowhere more striking than in magazines with primarily female audiences. The *Ladies' Home Journal*, like its big brother The *Post*, seemed to deny its modernity, reassuringly linking its reader to the familiar motifs of Sarah Hale's *Godey's Ladies' Book*. Like *Godey's*, the *Journal* at times seemed a thing of ladies, doctors, and ministers (the triumvirate of "feminized" Victorianism), running fashion plates, poetry, fiction, and editorial chitchat. But in fact the *Journal* departed significantly from the sentimental ethical basis of Victorian ideology. Whereas Hale had appealed to the "thousands of fair and gentle readers" to use their "moral power" in the "holier vocation" of prompting goodness and "purity" in their husbands—and advised that "the elevation of the sex will not consist of becoming like men"—the *Journal*, conversely, deemphasized the importance of literary cultivation in favor of domestic efficiency and civic activity. The way to lead women to the appreciation of beauty, Bok told one writer, was "not to print an essay by Ruskin but to tell them how many packages of flower-seeds you can buy for fifteen cents, and print a diagram of how to plant them." Bok also waged a private war against the old-style "self-culture" of women's clubs.[39]

The magazine was conceived in a marriage quite like the one it advocated. Originally, the *Journal* (first called the *Ladies' Journal and Practical Housekeeper*) was the brainchild of advertising innovator and publisher Cyrus Curtis and his wife, the former Louisa Knapp. While Mr. Curtis, in private business meetings, seemed to belittle editorial goals in favor of advertising objectives, Mrs. Curtis spoke of the magazine as a household adviser, offering domestic fiction, "Side Talks with Girls," "Everything About the House," "Hints on Home Dressmaking," "Floral Helps and Hints," and the like. "We propose to make it [the *Journal*] a household necessity," she wrote, "so good, so pure, so true, so brave, so full, so complete, that a young couple will no more think of going to housekeeping without it than without a cook stove." The goals of publisher-husband and adviser-wife went hand in hand. For instance, when the magazine secured a story from Marian Harland, a popular writer of domestic fiction, Cyrus financed it by securing an ad from an eggbeater manufacturer who admired her work. Cyrus knew that advertisers sought a magazine that would be used by the practical homemaker regularly, just as, it was hoped, products would be.[40]

Mrs. Curtis offered the *Journal* as a "regular visitor, entertaining, practical and helpful." She was convinced that what the world needed was "fewer wasp-waisted women" and more efficient homemakers. Traditional interests like dress or etiquette were always put to the acid test of utility. Curtis's ideal reader was a woman who rolled up her sleeves, trained her young daughters in practical affairs, and became a successful house manager. "No woman is educated," she wrote, "who is not equal to the successful management of a family." Bok continued this theme, adding his own emphasis on the value of common sense. He argued for simple, "sensible" dress; for "system in shopping"; for young girls to learn "application"; and for a wife to be as conversant with money as her husband. Summing up the new accent, feature writer Octave Thanet advised readers to accept their role as the "bread of existence" rather than *Godey's* "elixir" of reform—in other words, to be their husband's aide-de-camp rather than his moral inspiration. Bok likewise said he aimed his magazine at a woman who "did things"; sense was something men liked in their wives, if not, it was noted rather dryly, in their sweethearts.[41]

The ethos of managerialism reoriented magazine fare to "practical," work-oriented, and "timely" issues; the magazines, in turn, offered themselves as manuals in how citizenship, occupational life, and domesticity could be better "managed." But what was also different about these magazines was the way this advice was conveyed. In part it was their new "realistic" voice—colloquial, forceful, direct, and seemingly personal. But the magazines also employed "realism" in a broader sense: in design strategies and narrative devices designed to enhance the aura of authenticity by exerting greater influence over the reading process. Page recognized that a reader's tendency was to wander; *McClure's* implicitly acknowledged that a reader might be alienated by political stands; Bok and Lorimer were remarkably cognizant of readers' tendency to simply read a magazine and throw it away. In other words, editors intuitively recognized that to succeed fully the magazine had to generate trust, a sense of participation, and even proprietorship in the mind of the reader. This was best accomplished by a careful balance of the new and familiar that both stimulated the reader's attention yet reassured him—the lure of "new improved," the stability of product loyalty. A reader must come to look for something "fresh" (though pre-promoted) in each issue, yet he must also recognize the stamp of familiarity in his "favorite" magazine. Bok put this formulation in a characteristic analogy. "A successful magazine," he said, "is exactly like a successful store: It must keep its wares constantly fresh and varied to attract the eye and hold the patronage of the customers."[42]

At one level, designing of this kind derived from the new managerial style, in which the editor sought out writers and promoted their material in advance. Readers' expectations were thus set not only per issue, but also months ahead of delivery. But "anticipatory" production also surfaced in new design mechanisms of format and editorial presence that attempted to control reader response. Page, for instance—an advocate of scientific management in other realms—compared the editor to an "engineer" who, although he could not directly control the machinery he created, still set the magazine pace and direction. "His position," Page wrote, "is very much like the position of the locomotive engineer, he does not make the machine, but only guides it, he cannot make it go on any track except the track which was originally designed for it."[43] What Page implied here was that design was fundamental, and that the editor may *appear* "impersonal" and detached but, in effect, has already laid out the track the periodical will follow. Admitting that no journal could cover daily events like a newspaper, Page said once the editor was

spiritually baptized he has the discernment to see what sort of literature makes for progress and what does not, and his function is something like this: civilization goes forward always in a zig-zag course; it is never a uniform line of advance like a line of soldiers. . . . The magazine's duty is to take the foremost line, the foremost column and to put itself a little ahead of that and thus to invite its readers to a little broader vista so that men will see what is bound to come and it will inspire him to work to bring it to pass.[44]

Page's mixing of metaphors was especially revealing here. The editor, through his experience, acquires discernment which *allows him* to decide what literature "makes for progress"; his "column" ("inviting" in tone) puts itself ahead of the reader and convinces him to jump aboard a process that has already been portrayed as practically "inevitable."

Page built this desire to lead into the structure of his magazine. Whereas most Gilded Age journals had commonly placed editorial columns in the back pages, mixed in with letters, and often initiating new (or unrelated) topics of their own, *The World's Work* began with Page's own "March of Events." The effect of this "advance column" was to provide journalistic "lead-ins" to subsequent articles. Page not only influenced readers' expectations, he in effect sanctioned the veracity of the informative articles that followed by making them seem part of the "march" of progress itself.

Page's editorial "interpretation" thus provided an intervening lens between the reader and the material that followed. Page's principle of masculine prose also added substantially to the feeling of credibility. Although he approached issues rhetorically as "questions" or "problems," in fact he provided answers and opinions, in an authoritative tone he liked to call "profound earnestness."[45] This is supposedly why editorials, as he had said, could not be left to women: The soft sell of feminine "influence" would no longer do. Page's mode was "informative" rather than explicitly investigative. As his biographer John Milton Cooper observes, the magazine "sustained the impression in readers' minds that [The] World's Work was viewing events just the way they would if they were better informed." Rather than citing statistics, Page and his writers tended to bracket their opinions with knowing nods to "considerable or respectable body of opinion," "practical men who have long studied the problem," and so forth. In articles describing professions, the reader was not told how to do something—but he was shown how it was "intelligently" done.[46]

Page's main claim to authenticity was driven home further by printed photographs. In these early years, photographic reproductions probably had an element of irrefutability, and they shifted the journal's priorities further in Page's desired direction. By definition, photographs reinforced the shifting of content to things of the present. Moreover, photographs seemed perpetually to "up the ante" as to what, in the magazine's view, constituted "real life." As with *Life* magazine years later, readers came to expect not analytical photographs so much as those that offered new sights, new vistas, deeper looks into the March of Progress. Photos enabled editors like Page not only to define what was real, practical, or inevitable, but to endow his interpretation with an aura of romance and authority.

In contrast to *The World's Work*, *McClure's* lacked a visible editorial persona. But the muckraking journal also appealed to the reader's thirst for information—indeed, his sense of loss without it—by marketing its own variety of realism. In *McClure's*, the analog to Page's pitch of authority was an often "scientific" authenticity. For example, one of *McClure's* fondest memories was the "Human Document" series, which traced celebrities' lives through photo galleries (suggestively like a family album), and the "Real Conversation" series, which consisted of essentially modern interviews. In the Gilded Age, articles for the most part had existed in isolation; now they interlocked with actual "documents." Taking the traditional path through a celebrity's day— his habits, home, and personal library—*McClure's* gave it "realism" by emphasizing the element of photographic tangibility and real conversation. The relative novelty of the interview device was no better suggested than by the recurrent bafflement of the celebrities themselves. Even in these profiles, an element of the muckraking strategy can be detected—or perhaps muckraking's affinities with celebrity gossip. In either case, *McClure's* persuaded the reader that it had the "inside dope."[47]

The power of this appeal to "inside" authenticity became obvious when the magazine did, in time, turn to politics and social issues. "Before conditions can be cured they must be understood," the editors wrote in an introduction to a series on criminality:

. . . but the service does not stop there; the lukewarmness of the righteous is the stronghold of corruption, and about these reports there is something startling—a frankness, a closeness of contact like experience, a vital human picturesqueness, that makes abstractions real; and so they are calculated to win the readers that scorn preachments. . . .

That vital human picturesqueness has, too, a value apart from all its contingent immediate political significance. Here are human documents among the most curious ever brought forth; and even if we got all our cities cleaned up to the point of admiration, here would be good reading for all who delight in human nature and the contrarieties of the human scene for their own sake.[48]

Here the editors drew upon the expectations set by "Human Documents," making a claim Barnumesque in style ("among the most curious ever brought forth"). But also implicit in this introduction were two central editorial precepts about exposure. First, the "design" of the article's "frankness" is to startle the reader and raise his curiosity; second, "vital human picturesqueness" could often cover the risk of controversial political analysis. Realism served the dual purpose of attracting new readers and keeping old ones by basing its appeal not in politics but in style.

The "closeness of contact like experience" could be achieved in several ways. *McClure's* articles commonly combined an almost detective-like factuality with photographic reproductions. In Lincoln Steffens's "Shame of the Cities" series, the magazine printed actual city ledgers. Likewise, Ray Stannard Baker wrote in his portrait of Kaiser Wilhelm that the American visitor to Germany would "discover that his imagination in picturing the Kaiser had followed the exaggerations of the caricaturist rather than the sober reality of the photograph" (which, of course, appeared on the opposite page). In other instances, authenticity was acquired by printing either an "authorized" account or the wisdom of a well-known expert.[49]

Outside work could be both costly and unpredictable, however. A staff system such as McClure created, on the other hand, could control costs and meet deadlines. But to retain the feel of expertise, the staff attempted to evolve a professional style or manner within articles. In the case of Steffens and William Allen White, for example, investigative realism imported the aura of popular science. Whereas Page conveyed the authority of those "in the know," *McClure's* often sought irrefutability through the feel of scientific documentation. Once again, the appeal of "Human Documents," popular science, and muckraking all overlapped in a promise to show, with "facts," how things were really done—how they operated.[50]

Realism, however, could come in a variety of guises. At Lorimer's *Post*, the variety aimed for was one of "common sense" rather than informed opinion or scientific objectivity. Lorimer's *Post* essentially inherited the tenor of gossip that enhanced the comforting feel of its pages. Lorimer's "Who's Who" feature, for example, regularly contained a "Hall of Fame" subsection, within which the *Post* revealed who played golf with whom in the capital, a particular personality's nickname or habits (e.g., "Friends of Admiral Dewey says he's the best-dressed man in Washington"), and the like. Other regular features like "In the Bookshop," or even the fillers used to adjust column space,

often contained aphorisms balanced with anecdotes of humorously trivial import. Lorimer hardly apologized for this fascination with gossip
for its own sake; on the contrary, he defended it as a form of popular
literature. "Gossip is the ordinary man or woman's chief literary amusement," he said. "What people are, what they have done, what they are
doing or going to do—that is the prime interest of every normal
being."[51] The claim of "normality" justified the *Post*'s gossip on the
grounds that it was both entertaining and "inside dope." It was also the
Post's equivalent of *McClure's* "vital picturesqueness" in a lower key:
Readers potentially alienated by opinion would be held by the charming
contrarieties and eccentricities of (in a title later prominent) "people."
Even as it glamorized it trivialized: Gaps of power and privilege were
glossed over with a view of society as a "mass of humanity," a classless,
commonsensical place akin to a country town. Even forty years later,
the *Post* had a backwater feel.

Finally, in the other Curtis house periodical, the *Ladies' Home
Journal*, "realism" appeared in the form of helpful, intimate "confidences" between the reader and the magazine. Like other varieties of
inside dope, the *Journal*'s appeal was based in a sense of authenticity—
but more to the point, of "being inside," of belonging. Curtis Publishing's promotion drew the crucial connection. "The final tests of a magazine's excuse for existence," it wrote, "are the confidence which its
readers accord it, and the confidences they bring to it." The *Journal*
not only carried a good many pieces about what it called its own "family" of authors, but also printed reams of letters from readers, who wrote
in to various columns and editors with questions, opinions, and advice.
This latter strategy, a *Journal* trademark, had several functions. First,
it both enlarged and assured the continuity of readership, a strategy
that was essential to the building of large circulations. Second, the
letters provided the germ of market research; often Bok polled readers
before taking an editorial stand. Third, and most important, letters
enhanced what Bok liked to call the "sense of proprietorship" a reader
felt in the magazine. Bok likened his readership to a plebiscite, as policy
was presumably given a mandate if circulation rose. Letters gauged
reader response and helped plan future content; replies reinforced the
magazine's "intimacy" and advisory role. The *Journal* kept a full-time
staff just answering letters. These institutional strategies created the
opening for the gossip-like intimacy Bok claimed to create with his
editorial persona. "I want you to look upon us," he wrote, "as if we
actually came in person to your home. . . . And just as you would talk
to us if we were in your home, tell us when we fail to meet some want
in your daily life."[52]

Once again, Bok's editorial goals complemented those of Cyrus
Curtis. A corollary of being "practical," as far as the *Journal* was con-

cerned, was careful scrutiny of the marketplace of goods. Mrs. Curtis thus inaugurated a program that encouraged her readers actually to *read* the magazine's ads. The "way we would have it," she wrote, was if readers read the "paper clear through, advertisements and all." That, she said, was the secret of her success. The Curtis organization paid strict attention to the format and presentation of ads. Curtis, Bok, and Lorimer supervised their writing; advertising manager John A. Thayer inaugurated the process of actually designing ads and selling them to advertisers.[53] But the real keynote was struck by Bok in 1896 when, probably mimicking newspapers again, he began the practice of "ad-stripping" or "tailing." In this format, the magazine cut up fiction and other features and ran them into columns in the back pages, thus drawing the reader's attention back to ads otherwise ignored.[54] Here was a literal implementation of the trend that Dunne, *The Nation*, and others satirized: Magazine articles now "advertised" for ads.

Here again, Curtis Publishing realized that it was not enough simply to have the readers' eyes directed at ads. The readers must also trust what they read—the second half of "confidence" in the *Journal's* terms. Bok, for instance, later inaugurated a campaign against misleading patent medicine advertising—only, it should be noted, after readership polls supported his position. But even earlier, the *Journal's* editors announced that there was "no room for swindlers in our family," and promised to reimburse any reader who reasonably felt cheated by an advertiser. In an editorial called "Confidence in our Columns," Mrs. Curtis summed up her overall intent:

We intend to furnish the best practical and helpful domestic journal ever yet produced. . . . To do this we depend upon a good advertising patronage, and, to induce our subscribers to read and answer to the numerous and interesting announcements found in these columns each month, we *strive to secure their confidence* by inserting none but what we believe to be trustworthy and reliable. . . . We guarantee our subscribers against loss from any advertisement found in the *Journal*, and ask our readers, as a favor to us, to patronize our customers as often as possible, and *always* mention the *Journal* when writing. Don't forget that.[55]

This campaign against advertising irresponsibility is often taken as evidence of Bok's "reformer" status. But like Bruce Barton, Robert Lynd, and other apparent critics of consumerism, Bok's reformism only contributed to the long-term viability of consumer culture. In announcements like the one quoted above, the benefits of the guarantee to the *Journal* itself were tacitly acknowledged. First of all, advertisers could hardly find a better medium for their messages: The pledge not only "safeguarded" readers (if it did); by generating consumer confidence, it enhanced their willingness to buy. Ultimately, the reader was inclined to rely upon her "friend" and adviser, the *Journal*, to do the real scrutinizing. Secondly, the guarantee also helped to reinforce the adviser role of the *Journal* within its regular, non-advertising columns. Everyone belonged to the same family: reader, editor, writer, and advertiser. Here the consumer rhetoric doubled back upon itself: Once mimicking the language of the "well-managed store," the *Journal* now returned the favor and made buying a form of belonging.

IV

The topical magazines' rhetoric of practicality, "inside dope," and proprietorship came naturally to a status-conscious group of managerial "outsiders"; through the magazine, they imported this language to other quarters. We cannot precisely gauge how this new agenda was received by American readers. But I think we can legitimately infer an implied readership role that, beneath all the bluster about "activity" and "intimacy," described more accurately the kind of reading the magazines offered. One might say the new magazines were a bit like Coney Island. On the surface they enticed the reader with a flair for the exotic, with a sense of escape from the sterility of Victorianism, with the excitement of change; in the words of the historian John Kasson, they seemed "charged with a magical power to transmute customary appearances into fluid new possibilities." But like their amusement park counterpart, underneath lurked the "reality of control," a world of manipulated responses and "pageants" that invited passivity and anomie.[56]

The engineered "realism" of the topical magazines threatened to deepen the passivity of the reader in several senses. In the main, it tended to encourage the idea that "real life" was beyond the pale of the reader's existence. Although Page, for instance, often spoke of the common or humble life, in fact the life he displayed was something remote from most people's lives—international, always progressing, always uplifting. The effect, therefore, was to create the feeling that *others* experienced the real—the sense that the reader, too, was an outsider looking in. Rather than being called upon to offer insight into the world's workings, the reader was first awed by its complexity and then counseled by "experts" ostensibly closer to the action. Instead of promoting participation, the magazines elevated "seeing"; instead of encouraging readers' criticism, the editors interpreted for them—told them simply to "stay informed." Even *McClure's*' whirlwind of vital facts and documentary "feel" may have only mired the reader in spectatorship. Once editors realized that the appeal of exposure lay in "vital picturesqueness" rather than political ideology, muckraking by definition became a matter of style, a literary strategy rooted in the often vacuous process of stimulating and unveiling for its own sake—for the curiosity value of the operational aesthetic. If Barnumese invaded political analysis, the logical equation was that citizenship was akin to spectating. Even as these editors avoided advertising in their magazines, they reflected its logic in their editorial program: They marketed "being informed," like buying, as a glamorized product that only highlighted the gap between the reader's supposed ignorance and the power of those "in the know." [57]

One might object that the cracker-barrel feel of the *Post* and the *Ladies' Home Journal* seemed hardly glamorized. But as I have argued, the convertible strategy of "humanizing" was only the flip side of celebrity-making. Like Page and McClure, Bok and Lorimer's "family" offered a passive readership role; critics were right in calling the *Post* "homogenizing." Bending levels of power and privilege into a common humanity, the *Post* invited self-satisfaction in its readers by conveying the comforting message that bosses or political leaders were, despite their worldly experience, simply "regular fellows" like themselves. Bok's reassuring confidences, likewise, lumped advertisers, experts, editors, and readers into a commonality of interest, within which each could trust the other completely: The *Journal*, the reader was told, would do all the necessary weeding out of the unworthy. And just as the *Post* narrowed the reader's outlook to the tunnel vision of "safe and sane" upward mobility, the *Journal* introduced its own restrictions on the female reader's sphere. Mrs. Curtis's periodical had hardly been feminist, but it had retained the nineteenth-century faith that there was no single "woman's sphere"—in essence, that the management of the home qualified the woman for anything. But Bok wrote that "there are no two greater factors in human life to-day than woman and home. . . . Separate the two, and they become like two divided parts of a pair of scissors." Resisting suffrage all along, Bok longed for the days when womanhood was free of modern pressures, when "she sought not the ballot, because she intuitively knew it was not made for her hands." Bok's alternative programs—for civic beautification, for suburban home design, for moderate sex education—revealed that when he said he aimed at the woman who "did things," he meant "doing" in a circumscribed arena—to a large extent, one sanctioned and directed by the *Journal* itself. [58]

A passive readership role was implied even in the efforts of Page, McClure, Lorimer, and Bok to create a personable, colloquial, and "inviting" editorial voice. This idea clearly reflected a modern notion of "personality" that saw the editorial presence as a "persona," or mask, to be manipulated to meet the reader's needs. "Appearances are deceitful, I know," Lorimer's self-made merchant admits, "but so long as they are, there's nothing like having them deceive for us instead of against us."[59] Again, this was a motive derived essentially from the salesman's pitch. Yet in Lorimer's advice that the key was to make others' "inferiority" look like "equality," or Frank Munsey's allusion to the reader's "blood," or Bok's remarks about "vital needs," can be found the seeds of the elitist notion—later visible in market research, in certain branches of social science, or in political campaign packaging—that the consumer is an easily manipulated, irrational creature of "attitudes," hardly worthy of true intellectual exchange. Evaluating his career in *Twice Thirty* (1927), a memoir that his family reportedly recognized as "more like Edward," Bok's true feelings emerged:

It was simply not a work which from its very character I would have chosen to express my real self. There are undoubtedly acute problems which concern themselves with the proper ingredients in cooking recipes, the correct stitch in crocheting or knitting, the most desirable and daintiest kinds of lingerie, and the momentous question whether a skirt should escape the ground by six or eight inches. These are vital points in the lives of thousands of women, and their widest solutions should be given by the best authorities. But is it too much to say that they are hardly of a nature to develop and satisfy the mental and spiritual nature of man? At least, not for a lifetime.[60]

Here, Bok's program was revealed to have all the intimacy of "Dialing for Dollars."

Finally, for all of their efforts to streamline and manage the reading process, the magazines may have also generated a considerable amount of anomie. Not only was a single magazine often a matter of conflicting signals; one can imagine the confusion of a reader who subscribed to more than one. The new emphasis on "practicality," for instance, contained an anti-intellectualism that undermined their reverence for expertise; their fascination for "inside dope," as in the muckraking vogue, often ran counter to their overall program of civic "uplift." Denigrating literature in favor of more "serious" concerns, editors then turned to marketing gossip. The magazines often subjected the reader to a baffling, ever changing cycle of "researched" needs, stimulated demand, and oversupply; of public image making and then exposure, "seriousness" and gossip, anxiety and then advice, making someone into a celebrity only to make him human again. Being "timely" meant always changing; being informed meant staying tuned; and both meant never being surfeited. A reader's needs and ignorance were constantly exposed, but "knowing" was always just out of reach—

one issue away. Born in the hit and run of the traveling salesman, the new rhetoric inherited and promoted the mode of planned obsolescence. The cumulative effect may have been to exacerbate the very perplexity, anxiety, and inattention these editors hoped to eradicate.[61]

These qualifications cast serious doubt upon the success of the cultural program the new magazine claimed to underwrite: the overthrow of the passive, sentimental ethos of Victorianism. If anything, these magazines suggest that the pitch to "practicality" and masculinity masked a deepening of consumer and citizen dependency—a deepening, a fragmenting, a proliferation of his supposed "needs." We might, in closing, consider the testimony of a lone reader who wrote to *The Atlantic* in 1906. Surveying the publicly acclaimed demise of sentimentalism, this female observer suggested that this era actually marked the onset of newer, more modern forms of victimization. She limited her remarks to the optimistic Woman's Page, which promised to change a "maid forlorn" into a "beautiful and engaging" princess; her message applied, however, to other departments.

There are recipes for everything . . . my good is sought in a thousand ways; in columns of Don'ts; in pithy paragraphs of Useful Information; in exploitations of the fashions; in Health Talks and Beauty Hints. My good, I say, for there is in it all something so pointedly personal. . . . A pseudo-conscience calls me to its perusal from masterly leader or thrilling news-story; from high politics or current history.

Here, after all, was the pathos of the modern consumer: endlessly enticed and dissatisfied, reminded of one's shortcomings, set "free"—and yet guided by a "pseudo-conscience."

The Woman's Page . . . pursues me, weighs me, and finds me wanting, without my invitation. . . . Quite against my will, I am spurred to the performance of imperative duties galore. . . . It is without my real privity and consent that I am prodded with precept and stirred to teasing ambition, that I am moved to the painful storing of bits of alleged useful information, and am made uneasily aware of the latest collar and the newest style of hair-dressing—destined to change ere I can make them mine.[62]

Here, perhaps, was the price exacted by the new "realism" later replicated in other cultural media: the endless prodding and stimulation of advertisers and experts, the manufactured "pep" of the modern thriller, the shallow intimacy of speakers "right in your living-room tonight."

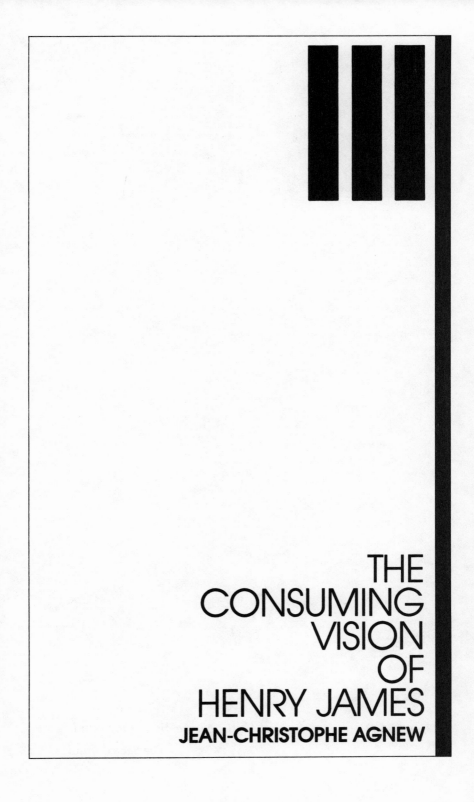

THE CONSUMING VISION OF HENRY JAMES

JEAN-CHRISTOPHE AGNEW

"The satisfaction of my curiosity is the pacification of my mind."

—*The Sacred Fount* (1901)

Commodities appear in virtually every space twentieth-century American culture affords. They have materialized in the physical landscape and branded its built environment. They have entered into our rites of passage and rendered them inseparable from the more or less predictable passages of style. They have become associated with the themes of family, sexuality, and individuality as vehicles for the fulfillment of each. Their presence has confused electoral politics with acts of purchase and has converted moments of communal affirmation into what one historian has called "festivals of consumption." In short, commodities have become—in life, in film, in literature—the givens of our existence, though it is of their essence that they are not free. That is, we take their collective presence for granted, though each commodity introduces itself as precisely that which cannot be assumed, as that which we do not as yet possess, as that which we must in fact acquire to remain full participants in our culture. So runs the critique of consumer culture in its broadest formulation.

Yet even if we acknowledge the general accuracy of this indictment, we recognize at the same time its familiarity; and in noting its familiarity, we prepare to exempt ourselves in particular from its strictures. Here the traditional, aesthetic critique of consumer culture collaborates with the personalized messages of that culture to convince us of our own individual immunity to the blandishments of the commodity form. Not only do we wish to distance ourselves from the materialism associated with acts of acquisition, but we are even more anxious to deny any semblance of the vulgar and debased symbolism of needs that cultural critics have so persistently associated with consumer culture. The impulse to deny complicity, one suspects, is almost as strong in the world of goods as in the world of sex. And nowhere is this denial better illustrated than in the question of historical origins. The written history of consumer cultures scarcely compares in breadth or depth to the written history of industrial cultures; it is, if anything, a conspicuous absence. When asked to draw the outlines of a consumer culture, historians have complied. When asked to sketch in its configuration of meanings and inward dynamic of growth, historians have, by and large, drawn a blank.

What follows is, first, an effort to explain this curious default as a consequence of the methods and priorities adopted by historians; second, an attempt to indicate the characteristic perspective of consumer culture as one of "acquisitive cognition," that is, an appropriative view of social meanings as fungible "things"; and third, an endeavor to illustrate the development of this perspective in the life and work of one of American consumer culture's earliest critics, Henry James.

In selecting James, I am aware of choosing a figure who demands to be taken on his own terms rather than on those of the culture from which he so imperiously held himself aloof. Part of the burden of this essay, then, will be to show those terms as the product of an extended negotiation between James and his contemporaries: his family, his class, and his culture. Yet I shall show this negotiation wholly from its interior, that is, from within the projected world of James's autobiographies and novels. Since this inquiry is most concerned with the possibility of a motive peculiar to cultures of consumption, it will inevitably sacrifice breadth for depth. It will trace the social and cultural pressures at work upon James only as they registered themselves within his consciousness, not as they appeared across the landscape of Anglo-American society.

I will be treating James's writings as clues to the ways that feeling and perception were restructured to accommodate the ubiquity and liquidity of the commodity form. If I leave to the companion essays in this volume (and to the reader) the task of measuring the degree to which James's insight into the commodity relations of his time was shared by his class and culture, I will nonetheless insist on the sharpness of his foresight into the commodity relations of our own time. A shorthand sketch of those relations appears in the first portion of this essay, against which James's own rendering of the commodity world can only stand as a rich and profound meditation. His revelatory powers came from an immersion in that commodity world from whose grasp this essay and this book seek to emancipate themselves. My aim is to document at close range the emergence and articulation of a new way of seeing the world peculiar to the felt presence of commodity forms and to suggest that way of seeing as a model of the ways in which Americans have acclimated themselves to the world of goods. It is only a model, of course, and its plausibility remains to be tested. Yet such sweeping cultural shifts as are implicated in the embrace of the commodity form involve significant collective redefinitions of plausibility— redefinitions of what is to count as an adequate cause or motive in our understanding of history. This essay seeks, above all, a point of entry into that inward process of cultural change whereby commodities become the unacknowledged reference points for the accounts we give of ourselves.

I

Historians have taken the world of goods for granted. More precisely, they have taken that world as the outcome of other historical developments—industrial capitalism, for example—that are felt to be more compelling. Treated as by-products, commodities have become the gauge by which allegedly more important historical developments are to be assessed. Thus, historians have used the quantity of consumption —broadly defined as the "standard of living"—as the scale in which to weigh the achievements of industrialization.[1] Their reluctance to go beyond such measures is not difficult to understand. To inquire more deeply into the social and historical formulation of such "standards" is to broach unwanted and unwieldy issues of subjectivity. To call for a more detailed account of those values, conventions, and expectations within which and against which industrial society was formed is to threaten the classic linear movement of historical narrative. Indeed, to demand a "thick" rather than "thin" description of the symbolic world of goods is to open up vistas of interpretation that are almost vertiginous in their potential complexity.[2]

When the head whirls, one reflex is to begin counting. And so it has been with historians. For they have found no more reliable way to count upon the presence of a simplified, homogeneous consumer mentality as a backdrop for industrialism's "story" than to treat that mentality as something to be counted. In this way, infinitely qualifiable attitudes are reduced to finitely quantifiable appetites. Another reason, then, for historians' silence on the formation of consumer culture is their inclination to see it in the shape of a bottomless pit of "demand" into which are thrown the effluvia of industrialism. One need merely stand at the edge of the pit, clipboard in hand, to count and catalogue the objects as they tumble in.[3]

Consumption is for most historians a consummated rather than a contemplated act. It is to be understood through measurement not only because appetites are more easily comprehensible in this way but also because sales figures are among the most precise textual records that consumer society leaves behind. Here, historians traditionally defer to the methods, approaches, and, more important, to the actual findings of social scientists and market pollsters. Such deference is understandable. Census schedules, probate records, and city directories—the basic resources for social historians—rarely approach the richness of detail available in market research. But while this research is a valuable and relatively unmined resource, it remains couched in the barren language of aggregates, averages, and marginality.[4]

With this language as a point of departure, some social scientists have nonetheless ventured beyond the notion of consumption as a completed act. Recognizing perhaps that contemplated acts of purchase remain the ultimate interest of the manufacturer, these investigators rely on more sophisticated and open-ended methods of polling to move inward, so to speak, from the actual purchase through the implied preference to the imputed want.[5] But a curious process occurs as these investigations refine, divide, and multiply the aspects of the commodities against which consumer wants are to be tested. The objects of these wants lose their initial connection to particular commodities. Instead, the *characteristics* of commodities (texture, convenience, or packaging, for example) emerge in marketing theory as the real objects of consumers' desires.[6] The very solidity of the commodity appears to dissolve in the presence of the newly acquired weight of the characteristics the commodity shares with other goods. These characteristics become objectified, reified.

Part of the impetus behind this recent refinement of marketing techniques grows out of a shift in economic theory toward a more complex treatment of the variables of consumer behavior. This development, in turn, parallels the increasing urgency felt by advertising firms to reduce the costs and risks of their national campaigns. In addition to the constant "improvements" of current commodities, there are the 1,200 to 1,500 new commodities that appear each year. These commodities, together with the advertising campaigns designed to introduce them, are subjected to intensive market testing. In this respect, consumers are seen as buying both a product and its marketing strategy. Marketing theory and practice thus converge to eliminate the conventional social and material boundaries marking off the individuality of commodities. Marketers fill trial balloons not with specific and discrete commodities (margarine, cereal, or deodorant, for example) but with assorted, interchangeable bundles or clusters of attributes (nutrition, freshness, or streamlining, for example), each of which is detached from the familiar earthbound associations that particular commodities have acquired over the years. The cable linking these "bundles of attributes" to the grasp of the classically insatiable consumer is severed almost imperceptibly by the marketer, leaving the balloon to drift over a landscape of infinitely divisible wants. Those wants found clinging to the cable at the end of each trial run are then counted so as to determine the prospects of success for both the product and its appropriate marketing campaign.[7]

Despite the insistence of marketing theorists that the commodity attributes in question be defined as physical and therefore quantifiable, their readiness to elevate commodity attributes over their particular embodiments represents a significant step away from the utilitarian tradition of "one good, one want" in which the earliest analyses of consumption were born.[8] Theorists have unintentionally opened up the possibility of the very demand for *non*quantifiable attributes—that is, symbolic properties—which the case for measurement was intended to remove. The ground of measurement upon which the historians of consumer society have hesitantly placed their feet turns out on closer examination to be a surprisingly unsettling terrain.

It may well be as unsettling for the consumer as for the historian. For to liberate commodities' attributes as commodity forms in themselves—forms by whose combination new products are constructed and reconstructed—is to dissolve those attributes as the identifiable properties of particular human artifacts. Descriptive qualities (sweet, low, wet, dry) replace brand and generic titles as the names of products. Singular and discrete use values are translated into multiple and interchangeable exchange values. Commodities become, in William Leiss's words, "progressively more unstable, temporary collections of objective and imputed characteristics—that is, highly complex material-symbolic entities." This "disintegration of the characteristics of objects," as Leiss notes, produces in its turn a progressive "fragmentation of needs."[9] Not that these needs become false needs in some moral or metaphysical sense; rather, they—like the characteristics they take as their objects—become infinitely divisible and divorced from any cognitively stable context. Neither the commodity nor the consumer remains definable in terms of some steady or persisting nucleus of traits or needs. The result, according to Leiss, is a " 'brownian movement' of particular consumer needs within the fluid medium of the market," a seemingly random movement of detached and fragmentary motives and goods through a radically defamiliarized material and symbolic landscape. "All that is solid," as Marx put it, "melts into air."[10]

While it is tempting to treat the market itself as the historical agent of this cultural defamiliarization and decomposition, the case is somewhat more complex than that. In economies based on household production, markets often operate to anchor the symbolic structures of communities, not only by establishing the conditions of personal accountability and identity among buyers and sellers but also by separating discontinuous spheres of social exchange: gifts versus commerce, prestige versus material goods.[11] But when production becomes production for exchange, markets grow both more intensive and extensive. The commodity form moves outside its traditionally designated enclaves, with a corresponding impact upon culture as a whole. Spheres of exchange collapse into one another; the gap between purchase and sale widens; and the problem of identity and accountability intensifies as buyers, sellers, and their goods grow in anonymity. In the measure that society itself becomes a marketplace, social relations, as one historian puts it, lose their "transparency."[12]

To understand the formation of specifically consumer cultures, we need to reverse Karl Polanyi's argument that market economies have been "disembedded" from their religious and symbolic ground. We are better advised to treat a consumer culture's symbolic representations as themselves "disengaged, disembroiled, disencumbered"—to use Henry James's words—from the specific and immediate needs of material life. Indeed, economics presents itself as an effort to control, restrict, and order the promiscuity of symbolic relations to which market exchange lends itself.[13] Cultural symbols are always polyvalent, but commodified symbols are infinitely so. In the setting of the high-intensity market, the original incongruities of the commodity form—that is, the measured equivalence of qualitatively incommensurable forms—are multiplied by new incongruities introduced by the successive combinations of commodity characteristics freed from any customary association with specific objects. The "fluid medium" of the mass market dissolves the social and cultural sediment in which symbolic forms are embedded; it continually and systematically dislodges the meanings that humans have always expressed through and attached to their own artifacts.

Given this defamiliarizing impact of intensive and extensive market exchange, the advertising industry acquires cultural burdens that are inseparable from its economic mission of stimulating wants for goods: It must refamiliarize or recontextualize these goods, or more accurately, these "bundles of attributes" in the commodity environment. "You are where you advertise," reads an ad for the *New York Times*. "A message is only as good, only as credible, only as believable as the environment it appears in." For this very reason, however, one Los Angeles firm prefers to market its clients' goods not through the self-conscious selling media of newspapers or television, but rather through the self-consciously non-selling vehicles of motion pictures, where products may be introduced in the guise of props. According to the firm's founder, products appear more "real" or "natural" in films because they are invariably situated in a "cluster of other brand-name products." Conversely, television dramas appear that much less vivid or real because "they are prohibited from showing the brand names that are an integral part of everyone's lives."[14]

The average consumer, according to yet another marketing specialist, has a "lifetime of experiences" in this trademarked environment "stored within him." "A commercial," he adds, "can provide the stimuli to regenerate those experiences, bring them into the foreground, and associate them with the product." But, as these examples suggest, advertising must root these commodities in a mercurial symbolic setting that is itself increasingly composed of goods. So that if metaphors snap under the strain of the symbolic incongruities that marketing requires —as happens, say, in the recurrent effort to label as "natural" or "real" what is clearly artificial—then they must be repaired or new ones improvised. As consumers we are thus not only sold goods, we are sold the characteristics of goods; and not only characteristics but relations among characteristics lodged in collections of commodities, whose total pattern it is the obligation of the advertisement to represent in the most aesthetically economical and psychologically plausible way.[15]

An advertisement markets a version of reality whose plausibility underwrites the value and significance of the commodity placed in its foreground. But since the foreground and background of all marketing images are alike composed of commodity attributes, plausibility is always a precarious victory. The continuous process of foregrounding within advertisements as a whole calls the long-term success of any particular ad into question. Each attempt at reorientation is at the same time a process of disorientation; each reshuffling of commodity characteristics across the spectrum of goods recontextualizes and thus redivides the needs and wants of its audience.

Under such conditions, it is extraordinarily difficult to sort out needs and wants. But if it is commodity contexts that are sold and consumed, as the theory and practice of contemporary marketing suggest, then one motive that an advertisement or commercial can be said to call out in every instance is a cognitive one: the desire to master the bewildering and predatory imperatives of the market by an acquisitive or possessive gesture of the mind. Here, cultural orientation becomes one with cultural appropriation. We read clothes, possessions, interiors, and exteriors as representing more or less successful accommodations to a world of goods, and in so doing we rehearse in our minds the appropriation of that social world via the commodity. We consume by proxy. We window-shop.

To shrug off such rehearsals as vicarious ventures is to neglect the powers at play in this mental consumption. On the one side stands the marketer, arranging and framing the display so as to refamiliarize and resituate the commodity. On the other side stands the consumer, at once distanced and absorbed in the visual appropriation of texture, color, status, and history. Each display invokes, satisfies, and reinvokes a cognitive drive, what Jean Baudrillard calls "the passion for the code."[16] Each advertisement promises a fix on the complexities of the market by appealing to the power of purchase as a mental power, a matter of possession and leverage in an indeterminate situation. For every actual purchase, countless contemplated purchases prepare the way. A habit of mind thus develops that uses the commodity without, in the conventional sense, using it up. What modern consumer culture produces, then, is not so much a way of being (profligate, miserly, reserved, exhibitionist) as a way of seeing—a way best characterized as visually acquisitive. In short, modern consumer culture holds up the cognitive appetite as the model and engine of its reproductive process.

The word "modern" needs to be emphasized here since consumer cultures in the broadest sense are as old as human society itself. Archaeological and anthropological evidence indicates that the earliest forms of societies were those organized around the acquisition, exchange, redistribution, and use of material life, rather than around the production of goods. Hunting, gathering, and nomadic societies are appropriative societies to the modern view because they take rather than produce their living. Yet as cultures, these societies display few of the appropriative fears and desires that we have come to associate with contemporary consumer society and that we can already see at work in societies characterized by such features as plow agriculture, household production, and patriarchal organization. There, in fact, we do find evidence of an appropriative vision, or at least evidence of its cultural recognition in the form of the "Evil Eye." But these recognitions differ significantly from our own and, as I shall try to show, from Henry James's. First, the defenses against the Evil Eye are invariably ritualized appeals to a protective authority, whether symbolic or real. The protections sought remain fixed with the social hierarchy that occasioned the fear. Second, the dangers of the Evil Eye's consuming vision imply an older notion of consumption as waste or destruction (rather than acquisition or appropriation); they refer to the destruction of crops, the death or deformity of children, the sterility of the womb. The Evil Eye can be a weapon for peasant societies, but it is almost always an unwanted faculty and at times a disease, a miasma.[17]

It is at the point where consumption converts its meaning from a disease into a cure that we may begin to speak of a consumer culture in the sense we experience it. How and under what particular conditions that point is passed is a difficult historical question, the answer to which this essay will confine to the life and work of one man: Henry James. Nevertheless, at the broadest level, it is possible to see consumer culture as an episode in the history of market societies, and, furthermore, to see that culture as increasingly organized around a model of possessive or acquisitive cognition—a motive that reproduces what it aims to reduce: the defamiliarizing dynamic of the market medium.

II

How we approach this cognitive appetite may depend in part upon the intellectual traditions within which we seek to understand it. If, for example, we turn to the utilitarian tradition of political economy, we may find ourselves agreeing with Adam Smith that the hungry eye of market societies is the driving force behind their growth into civilizations. If, on the other hand, we turn to the romantic tradition of philosophical anthropology, we may find ourselves agreeing with Rousseau and the early Marx that such civilizations are proportionately impoverished with every increment in possession. Where Smith sees commodities as enlarging and refining the human sensibility by multiplying its objects, Marx sees them as alienating it through the forms in which its objects are appropriated. Within a commodity world, Marx argues, "*all* the physical and spiritual senses" are replaced by "the sense of *having.*" Consumption is in Marx's account and to some degree in Smith's account neither a by-product nor an end product of production; it is rather a reenactment within consciousness of accumulations forged within the material world. It is, in Raymond Williams's phrase, an act of "internal capitalisation." [18]

Cryptic as such phrases may appear, they nonetheless point toward a horizon where the planes of social consciousness and economic activity seem to meet. They suggest connections between ways of appropriating the material world and ways of seeing or sensing it. They pose consumption as a cultural question, as a question of the social conditions of meaning under which particular commodity relations reproduce themselves. The term "internal capitalisation" may strike us at first as no more than a catch phrase, but what it attempts to catch is just that which has eluded historians: the systematic description and historical analysis of the lived world of commodities, the world of goods produced for exchange, the world in which consumption appears as *the* consummatory act.

Yet if the languages of rationalism and romanticism do no more than allow us to gesture at the horizon where consumer experience and consumer behavior meet, where then may historians look for the kinds of evidence and instrumentalities that might bring that horizon into closer focus? The possibilities are numerous. We might for example look to memoir or autobiography, sources conventionally associated with the education of sensibility. Or we might look to the history of theology and social theory, disciplines aimed at bridging the gap between private meanings and collective consciousness. Or we might look at imaginative literature, particularly at the point where the conventions of the genre open themselves up to the possibility of a defamiliarized world. [19] Specifically, we might look at that extended moment in American literature—a moment coextensive with the emergence of a consumer culture among the middle class—when the claims of romance and the claims of realism were still in the balance. We might look, in short, at the literature of late nineteenth-century America.

Henry James, whose literary career spanned a considerable portion of that "moment," does not at first glance offer historians much more than a grudging acknowledgment of the tawdry spectacle of consumer culture. Indeed his revulsion from it is celebrated. Like his brother William, Henry displayed a seemingly "instinctive repugnance" toward the strident entreaties of the Age of Barnum—a repugnance so lively as to have stirred him eventually to flight.[20] Something akin to a note of embarrassment runs through those rare passages in James's writings that explicitly take up the question of the commodity world: the world of goods, newspapers, and advertisements. That note in turn reverberates upon an even more deeply felt sense of violation, one that James consistently associates with the shamelessly intrusive appeals of the market. What James sees violated in almost every case is "privacy," a term he uses quite broadly to refer to the indispensable conditions of familiarity upon which the fragile structure of human communities is formed. What dissolves the foundation of this familiarity is almost invariably "publicity," a word he uses with equal expansiveness to refer to the values and instrumentalities of a market society: the traffic in commodities, the habit of display, the inclination to theatricality, the worship of novelty and quantity.

Given the prominence of these themes, James's fiction appears as an ingeniously contrived and meticulously sealed shelter thrown up against the loud and discordant appeals of a commodity culture. The "house of fiction"—James's celebrated metaphor for the achieved literary form—figuratively expresses what James's English home—the isolated and tranquil Lamb House—materially represented: a sanctuary built by and for the creative imagination. A venture outside this enclave was always for James a calculated risk, yet it is only in such ventures that we find him confronting in a more or less direct fashion what he labeled as "the unredeemed commercialism" of his homeland's "vast crude democracy of trade."[21] *The American Scene* (1907)—James's memoir of his visit to America of 1904–5—provides the single most explicit judgment on his encounters with consumer culture. As such, it serves as a point of entry into the more complex relation between the writer and the world of goods.

In the opening section of *The American Scene* James recalls his first tremor of apprehension about his "new" world when, upon stepping off the boat, he inhaled "the air of unmitigated publicity, publicity as a condition, as a doom, from which there could be no appeal." On land, he feels himself at sea. Steeped in this all too public medium of trade, James can find no model, no inward projection, "no image, no presumption of constituted relations, possibilities, amenities" in the American social order. It is, he concludes, "as if the projection had been so completely outward that one could but find oneself almost uneasy about the mere perspective required for the common acts of the personal life." Here James's sharp and sudden sense of disorientation appears to grow from an impression that the symbolic constituents of personal relations have acquired an impersonal, public currency. This impression, in turn, adds to his quickening conviction that in America the wage relation (and what it fetches) has altogether replaced the more familiar and established reciprocities of manners. Public and private spheres have collapsed; "the market and home therefore look alike dazzling, at first, in this reflected, many-coloured lustre" of a life constructed out of commodities.[22] And nowhere is this feeling of bedazzlement more insistent than in the institution where home and market have been effectively merged: the hotel.

"One is thrown upon it," James writes of the Waldorf-Astoria, "as straight upon the general painted scene over which the footlights of publicity play with their large crudity, and against the freely-brushed texture and grain of which you thus rub your nose more directly, and with less ceremony, than elsewhere." The violence of James's language is unusual in itself, yet at the same time entirely consonant with the intimations of violation he has elsewhere associated with the effects of "publicity." The New York hotel is for him a monstrous incarnation of self-promotion and self-aggrandizement and, as such, embodies the "American spirit most seeking and most finding itself." It is the stationary Pullman of a "hotel civilization," an extraordinary maze of seemingly random encounters and exchanges whose totality threatens to engulf the single "visionary tourist." The Waldorf is for James nothing less than the "conception of publicity" organized as "the vital medium" of human relations.[23]

Feeling himself stirred about within this fluid medium of hotel life, James nonetheless suspects a hand or hands behind the movement. "Master-spirits of management" he calls them, powers whom he imagines in the form of "some high-stationed orchestral leader . . . keeping the whole effect together and making it what it is." James sees the American scene, then, "in its crude plasticity, almost in the likeness of an army of puppets whose strings the wealth of his [the conductor's] technical imagination teaches him innumerable ways of pulling, and yet whose innocent, whose always ingenuous agitation of their members he has found means to make them think of themselves as delightfully free and easy."[24] It is for James both an appealing and an appalling image.

It is at the same time an extraordinarily prophetic image of the managed freedom of consumer societies. The passage, indeed the whole of *The American Scene*, foreshadows the modern critique of the consumer culture industry as "mass deception."[25] And like that critique, the book seems to look backward as well to the romantic tradition within which Marx first ventured his views on the human impoverishment of possessive individualism. For just as James discovers a new form of mobile, consumable wealth in midtown Manhattan, so he finds a new form of mobile, consumable poverty on the Lower East Side. There "the wants, the gratifications, the aspirations of the 'poor,' as expressed in the shops" signify for him "a new style of poverty," a shop-bought and shop-worn poverty thrusting itself "out of the possible purchasers" he encounters on the street and making them, "to every man and woman, individual throbs in the larger harmony." James recapitulates his orchestral metaphor, to which he adds the contrapuntal relation between the properties available in the ghetto shops and "the living unit's paying property in himself"—the relation, in short, between goods and labor. The Hester Street laborer's "property in himself"—his new and alien form of self-possession—has for James a defiant and abrasive side: the insolent liberties taken by free workers. But it has its pitiable side as well, since whatever deference or manners the wage has displaced, its earner still bows before the power "of the new remorseless monopolies." The laborer's property in himself now stands in relation to "properties overwhelmingly greater . . . that allow the asking of no questions and the making, for coexistence with them, of no conditions." The conclusion seems inescapable to James: "There is such a thing, in the United States, as freedom to grow up to be blighted, and it may be the only freedom in store for the smaller fry of future generations." [26]

Taken together, these observations constitute for the historian one of Henry James's grimmest and most pointed forays upon the terrain of social and cultural criticism; also one of his rarest. Whether out of revulsion or pity, James kept the forms of consumer culture he found in America's hotels and ghettos firmly confined to the outskirts of his fictive settings, muffling the cries of the market behind the ancient walls and hedges of private villa and country house. This aloofness saps the analytical force of his reportage upon consumer culture. His prescience becomes for us altogether facile, and thus suspect. For if his observations do anticipate the critique of mass culture imported to America three decades later, they also open themselves to the charge of elitism. Revulsion and pity, after all, are alike forms of condescension, and despite James's misgivings upon the corruptions of Europe, he was never loath to use the heritage of the Old World to touch the raw nerve of the New. However promising his judgments of America's market world may appear to the historian, they nonetheless assert themselves as the judgments of an outsider.

No one did more to sustain this image of remoteness than James himself. Reflecting on his own sense of disorientation in *The American Scene*, he attributed it less to departures from a scale of life he had grown up with as a "small boy" in America than to departures from a scale of life he had embraced as a young man in Europe. "Importances," he found, "are all strikingly shifted and reconstituted, in the

United States, for the visitor attuned, from far back, to 'European' importances."[27] The image is true to the letter of his experience but not to the substance. James had indeed been "attuned" to European importances from far back, but the manner in which he had thus acclimated himself had been eminently American and preeminently consumerist. The "hotel civilization" that he found so unsettling in turn-of-the-century America was the same medium through which he had first become acquainted with mid-century Europe. James's celebrated posture of detachment—his conjoined attitudes of icy aloofness and intense scrutiny—may have had as much to do, in the end, with the emotional and intellectual proximity he once felt to a burgeoning mass-market society as with the distance he eventually adopted.

The possibility is worth exploring. For if we treat James's detachment as something more than a convenient ground for accepting or dismissing his particular assessments of the Age of Barnum; if, in fact, we treat it as a part of an age that requires explaining, then we may find ourselves better able to unpack the historical significance of that literary baggage of James's late style, which has remained for so long within the particular jurisdiction of formalist critics. We may be able to break the seal of historical solipsism and idiosyncracy surrounding James and treat the record of his sensibility as the remarkable document it is. And we may trace through that sensibility a route of access to the very culture of consumption from which it is assumed to have recoiled in dismay.

We may see this route toward the commodity world first figuratively inscribed within James's consciousness as the great avenue leading out of the "small and compact and ingenuous society" of his youth, the society of New York's Washington Square. "Broadway was the feature and the artery, the joy and the adventure of one's childhood," James recalls in one of his autobiographies, "and it stretched, and prodigiously, from Union Square to Barnum's great American Museum by the City Hall." His is if anything an affectionate memory of a boulevard crowded with theaters, confectioners, and "vast, marmorean, plateglassy" department stores—a peripheral world "bristling" with goods "heaped up for our fond consumption." A prodigiousness of avenue was matched by a prodigiousness of childlike appetite, the two of which are joined retrospectively in James's autobiography as expressions of a bucolic America's "Edenlike consciousness." "We ate everything in those days," James confesses, "as from stores that were infinite."[28]

But if it is innocence that James wishes to conjure up as the theme of his (and by extension America's) childhood, it is a characteristically mindful innocence. His child's consciousness selected and weighed even as it prepared to consume. And more than any other feature of the Broadway experience, it was Barnum's Museum that evoked in the young James this market-wise balance of hedonism and detachment, of psychic investment and psychic withholding. Would he scatter his allowance "in the dusty halls of humbug, amid bottled mermaids, 'bearded ladies' and chill dioramas," he asked himself, or would he hold out for the drama of the lecture room? "The impression appears to have been mixed," he remembers; "the drinking deep and the holding out, holding out in particular against failure of food and of stage-fares, provision for transport to and fro, being questions equally intense."[29] Such rudimentary appreciations of his own consumer preferences—his own demand schedule—were but one aspect, however, of a detachment he felt in the midst of his intense attraction to the "Barnum association." Indeed, it was this detached perception that was at bottom the source of James's enchantment with a carnivalesque setting he otherwise regarded as sordid and impoverished.

For James does remember the "Barnum picture" as "above all ignoble and awful, its blatant face or frame studded with innumerable flags that waved, poor vulgar-sized ensigns, over spurious relics and catchpenny monsters in effigy." He remembers as well the "audible creak of carpentry" and properties upon the stage of Barnum's theater and envies "the simple faith of an age beguiled by arts so rude." Such makeshift arts failed to work their fascination upon the youthful James because *his* fascination lay entirely with the workings of the illusion. As he puts it in *A Small Boy and Others* (1913), "The point exactly was that we attended the spectacle just in order *not* to be beguiled, just in order to enjoy with ironic detachment and, at the very most, to be amused ourselves at our sensibility should it prove to have been trapped and caught." The small boy found himself absorbed not so much by Barnum's theater as by Barnum's theatricality; if he identified himself with any of the figures in *Uncle Tom's Cabin*, it was not with the characters but with the actors, perhaps even with the producer-director.[30] Thoroughly absorbed, James's mind was at the same time thoroughly divided. Thus divided, he found a doubled appreciation of the scene. He had been sold a (play) bill of goods—the crude scenic contextualizations of Barnum's drama—only to have restored its value by recontextualizing the play as an exercise in theatricality, a hoax in cheap clothing. He had, in his words, enjoyed an "aesthetic adventure" at the painless price of intellectual condescension.

James's condescension, however, was as misplaced as his mock envy for the "simple faith" of Barnum's audience. For as Neil Harris has noted, Barnum had built his success less upon the credulity of his public than upon its suspicion.[31] His wild promotional schemes tested the limits of plausibility in order to goad his audience into discovering (for a price) the mechanics of his deceptions and into measuring their sense of the "trick" against that of their companions. Barnum thus doubled his fortune by doubling his public's curiosity, or, more accurately, by importing the manipulations and suspicions of Yankee peddling into the sphere of entertainment. This lesson of the master imprinted itself deeply, if obliquely, upon James's mind, upon a "consciousness," as he puts it, "that was to be nothing if not mixed and a curiosity that was to be nothing if not restless." The sordid commodity world of Barnum's museum became for James "a brave beginning," a "great initiation" into the "possibility of a free play of mind" over its objects.[32] The battle of wits of the country store, translated by Barnum into the cognitive game of the popular museum, was recast once more by James into the leitmotif of his life and work: his concern with the play or presence of mind, with the struggle of sensibilities that could be "trapped and caught."

To locate the cultural and historical sources of this agonistic strain within James's early aesthetic awakenings is to understand the peculiarly active and powerful inflection James gives to the word "spectatorship." His is a vision that, in an almost physical sense, "takes in" the world; takes it in so as not to be taken in by it. He describes his youthful hunger for impressions as "a visionary ache," and speaks of this ache as a "dark difficulty at which one could but secretly stare—secretly because one was somehow ashamed of its being there and would have quickly removed one's eyes, or tried to clear them, if caught in the act of watching." He remembers his state of mind as a consciousness "positively disfurnished" of business sense—a want of knowledge that he experienced as a form of exposure. He sees himself as having drawn upon others' experience, upon his brother's in particular, filling himself on "the crumbs of his feast and the echoes of his life." In *A Small Boy and Others* he compares himself to William as "some commercial traveller who has lost the key to his packed case of samples and can but pass for a fool while other exhibitions go forward." In sum, Henry James portrays himself as a vicarious, voyeuristic consumer always living near "the constant hum of borrowed experience."[33]

Obeying his father's injunction to "convert" his impressions into more "soluble stuff," the small boy window-shopped his way through Europe during the 1850s as his nomadic family—"housed and disconnected"—moved from one lodging to another. His visual appropriations of the European scene accumulated at every step until, as he recalls, his "small uneasy mind" felt like "a little jacket ill cut or ill sewn," a garment "bulging and tightening in the wrong, or at least in unnatural and unexpected places." The natural cornucopia of the New World soon paled in comparison to the accumulations of the Old. Europe was for the young James a "thick" rather than a "thin" wilderness, and he gloried in the power of converting any residual thinness into thickness, into density.[34]

"Housed and disconnected," James's active mind sought to embody itself by attaching its "gaping view" to "things and persons, objects and aspects." He became for all intents and purposes an entrepreneur of observation. "I take possession of the Old World," he exclaimed upon his arrival in England in 1875. "I inhale it—I appropriate it." Later he reported himself able "to carry all England in my breeches pocket." The images are arresting, suggesting as they do the almost visceral sense in which James felt himself to have incorporated the world he had "taken in" through his vision. And having thus incorporated this world, he was correspondingly reluctant to leave it. Nearly four decades after his arrival in England, James refused an invitation to return once again to America. "You see," he wrote his friend William Dean Howells, "my capital—yielding all my income, intellectual, social, associational, on the old investment of so many years—my capital is *here*, and to let it all slide would be simply to become bankrupt."[35]

James was hardly the first American capitalist, figurative or real, to acknowledge his dependence on British accumulations, but the lesson of their conversion into more "soluble stuff" had been learned at home. The story of James's life, as of his art, is the story of relentless commitment to acquisition, an unceasing *furnishing* of his "inward life" with objects whose properties—personal, material, theatrical—formed the capital of his imagination.[36] His envy of those more active than himself, such as his "soldier-brothers" of the Civil War, was not directed at the celebrated benefits of the strenuous life. What he envied above all was their "wondrous opportunity of vision"; not their stand at one or another battle, but their standpoint. Vision, he concluded, would do "half the work" of carrying him through life, so much so that the moment one ceased "to live in large measure by one's eyes (with the imagination of course all the while waiting on this) one would have taken the longest step towards not living at all."[37] No more poignant expression of James's own consuming vision of life may be found, outside his novels.

By hinging his own sense of survival upon the power of his possessive outlook, James may have been expressing—perhaps more than he knew—the anxieties of a middle class accustomed to affluence yet no longer secure in its proprietary powers; a class seeking to replace an older set of resources (ownership of the means of production and distribution) with another (control over the means of communication and service).[38] Born into a wealthy family at odds with the thought of its own material possessions—a home intensely familial yet intensely defamiliarizing—James felt himself painfully exposed from an early age.

Urged "to be something, something unconnected with specific doing, something free and uncommitted," James turned his own apprehensions about the world into apprehensions of it.[39] Spectatorship, understood as an appropriative gesture of the mind, belies its outward semblance of passivity; it is rather a vision armed to meet a wilderness, thick or thin, where sensibilities may be "trapped and caught." James's reminiscences reveal what we might call the social construction of a motive: an overwhelming desire to possess as knowledge springing out of the experience of an idiosyncratic childhood, a transitional class formation, and an embryonic consumer culture.

James would never have seen himself in this way, of course. The image he had selected for himself was in his eyes unique and unshareable. "I had not found him in the market as an exhibited or *offered* value. I had in a word to draw him forth from within rather than meet him in the world before me, the more convenient sphere of the objective, and to make him objective, in short, had to turn nothing less than myself inside out." In a sense, this reading is quite true. Threatened by a sense of his precarious position in a market society, James had fallen back upon his own resources. But those resources and the method of their acquisition had had everything to do with the market he otherwise found so empty and sterile. He had learned the lessons of his peculiar upbringing all too well, too well indeed to accept any crudeness in their expression. So deeply and finely had he internalized the social world of goods as the foundation of his own psyche that any material expression of it loomed before him as a horrifying yet fascinating extraction of himself, a fragment of an encompassing alter ego.[40] Publicity affronted him because it confronted him with a reflected image, albeit gross and deformed, of the "densities" he had accumulated within himself, accumulated in order to turn them, once again, inside out.

The critique James developed against America's burgeoning consumer culture was thus an immanent critique, a critique from within rather than from without. He may have detested the Age of Barnum, but from it he drew the rules of humbug to which he subjected his characters and, at times, his readers. Popular romancers might see their novels as requiring the creaking paraphernalia "of boats, or of caravans, or of tigers, or of 'historical characters,' or of ghosts, or of forgers, or of beautiful wicked women," but not James. Though each of these devices did enter into his fiction at one time or another, they did so largely as metaphors for more "common and covert" dangers that to the unarmed eye "look like nothing" but which "can be but inwardly and occultly dealt with."[41] In the dense and bristling "forest of symbols" that was Phineas T. Barnum's and Henry James's preserve, the impresario and impressionist alike appointed themselves as scouts of the mind, as Pathfinders for an inquisitive, acquisitive cognition. If the setting was deceptive and confusing, so much the better; for James, like Barnum, was prepared to use his peculiarly doubled vision—personal and fictive—to point the way to the egress.

III

James's autobiographical recovery of his childhood experiences was undertaken at roughly the same late point in his life as the re-*visions* (as he liked to call them) of his novels, and both ventures betray the imposed continuities of his afterthought. Only from the unrevised works themselves may we glean something of an evolution in James's relation to consumer culture. These works reveal a deepening awareness of the commodity world, an awareness that becomes by the end of his life wholly critical *and* wholly complicit. The contradiction is a fertile one, for through it we are able to glimpse the process by which an American bourgeoisie created and contested a culture of consumption at the turn of the century.

The "consuming vision" as such appears first as an ambiguous but often sinister theme in James's early work, reemerges as a disruptive force within the writing of his middle years, only to end as the constitutive power of his last complete novel. James's oeuvre thus offers us a rich document of internalization, an example of the lived density and historicity of consumer culture. Indeed, the historicity or periodicity of James's work may be calculated as a matter of the successive and cumulative ways in which he managed to impart density to what are in every other aspect the most intangible, insubstantial relations. The thickness of Jamesian description grows over the sequence of his novels at the same time as the proportion of direct reference to material life declines. The only things Jamesian characters actually produce are effects. A person's effects are always contrivable, alienable, acquirable in James's fictive world. And in the measure that social life approximates a traffic in effects, the social selves generated therein acquire the durable and resilient features of goods. Over time, the ensemble of a person's effects—the product of the mutual effort to appropriate and to *be* appropriate—congeals into character. Character is, in turn, "internalized as a possession," that is, "as something which can be either displayed or interpreted," and the circle is completed—a circle that Raymond Williams describes, in his etymology of the word "character," as "an extreme of possessive individualism."[42]

The Jamesian character does not so much express a type, then, as he creates one through the sedimentation of cumulative effects: a mask or shell or collaborative manufacture that solidifies with every representation. Theatricality and commerce mix themselves in James's writing so as to suggest that conspicuousness itself—the exposure of stage or shop window—burnishes its human objects. James offers a vivid example of this process in the image he gives to the old actress Honorine Carré of *The Tragic Muse* (1890): "Her whole countenance had the look of long service—of a thing infinitely worn and used, drawn and stretched to excess, with its elasticity over done and its springs relaxed, yet religiously preserved and kept in repair, like an old valuable timepiece, which might have quivered and rumbled, but could be trusted to strike the hour."[43] In Carré's world, life more than imitates art; it borrows, exchanges, and fabricates itself through art. It embodies itself in a social marketplace whose recurrent acts of representation (and misrepresentation) bestow upon their agents the plastic or brittle properties of commodities.

Part of what brings people to this marketplace, James suggests in his early novels, is the sheer desire to please. Such at least appears to be the case with characters like Felix Young in *The Europeans* (1878), Isabel Archer in *The Portrait of a Lady* (1881), and Verena Tarrant in *The Bostonians* (1886). Yet each of these characters remains an expressive and independent being whose complaisance pales besides the febrile social sensibilities of James's early villains. The character of Madame Merle is perhaps one of the most celebrated instances of an achieved marketplace identity. Isabel Archer finds it impossible to think of Madame Merle "as an isolated figure." She seems to exist "only in relations with her fellow mortals." Her angles are "too much smoothed," her character "too flexible, too supple . . . too finished, too civilized . . . too perfectly the social animal that man and woman are supposed to have been intended to be." Madame Merle, for her part, instructs Isabel:

When you have lived as long as I, you will see that every human being has his shell, and that you must take the shell into account. By the shell I mean the whole envelope of circumstances. There is no such thing as an isolated man or woman; we are each of us made up of a cluster of appurtenances. What do you call one's self? Where does it begin? Where does it end? It overflows into everything that belongs to us—and then it flows back again. I know that a large part of myself is in the dress I choose to wear. I have a great respect for *things!* One's self—for other people—is one's expression of one's self; and one's house, one's clothes, the books one reads, the company one keeps—these things are all expressive.

Isabel's offended response allows James to draw more sharply the contrast between the two social types: "I don't know whether I succeed in expressing myself," she replies, "but I know that nothing else expresses me. Nothing that belongs to me is any measure of me; on the contrary, it's a limit, it's a barrier, and a perfectly arbitrary one."[44] For our part, we may label this dichotomy of character in any number of ways: Arminian/antinomian, pragmatic/transcendent, other-directed/inner-directed. But the dichotomy itself remains an irreducible and irresolvable feature of James's early work, infusing the narratives with a Manichean conflict.[45]

Within the framework of this conflict, a character's perfected sense of the appropriate often signals a less visible but no less developed appropriative vision. Unable to produce "an impression which she knew to be expected," Isabel Archer is matched against Gilbert Osmond, whose life is "altogether a thing of forms, a conscious, calculated attitude." Osmond's propriety is, in its core, proprietary: He imagines Isabel's intelligence as a "silver plate" upon which he might heap up the fruits of conversation. In his mind's eye, he can "tap her imagination with his knuckle and make it ring." And it is their liaison, with its mixtures of deception and self-deception, that first transforms Isabel's face into a "fixed and mechanical" mask, a representation rather than an expression of serenity.[46] Her ultimate triumph comes only when she casts off her mask and recovers a serenity that has become hers by virtue of an act of self-conscious renunciation, an act that raises her above the sorts of exchange to which she is, in form, submitting by her marriage to Osmond. In filling the frame of the portrait so many have constructed for her, Isabel discovers within herself a plenitude that defies its constraints, a plenitude that resists the consuming vision. She remains James's character, but as a type, she is no longer a "Jamesian" character.

Few of James's early novels—novels of the 1870s and early 1880s —fall so neatly into the typology of *The Portrait of a Lady*, his acknowledged masterpiece of the period. The appropriative vision inhabits these works but doesn't consistently animate them; it mingles itself with other Jamesian interests. To the international and aesthetic themes James adds the social themes of his middle period, the period of *The Bostonians* and *The Princess Casamassima* (1886). His fictive world widens to embrace a panorama of characters—feminists, philanthropists, anarchists, actors, publicists, politicians, and bookbinders—with the result that his novels become distended and occasionally disorganized. Possessive struggles are still decisive ones, but the contests are themselves so pointed, even naked, in their character as to crowd out the more "common and covert" dangers of the social marketplace: the town house and the country house. Where the proprietary vision once threatened, it now finds itself threatened. "Consumption" recovers some of its earlier, destructive connotations in *The Princess Casamassima* as the specter of expropriation haunts the appropriative spectator. This is in fact the plight of James's aesthetic revolutionary, Hyacinth Robinson.[47]

The suicide of Hyacinth in *The Princess Casamassima* is for James the death of the pure renunciatory act as an adequately redemptive response to a possessive culture. Henceforth in James's fiction there is a gradual movement from the renunciatory to the retaliatory impulse.[48] Renunciation itself becomes an increasingly ambiguous act as it acquires some of the aspects of reprisal; it becomes a gesture not of forgiveness but of foreclosure, a denial of possibilities in response to the betrayal of a pledge—a return, so to speak, in kind. Gradually, inexorably, a principle of transcendence gives way to a principle of symmetry —moral, aesthetic, social—a principle that James refines to its intensest pitch in his final novels.[49] The elusive and collusive relations among the characters merge indistinguishably with the relations between author and reader, an effect heightened by James's removal of author surrogates (the Rowland Mallets and the Ralph Touchetts) and his focus on central narrators or points of view. (Fanny Assingham in *The Golden Bowl* is an exception to which I shall return below.) As those points of view are themselves challenged within the text, the reader is made to share, often unwittingly, the characters' hunger for knowledge.

The consuming vision implants itself at the heart of James's fiction in the years after 1886. An appetite once thematised within the novel now thematises the novel as one of a variety of its representative forms. What was once a problem within the novel is now its problematic: its defining set of questions and motives. But what can define can as well undermine. The pressure of external events—the pain of social injustice—that is at work in *The Princess Casamassima* gives way to the internal pressure—the "visionary ache"—of James's subsequent novels. His struggle during the "treacherous years" of the 1890s and after is, in a sense, a struggle to find a vessel, a container adequate to the insistent, accumulative pressure of his proprietary vision. Such redemption as occurs within the novels becomes the redemption not of characters but of form, the commodity form.

The imprint of James's "visionary ache" is legible as early as 1888 in his short novel, *The Aspern Papers*. Its unnamed narrator, an editor, engages in an elaborate imposture to secure the papers of a dead American poet from Juliana Bordereau, the poet's former mistress, who lives a secluded existence in a Venetian villa. The narrator's entry into Venice, in which he "besieges" the city with his eyes, prepares the reader for the literary pillage he is contemplating, while the deployment of his eyes over the room of the dying woman, "rummaging with them the closets, the chests of drawers, the tables," rehearses his actual attempt at burglary. The editor's eventual detection by the poet's former mistress is similarly foreshadowed in her habit of wearing a "horrible green eyeshade" that serves her "almost as a mask," a device for scrutinizing the narrator without herself being seen. The eyeshade has its figurative parallel in the aged woman's house, whose "motionless shutters" become for the inquisitive narrator "expressive as eyes consciously closed," themselves invisible yet seeing all "between the lashes." Through the vehicle of the narrator's consuming vision, the reader is made an interested accomplice in the violation of this masked, enclosed world: the piercing of Juliana's shuttered house and the (mis)appropriation of its contents. But the only spoils recovered are the elements of the story itself. Thwarted by Juliana's spinster niece, who burns the poet's letters after her aunt's death, the narrator feels for a moment "a real darkness" descending upon his eyes.[50] If this is renunciation and not retribution, it has about it a Mosaic, if not oedipal, complexity.

A decade later, in *The Spoils of Poynton* (1897), "The Turn of the Screw" (1898), and *The Sacred Fount* (1901), the faculty of sight acquires a power sufficiently intense and sufficiently expansive to infuse its projected landscape with its own appropriative intentionality and thus to find unfamiliar and unwanted eyes at *its* windows. In these years James's consuming vision threatens to erupt within the novel, to press its forms into the service of its own needs, and thereby to convert his controlled psychological realism into a species of uncontrolled sociological surrealism. Never does this threat come closer to fulfillment than in *The Sacred Fount*, a novel whose suggestions of the occult are far more metaphysically frightening than those of "The Turn of the Screw" precisely because they are so deftly lodged in the ordinary world of Jamesian intercourse: the traffic in social selves. What are *dis*lodged are the conventions of placement—the signposts of identity, motive, and circumstance—that orient the reader. Without losing an ounce of civility, James briskly and methodically defamiliarizes the most familiar of his fictive worlds.

The novel's opening scene, set in a busy train station, is filled with premonitions of estrangement and predation. Its unidentified narrator uses the occasion to "look out" for "possible friends and even possible enemies," finding in the scene before him only one recognizable face yet acknowledging at the same time the possibility that its familiarity may be the projection of his own need. As the narrator prepares to embark for a sociable weekend at Newmarch, a country estate, he prepares the reader for the world to be found there: a world of careful concealment and consummate display, of studied privacy and restless curiosity, of suppressed anxiety and misplaced confidence. The narrator never identifies himself and offers the reader barely enough information to sustain the identities of the novel's other characters. Indeed, their substance seems to ebb and flow with their movements, the orbits and collisions of which compose the structure of the novel. This almost impersonal ebb and flow, so like the public life of the station, forms the central theme of *The Sacred Fount*. What the narrator refers to as the "pleasant give-and-take of society" becomes for him the literal problem —the problematic—on which his eye and, with it, the novel, turns.[51] Half flaneur, half anthropologist, the narrator sees about him at New- march figures who appear to gain visibly in youth or wit at the expense of others, and so he sets himself the task of discovering the principle at work and, through it, the human sources—the "sacred fount"—from which any particular character draws his or her new vitality.

The narrator's sense of this physical and intellectual "give-and- take" is quite vivid. Of one of its victims, May Server, he observes that he had "never seen before what consuming passion can make of the marked mortal on whom, with fixed beak and claws, it has settled as on prey." She reminds him of "a sponge wrung dry and with fine pores agape." "Voided and scraped of everything, her shell," strikes him as "merely crushable." She has been emptied of her substance, her wit and intelligence, and turned into "an old dead pastel under glass." But by whom? for whom? and upon what principle? The riddle puzzles the narrator as it has James's critics. Leon Edel treats the relations among the characters as a form of cannibalism or vampirism, terms that plainly fit the narrator's "portrait" of Mrs. Server. But those metaphors may be seen, in turn, to animate the controlling market imagery within which the novel situates the effects of the characters' "consuming passion." "One of them always gets more out of it than the other," the narrator's nemesis (Mrs. Briss) observes of a Newmarch couple. "One of them— you know the saying—gives the lips, the other gives the cheek." It is a chilling observation, but one to which the narrator rises with equanim- ity. "One of the pair," he notes, "has to pay for the other. What ensues is a miracle, and miracles are expensive."[52] The act of observation thus becomes for the narrator and for the reader a kind of mental bookkeep- ing, an extended, finely tuned audit of the characters' exchange rela- tions.

This audit has its own appropriative dimension, of course. Throughout *The Sacred Fount* the narrator's vision swells in power and confidence, grows till it can toy quite literally with the idea of its divine omniscience. The suggestion of paranoia, broached in the opening scene and whetted upon the sharp, pointed, penetrating gazes of the Newmarch gathering, finds its extension in the delusions of grandeur that the narrator begins to entertain. He feels "an undiluted bliss" in his "intensity of consciousness." He no longer needs to test his hypoth- esis of the social "give-and-take" or his list of suspects on anyone. He knows the "joy of the intellectual mastery of things unamenable, that joy of determining, almost of creating results." He incorporates the world of Newmarch, steeps himself up to his "intellectual eyes" in the "grossness" of its luster and the "thickness" of its medium, and settles himself within its "crystal cage."[53]

The narrator remains nonetheless unsettled. Though he sees the "opposed couples" at Newmarch as "balanced like bronze groups at the two ends of a chimney-piece," he yet wonders whether he has not imposed this "fine symmetry" upon them. He has always acknowledged his "idle habit of reading into mere human things an interest so much deeper than mere human things were in general prepared to supply"; but he has acknowledged the habit only to dismiss it as "the common fault of minds for which the vision of life is an obsession." "The obsession pays," he notes, "but to pay it has to borrow." And indeed the narrator's vision borrows more ruthlessly and more recklessly than any other in the novel, literally seizing each of its chapters as yet another installment on its curiosity. When the narrator suddenly finds himself overextended, one character (Mrs. Briss), recognizing his predicament, challenges his version of events and, by doing so, deprives it "of all value as coin." In panic, he feels himself age a thousand years and break into countless pieces. "I don't see," the narrator exclaims, "as I look about me, a piece I can pick up."[54] The novel ends abruptly in a scene of dismay and departure.

The Sacred Fount is itself a notable departure, as critics have remarked, if only for its willingness to indulge themes, pressures, possibilities that remain carefully controlled and contained elsewhere in James's work. To be sure, James makes no slips in the novel, as Edel has noted. The narrator's version of events loses its certitude without sacrificing its plausibility. The symmetry and surface of the Victorian novel are preserved even as its interior shell is fractured and split from within. *The Sacred Fount* strains against the pressure of its cognitive accumulations, despite James's dismissal of these accumulations (in a private letter) as "profitless" and "insubstantial."[55] His modesty in this case is more beguiling than becoming. James's novel strives to represent as an amusing fancy what his autobiography expresses as a disturbing fantasy: the "borrowed experience," the "bulging and tightening" mind, the "visionary ache," all of which constitute for him the "dark difficulty at which one could but secretly stare." If it is a state of poise that the novel's irony seeks to communicate, then it is a poise that constantly flexes and tenses the formal musculature of the narrative. James's posture suggests the precarious equilibrium of an obsession observed, an obsession allowed to run its course in literary harness, and thus an obsession exercised rather than exorcised. Self-indulgence and self-possession are inseparable in the appropriative world projected within the work, and within the life. James "letting go" is always James "taking in." *The Sacred Fount* is a monument to a consuming vision that in 1901 was far from entombed.

IV

If James's "visionary ache" was not exhausted in his "phantasmagorical" works of the late nineteenth century, it was in many ways assuaged in the magisterial works of the following decade. But it was only in *The Golden Bowl* that James achieved a kind of peace with his "consuming passion." There, in what Edel terms "the richest of all his creations," James drew together his creative powers and his major themes to produce what is, in effect, a deliberate and consummate reply to the manic and fragmentary fantasy of *The Sacred Fount*. The general visual avidity that threatens to disrupt the fragile and glittering world of Newmarch is transformed into an energy that both shapes and animates the equally precarious and lustrous world of Eaton Square and Portland Place, the world of *The Golden Bowl*. The very cognitive drive that from the outset is the problem of the earlier work is made to grow and flower into the solution of the later work. In this, *The Golden Bowl* offers itself as the first fully achieved literary expression of an American culture of consumption.

At first glance, the novel seems dense and massive. Yet the massiveness of the form conceals what is an altogether simple, almost slender, narrative scheme. A wealthy, expatriated American widower and his daughter (Adam and Maggie Verver) "acquire" spouses—a charming American woman and an equally charming Italian prince—who, unbeknownst to them, are former lovers. Encouraged by their renewed proximity and by the seeming complacency of both father and daughter, the two lovers resume their relationship. When the liaison is eventually discovered by Maggie, the widower's daughter, she uses her newfound knowledge to isolate the lovers from one another and to restore the forms, if not the substance, of her and her father's marriages. Each character is ultimately required to give up one relation in order to preserve another: The informal and "unnatural" attachments of implicit incest and explicit adultery are sacrificed to the formal and "natural" attachments of marriage. Here, *The Golden Bowl* is a work of almost perfect symmetry, a work in which the social and moral resolutions of the narrative blend imperceptibly with the aesthetic resolutions of the form; it is, in its own way, James's fulfillment of Flaubert's aspiration to write a formally exquisite novel about nothing.

There is of course much ado about this "nothing." The novel teems with "common and covert" dangers, dangers that the choric character, Fanny Assingham, delightedly and obsessively ponders. "One can never be ideally sure of anything," she observes at one point. "There are always possibilities." Against the skeptical attitude of her laconic husband, Fanny upholds the ideal of an exquisite presence of mind. Her eye for propriety is one with her proprietary eye, and it is through her eyes that the novel's four main characters initially seek to take hold of their situation. "I can do pretty well anything I *see*," the anxious Prince tells Fanny on the eve of his marriage to Maggie. "Therefore it is that I want, that I shall always want, your eyes. Through *them* I wish to look—even at any risk of their showing me what I mayn't like." [56] Fanny operates as the Prince's (and the reader's) scout, scanning the terrain so as to anticipate and forestall any misstep he or others might make. The ground of the novel is treacherous because it is invariably owned by someone; it exists only as a visual or cognitive possession of the characters, and, as such, it endows their movements across its landscape with intimations of trespass and piracy.

The novel, in fact, opens and closes amid images of gold and booty. Maggie likens herself and her father to a pair of "stage pirates" and her prospective husband, the Prince, to their treasure. "You're a rarity, an object of beauty, an object of price," she tells the Prince. "You're what they call a *morceau de musée*." The Prince takes the point, but James makes it the point on which the central triangle of his tale—the relation between Maggie, the Prince, and his lover, Charlotte—balances. The novel is, in this respect, one long speculation on the felt exchange value of the Prince, one that begins with the Prince's own ruminations:

It was as if he had been some old embossed coin, of a purity of gold no longer used, stamped with glorious arms, medieval, wonderful, of which the "worth" in mere modern change, sovereigns and half-crowns, would be great enough, but as to which, since there were finer ways of using it, such taking to pieces was superfluous. That was the image for the security in which it was open to him to rest; he was to constitute a possession, yet was to escape being reduced to his component parts. What would this mean but that, practically, he was never to be tried or tested? What would it mean but that, if they didn't "change" him, they really wouldn't know—he wouldn't know himself—how many pounds, shillings and pence he had to give? [57]

The Prince feels himself "invested with attributes" by Maggie and her father, Adam, but is unable to fathom the price they put upon them.

He is not to *do* anything for the Ververs; he is to *be* something for them: an exquisite "cluster of attributes." He is to be an object not of utility but of appreciation.

Appreciation—always an emotionally charged word for James— regains some of its earliest historical connotations in *The Golden Bowl*. Its Victorian associations with taste and esteem are continually subverted by James's use of the word to suggest appraisal or assessment: the setting, though not necessarily the naming, of a price. This at least is how the Prince experiences the appreciation of "the decent family eyes"—the eyes of Adam and Maggie—he encounters at Eaton Square.

This directed regard rested at its ease, but it neither lingered nor penetrated, and was, to the Prince's fancy, much of the same order as any glance directed, for due attention, from the same quarter, to the figure of a cheque received in the course of business and about to be enclosed to a banker. It made sure of the amount—and just so, from time to time, the amount of the Prince was made sure. He was being thus, in renewed instalments, perpetually paid in; he already reposed in the bank as a value, but subject, in this comfortable way to repeated, to infinite endorsement.[58]

But if he is purchased or consumed in relation to his wife and her father, he is in turn purchaser and consumer in relation to Charlotte Stant, the woman whom Maggie takes as a friend, Adam as a wife, and the Prince as a lover. In one of the earliest and most extraordinary episodes of the novel—the pre-nuptial scene at Fanny Assingham's in which the Prince is unexpectedly reunited with his former lover— James has Charlotte offer herself up to the Prince's vision "for his benefit and pleasure." The Prince's appreciative response amounts to a mental inventory of Charlotte's features.

But it was, strangely, as a cluster of possessions of his own that these things, in Charlotte Stant, now affected him; items in a full list, items recognized, each of them, as if, for the long interval, they had been "stored"—wrapped up, numbered, put away in a cabinet. While she faced Mrs. Assingham the door of the cabinet had opened of itself; he took the relics out, one by one, and it was more and more, each instant, as if she were giving him time. . . . He knew her narrow hands, he knew her long fingers and the shape and colour of her fingernails, he knew her special beauty of movement and line when she turned her back, and the perfect working of all her main attachments, that of some wonderful finished instrument, something intently made for exhibition, for a prize. He knew above all the extraordinary fineness of her flexible waist, the stem of an expanded flower which gave her a likeness also to some long, loose silk purse, well filled with gold pieces, but having been passed, empty, through a finger-ring that held it together. It was as if, before she turned to him, he had weighed the whole thing in his open palm and even heard a little the chink of the metal.[59]

The passage evokes the memory of the predatory Gilbert Osmond, but with this difference: The proprietary vision is no longer the distinctive feature of one character but rather the distinctive and constitutive relation among *all* the characters. Even Adam, the "consummate collector" of art, cannot forbear from seeing in Maggie "the appearance of some slight, slim draped 'antique' of Vatican or Capitoline halls." He acknowledges this perception as a "trick" of his mind that comes "from his caring for precious vases only less than for precious daughters."[60] But such tricks are just the stuff out of which the novel (and its title) is made. Adam's authority comes not from his wealth alone—the creature comforts and security it affords—but from the power of that wealth to fulfill the appropriative habits of mind that collectively form the second nature, the social medium within which the characters have for so long operated. The world of Portland Place and Eaton Square cannot be more distantly removed from the crude and callous transactions of the marketplace (the place where Adam made his millions), yet it is nonetheless a world saturated with the imagery of the market, a world constructed and deconstructed by the appreciative vision.

Consequently, when the rare material transaction does enter James's narrative, it does not so much disrupt as fulfill the logical possibilities of a deeply internalized commodity world. Charlotte's and the Prince's sortie to Bloomsbury in search of a wedding gift for Maggie, Adam's and Charlotte's shopping trip to Brighton, and Maggie's solitary return to the Bloomsbury shop (all reminiscent of James's childhood journeys up Broadway), are instances of the quickening or heightening function of material exchange in *The Golden Bowl*. Charlotte uses the occasion of the Bloomsbury excursion—the occasion on which the flawed bowl is first proffered and rejected—to bind the Prince to her in a prefigurative act of collusion on the eve of his marriage. At the very moment of renouncing her earlier claim upon him, she plants the seed of their eventual adultery. Passion, in the conventional sense, is scarcely at issue; it is not sensual or affectional desire that prompts their secrecy, but secrecy that sets their desire in motion, in particular, the desire to *know*. In a fictive world of what economists concede as "imperfect knowledge," a shared lie becomes a shared tie. Deprived of its ordinary yet rich emotional meanings, intimacy reduces itself in *The Golden Bowl* to a conspiratorial community—in Lawrence Holland's phrase—of "knowledge and possession."[61]

The Prince himself muses on this peculiar sense of community in the solitary moments before Charlotte arrives to consummate their own affair. He has, for his part, quietly prepared himself for this possibility by treating it as the logical fulfillment of the tacit understandings by which the Ververs—father and daughter—have so good-naturedly arranged for the group's comfort and convenience. "This understanding had wonderfully," the Prince reflects, "the same deep intimacy as the commercial, the financial association founded, far down, on a community of interest." Commercial affairs thus acquire the same furtive and illicit undertones as love affairs; indeed the two sorts of relations are collapsed together in the novel as productive of the same sorts of satisfactions and the same sorts of shame. Adam's scheme to marry Charlotte—that is, to possess her as a "human acquisition" and a "domestic resource"—is a "thing of less joy than a passion." His drive to acquire, to collect, to consume must serve in place of love and lust; the result is that James has Adam propose to Charlotte only after an exceptionally lurid scene (for James) in which she is forced to watch as Adam transacts business with a Brighton art broker.

> She had listened to the name of the sum he was capable of looking in the face. Given the relation of intimacy with him she had already, beyond all retraction, accepted, the stir of the air produced at the other place by that high figure struck him as a thing, that, from the moment she had exclaimed or protested as little as he himself had apologized, left him, but one thing more to do. A man of decent feeling didn't thrust his money, a huge lump of it, in such a way, under a poor girl's nose—a girl whose poverty was, after a fashion, the very basis of her enjoyment of his hospitality—without seeing, logically, a responsibility attached.[62]

The restraints of delicacy and tact usually reserved for sexual misadventures are here transferred to the marketplace. And once again a material transaction prompts and figures a social one.

Maggie's purchase of the golden bowl—its hidden crack the symbol and "document" of all the flawed relationships—is the third example of the quickening effect of material exchange in the novel. With its acquisition, she is at last put into possession of "real knowledge." The disclosure of the object's curious history allows her to piece together the extent of her (and her father's) betrayal at the hands of Charlotte and the Prince. And when her discovery is challenged by Fanny (much like the narrator's confrontation with Mrs. Briss in *The Sacred Fount*) and the bowl is dashed to pieces, Maggie does not flee the scene. Instead, she uses the episode to impress the Prince with the extent of her knowledge and of his vulnerability. She begins, in a sense, where the narrator of *The Sacred Fount* leaves off. What was once the occasional "throb" of Maggie's curiosity now yields to "the perpetual throb" of her new "sense of possession," a pulse "almost too violent either to recognize or to hide." She no longer sees herself as an understudy thrust unexpectedly upon the stage with only a "humbugging smile" to mask her uncertainty; she is now the director, looking through the windows of the country house of *her* fiction, looking in to see the "figures rehearsing some play of which she herself was the author."[63]

Prices are finally named. Charlotte "bargains" with Maggie to assure her silence, but the standoff becomes in Maggie's hands a tradeoff: Maggie gives up her father to Charlotte in return for her full possession of the Prince; Charlotte gives up her lover in order to remain Adam's "domestic resource." The delicate balance of marginal utilities is recalibrated; the decision to part couples is made; and Maggie and Adam take a final inventory of their possessions:

. . . the other objects in the room, the other pictures, the sofas, the chairs, the tables, the cabinets, the "important" pieces, supreme in their way, stood out, round them, consciously, for recognition and applause. Their eyes moved together from piece to piece, taking in the whole nobleness—quite as if for him to measure the wisdom of old ideas. The two noble persons seated, in conversation, at tea, fell thus into the splendid effect and the general harmony: Mrs. Verver and the Prince fairly "placed" themselves, however unwittingly, as high expressions of the kind of human furniture required, aesthetically, by such a scene. The fusion of their presence with the decorative elements, their contribution to the triumph of selection, was complete and admirable; though, to a lingering view, a view more penetrating than the occasion really demanded, they also might have figured as concrete attestations of a rare power of purchase. There was much indeed in the tone in which Adam Verver spoke again, and who shall say where his thought stopped? *"Le compte y est.* You've got some good things."[64]

With exquisite grace and tact, Maggie brokers the concluding transactions of the novel; her appreciative vision rearranges the fragments of a shattered world and, in so doing, redeems the magic power of the commodity form. James's rare intrusion into the narrative—his "lingering" and "penetrating" view—indicates how deeply indebted he feels to a "power of purchase" that has restored the symmetry not only of Maggie's world but of his own. The manipulative treatment of persons as so much "human furniture" that was once a source of concern in *The Sacred Fount* is now a source of celebration. Maggie, like James, uses the characters as her "compositional resources" and, by her skill, makes of herself and the novel a "value intrinsic."[65] James, of course, is never to be wholly identified with his characters, but it is fair to say that he never gives more fully of himself to any character as he does to the triumphant Maggie Verver of the closing pages of *The Golden Bowl.*

But James's complicity in the commodity vision of his supersensible characters is more than a matter of his (and our) emotional identification with the unconquerable Maggie. For emotion itself takes on a peculiarly restricted form in James's later works: It becomes wholly submerged and exhausted in the act of seeing. The emotional intensity of the fictive relationships is raised to its highest pitch in *The Golden Bowl,* but the gain in affective power is achieved only at the loss of variety and richness of feeling. Emotions in the novel, like those in *The Sacred Fount*, are almost invariably cognitive or epistemic; they have entirely to do with a character's impulse to possess as knowledge. James's characters are alternately conscious and surprised, enlightened and benighted, engrossed and amused, aware and bewildered, bemused and interested, but they are seldom anything else. And the emotional nuance varies proportionately with the possessive status each term suggests. As Seymour Chatman puts it, "It is hard to think of an occasion in a novel of James when a real taste is tasted or a real smell smelled."[66] "All the physical and spiritual senses," to recur to Marx, are replaced by "the sense of *having*," a sense James implants deeply within the cognitive act itself.

The distinctive density and detachment of *The Golden Bowl* reveal the extent of James's immersion in the novel's projected commodity world. The density is itself the outcome of a consuming vision's merciless power to detach not only itself, but its objects: alienating them quite literally from their conventional associations and context and accumulating them as resources, as capital. The market metaphors that so infuse his later writings are more than mere conceits or occasional tropes. They define the very medium—the fluid medium or solvent—in which the characters and their relations dissolve. For it is not just that the *characters* feel themselves "invested with attributes." The reader is made to feel same sensation by means of a language that transforms active verbs into passive participles and participles, in turn, into nouns. In place of human actors engaging one another in a material environment, James substitutes their properties or characteristics—fully materialized, fully animated, and fully prepared to take on a life of their own. "Thoughts and perceptions in James's world are entities more than actions, things more than movements," Chatman writes in his study of James's later style. "They occupy a space—the mind; though intangible, they are 'things' *in* the mind. Further, there is established between them and the characters a relation not unlike the relation which characters bear to each other, indeed, one which may be livelier." In short, the world of *The Golden Bowl* is a reified world. James represents the relation between characters as a relation between things, luxurious and rarefied things to be sure, but things nonetheless. The result, to paraphrase him, is a "rich little spectacle of objects embalmed in his wonder."[67]

A universe in which the "properties" of goods and people imperceptibly mingle is a world of precarious substantiality. It is, to say the least, unsettling, defamiliarizing. It induces the same uncertainty and anxiety as that occasioned by "some bad-faced stranger surprised in one of the thick-carpeted corridors of a house of quiet on a Sunday afternoon." To read *The Golden Bowl*, as Ruth Yeazell observes, "is to suffer a kind of epistemological vertigo," not simply, I would add, because of the shocks that lie concealed within its plot but because of the incongruities that lie embedded within its form—the commodity form.[68]

For the world projected in *The Golden Bowl* is, in the final analysis, virtually identical with the world disclosed in contemporary market research, that is, a world constructed by and for a consuming vision. It is an imagined world, of course, but one in which imagination itself strives to gild, glaze, and ultimately commodify its objects. Here the psychological novel and the psychographic study meet. James's celebrated "balloon of experience," it turns out, contains the same "clusters of attributes," the same freestanding and free-moving commodity characteristics as the trial balloons launched by modern marketers. Whether taken as art or artifact, these two forms of inquiry into social relationships indicate the presence, in Raymond Williams's terms, of a "common conventional mode" or rule in which needs, satisfactions, and anxieties are understood as mediated through the commodity form. Indeed, as Williams points out, it is only when the commodity form has become the "dominant mode of human perception and interaction" that a basis develops for a culture (films, magazines, novels, programs, etc.) "which present[s] human beings and their detachable characteristics as commodities, either for purchase or, more generally and more discreetly, for window-shopping."[69]

To be sure, more than a half-century separates James's last complete novel from the marketing wisdom it so eerily prefigures. And while it is possible to adduce the presence of the commodity form as the dominant cultural form of our own time, it is quite another matter to take it as such in the year of *The Golden Bowl*. The lag is not unlike that between Einstein's special theory of relativity, published at roughly the same time as James's final work, and our own cultural accommodations to the theory's operative principles. The scientific analogy is not altogether farfetched. There was, after all, more of the ruthless, dissecting, microscopic reflex in Henry James than in his brother, whatever the former's disclaimers. And the peculiar events of his life do suggest the way in which James's own mind might have served as a laboratory in which the embryonic possibilities of a consumer culture could be incubated.

But if James was a scientist, he was a strange one, preferring as he did a parsimony of instances and a plenitude of explanations. Such science is more oracular than anything else, and it was as prophet that James ultimately preferred to think of himself. His preface to *The Golden Bowl* portrays him as a "seer," a self-conscious play on his own consuming vision. For his was, if anything, an acquiring as well as inquiring mind. "To criticise," he wrote, "is to appreciate, to appropriate, to take intellectual possession, to establish in fine a relation with

the criticised thing and make it one's own. The large intellectual appetite projects itself thus on many things, while the small—not better
advised, but unconscious of need for advice—projects on few."[70] By
allowing his imagination to play the market, by allowing his deepest
desires and fears to take their shape and course within an aestheticized
commodity form, in sum, by allowing the culture of consumption to
enter into the very form and substance of his discourse, James has given
us perhaps the most complex portrait of the lived experience—the phe-
nomenology—of American consumer culture. His work is more than a
grace note on Marx's score for the "fetishism of commodities"—it is a
masterwork in its own right.

I began this inquiry upon the premise that consumer culture in
America requires a more complex experiential account than historians
have been prepared to give. I found, in that connection, that market
research and economic theory had themselves affirmed the motivational complexity of the symbolic world of goods while attempting, at
the same time, to contain that complexity within the bounds of statis-
tically quantifiable phenomena. These efforts notwithstanding, I argued that the social world projected within this research was a
symbolically disrupted and fragmented one, one in which the capacities
of symbols to condense and represent were strained to accommodate
the infinite valences of the commodity form. Taxed in this way, the
material and individual presence of commodities—as objects of research and demand—dissolved into their diffusable and detachable
properties, properties freely and symbolically deployed by marketers to
elicit consumer response. Following William Leiss, I described the cultural consequences of this dissolution as a progressive fragmentation of
human needs and, in addition, their subordination to a more immedi-
ately compelling need to know, to *possess* as knowledge. It is in this
respect that I proposed the act of consumption as the constitutive act
not only of contemporary material life but of contemporary culture as
well. Modern consumer culture, I hypothesized, holds up the motive
of acquisitive cognition as the model of its reproductive process.

James's work offers us a window—to use his own image—on this
process of cultural reproduction. Through it we are able to see the
gradual and seemingly inexorable incorporation of the commodity form
by a consciousness disposed to it (and exposed to it) by the peculiar
circumstances of his childhood, his class, and his culture. In each of
these circumstances, James's consuming vision served as a homeopathic remedy for the malaise it induced, filling the void of "borrowed
experience" with its ceaseless appropriations. Indeed, his work, as I
have already suggested, spanned the historical "moment" during which
the word "consumption" converted its meaning from a disease into a

cure. So we should not be surprised to see his language, like our own, reveal the blindness and prevision with which Americans entered into the world of goods.

It would be well for us to remember James's ambiguous legacy in contemplating the culture of consumption in America. For if we look to other disciplines beyond history for aid in producing a "thick description" of the meanings that have for so long been repressed, we will find curious echoes of his novels. We will find literary critics who treat literature and culture as a cluster of texts "disengaged, disembroiled, disencumbered" from the inconveniences of history and biography.[71] We will find sociologists who insist that ritual actions and natural expressions "are commercials performed to sell a version of the world under conditions no less questionable and treacherous than the ones advertisers face." And we will find anthropologists who argue that "the essential function of consumption is its capacity to make sense," and that commodities, like Trobriand necklaces, are, above everything else, "good for thinking."[72]

But if we have learned anything from James's art, it is that the thinking that is done with commodities is significantly different from the thinking that is done with Trobriand necklaces, and that to see one culture as indistinguishable from another in this respect is precisely to naturalize the most denatured of experiences: our own. It is a historical re*vision* of the most dubious sort.

James, I suspect, knew this. His last novel does in fact close on a note of renunciation. In the final scene of *The Golden Bowl*, the scene following Adam's and Charlotte's departure, a chastened Prince enters the room where Maggie awaits him. She asks him whether he *sees* how Charlotte's pride—her determination to adhere to their contract—will aid their own reconciliation. But the Prince is once again Maggie's dazzling and dazzled possession and, as such, fails to catch her meaning. "See?" he asks. "I see nothing but you."[73]

And the truth of it had, with this force, after a moment, so strangely lighted his eyes that, as for pity and dread of them, she buried her own in his breast.

Blindness and death—portentous imagery for a writer who believed that when he had ceased to live by his eyes, he "would have taken the longest step towards not living at all." Having realized in *The Golden Bowl* what he called the "best" and "solidest" of his visions, James, like Shakespeare's Prospero, renounces it. Even at its most cryptic, then, James's work is a document that opens up the contradictory experience of the commodity world. If it appears hermetic to us, we need only recall that Hermes was, among other things, the god of trade.

IV

EPITAPH FOR MIDDLETOWN
ROBERT S. LYND
AND THE ANALYSIS
OF CONSUMER CULTURE
RICHARD WIGHTMAN FOX

I

The 1920s and 1930s were the critical decades in the consolidation of modern American consumer society. It was in those interwar years that the characteristic institutions and habits of consumer culture—the motion picture, the radio, the automobile, the weekly photo-newsmagazine, installment buying, the five-day work week, suburban living, to mention a few—assumed the central place that they still occupy in American life. The Depression and the Second World War, far from undermining the consumer ethos, merely delayed for many the day of gratification. The ideal of fulfillment through consumption and leisure was if anything furthered by the experience of involuntary deprivation. By the 1950s millions of working-class Americans could join the middle class in sampling the satisfactions advertisers had continued to hawk during the lean years. No wonder so many postwar social observers persuaded themselves that America was a uniformly middle-class society; wherever they looked they saw consumers. Whatever gaps might persist among Americans at work, at the point of production, all seemed united by their commitment to acquiring the mass-marketed tokens of "the American standard of living."

What makes the interwar years so pivotal in the development of consumer culture is not just the firm establishment by the middle class of patterns and ideals of living that it had begun to promote as early as the 1880s. It is also the emergence of a new consciousness of the centrality of consumption in American life. A wide array of commentators, activists, and authorities made Americans acutely aware of their new collective role as consumers. A vast literature—novels, social science monographs, government reports, magazine pieces, trade journal articles, reform tracts—documented and dissected, celebrated and abominated the new culture of consumption. Stuart Ewen is no doubt right that Americans came increasingly to regard themselves as consumers rather than producers in these years, but he is wrong to imply that they were hoodwinked by "captains of consciousness"—advertisers and corporate leaders—into elevating buying over making. Americans were not passive creatures subject to direct manipulation by wily agents of capital. They became consumers through their own active adjustment to both the material and spiritual conditions of life in advanced capitalist society. Through consumption, as Jackson Lears argued in the first essay, they continued the quest for "real life," which earlier generations had sought in the transcendent religious realm.

It is true that Americans were also "educated" in the styles and ideals of consumer culture. But the "class" that took the lead in redefining the American as consumer was much broader than the corporate and advertising elite. It included social observers of all stripes, including, ironically, those vociferous opponents of advertising and business practices who by the early twentieth century were urging buyers and voters to define themselves as a consumer interest group. Americans were the recipients of a pervasive conventional wisdom that portrayed them not as citizens engaged in the task of governing themselves, but as consumers engaged in buying—either passively in response to advertisers' blandishments, or actively in response to the advice of professional experts. And many of the professionals, academics, government bureaucrats, and activists who helped circulate that wisdom were scarcely working hand-in-glove with the business elite. Some considered that elite their sworn enemy. But whatever their conscious alienation from big business, the social experts of the "professional-managerial class" did not constitute a distinct stratum between labor and capital. They were active contributors to the long-term expansion of the capitalist marketplace into the whole of everyday life, and therefore the witting or unwitting servants of "capital" broadly conceived.[1]

In the creation of the conventional wisdom about the consumer a key role was played by social scientists, who along with other policy-oriented professionals were rising to positions of increasing prominence and even power in the interwar period. Whether they considered themselves reformers or neutral analysts, social scientists were in fact purveyors of advice—about the efficient management of institutions ranging from the family to the national economy. Whether they believed their clientele to be business, labor, government, or the public in general, they were united in their commitment to professional expertise—as a means both of furthering the scientific understanding of society and extending the market for their advice. The professional social analysis produced in the interwar years was designed not only to provide expert counsel but to prove the necessity of such counsel for the preservation of social order.

The complex interrelationship between the rise of consumer culture—of a culture of self-conscious consumers—and the growing prominence of social scientific and other professional groups has not yet attracted the systematic labor of American historians. This essay will try to shed some light on that connection by examining the career of a single sociologist, Robert S. Lynd, who with his wife, Helen, authored the most significant analyses of consumer society between the two wars. *Middletown* (1929) and *Middletown in Transition* (1937) were extremely influential in defining and spreading the idea of America as a consumer culture. Lynd was also a leading social scientist who in the course of his Muncie studies committed himself to the notion of social leadership by a caring elite of professional planners. His career is a particularly vivid example of the link between the emergent consumer culture and the ideal of a scientifically ordered, methodically managed society.

Focusing upon the life and thought of a single individual poses the obvious problem of representativeness. The experience of Robert Lynd is in some respects atypical, and the analysis of consumer culture in the Middletown series diverges from the work of other commentators. But his distinctiveness is as much an advantage as a drawback. Following the biographical development of a reflective person like Lynd helps to challenge easy generalizations about "social science," "consumption," or "class." Lynd himself struggled with these concepts, as he battled with the realities they meant to illuminate. He was a social scientist who bewailed much social science, a consumer activist who detested consumer society, a committed opponent of the American corporate elite who held a respected place in elite institutions throughout his life. What a biographical focus sacrifices in breadth or generalizability it can try to make up in depth—and in signaling the danger of historical arguments based on brittle, static concepts. Lynd is especially valuable as a test case because he was such a vigorous critic of the corporate and advertising elite. His career makes plain that taking the side of the consumer—for whom Lynd fought assiduously as an activist in the 1930s—was quite compatible with an analysis that reduced the actual consumer to social impotence. Lynd's odyssey can serve as one building block in the larger history of consumption and professionalization that remains to be written.

Moreover, it is only by studying Lynd's life—a task that this essay undertakes, however partially, for the first time—that we can make sense of the Middletown volumes themselves. They were not just original, influential studies of American consumer society, and key embodiments of the growing self-consciousness of consumer culture. They were also records of Lynd's own painful adjustment to the consumer world, and documents of his stormy relationship with the elite Institute of Social and Religious Research, which funded the first volume. That book had such an enormous and immediate impact on its thousands of readers because it caught the subtle tensions and confusions of the early years of consumer society in America. The reason it caught them so flawlessly was that Robert Lynd had spent a decade sorting out those tensions and confusions in his own life. The two Middletown volumes, along with Lynd's third and final book, *Knowledge for What?*, map his progression from Christian minister to secular sociologist, from cultural analyst to political activist, from outsider to member of the professional elite, from critic of American consumer capitalism to critic of the irrational American consumer. It was hardly a simple progression. Like Bruce Barton, Henry James, and other writers and thinkers whose work embodied certain key features of the culture of consumption, Lynd remained in important respects a dissenter from that culture—and a vociferous critic of his fellow social scientists. His career shatters neat historical formulas. The social scientific elite that played a central role in the establishment of consumer culture did not conspire as a body to reduce Americans to the status of consumers, any more than business-men and advertisers did. Professional experts were an internally warring group. Many sought professional status, as Lynd did, in order to combat business hegemony. Yet even in Lynd's career, where one would least suspect it, one finds clear expression of the group consciousness of the professional elite and of its effort to root itself as an indispensable party in the effective management of the American consumer. Lynd's cri-tique of consumption was a pivotal contribution to that effort.

II

Robert Staughton Lynd was born in New Albany, Indiana, in 1892, of old midwestern, Anglo-Saxon stock. Although he grew up in Louisville, just across the Ohio River from New Albany, he could honestly inform Muncie's residents thirty years later that far from being, as they guessed, a condescending East Coast sophisticate, he was a genuine Hoosier by birth. It was no surprise when after graduating from high school in 1910 Lynd set out for Princeton. His great-great-grandfather William Staugton had taken his D.D. there over a century before. And his father, a self-made banker of modestly affluent means, was a leading Presbyterian layman in Louisville. Princeton was the bastion of Pres-byterian orthodoxy in America. "I grew up in a responsible Presbyterian family . . . in a home that was happy and honest," Lynd recollected privately in the 1950s. "My father was one of the straightest men I ever knew. When I went off to Princeton my father shook hands with me at the train and said: 'Bob, when the Indians brought up their sons, they sought to train them to ride, shoot straight, and tell the truth.' That was all, but by God he meant it, and I knew he did." His father was the complete Calvinist, the perfect embodiment of the Protestant ethic. Serious, sincere, morally rigorous, he closely scrutinized his thoughts and actions while working his way up from modest beginnings to sub-stantial material success. The good life, he taught his son, was the methodical life, the life subjected to rational plan, underlain by a re-lentlessly probing conscience.[2]

For Robert Lynd, Princeton came nevertheless as a shock. His wife, Helen, later recalled that his midwestern style did not go over well with the Ivy Leaguers. "He was a friendly person who went around and said 'Hi' to everybody, which wasn't done. And he didn't make a frater-nity. He felt rejected and left out, and it had a great influence on him for the rest of his life. He was always inclined to emphasize derogatory things, and to deemphasize laudatory things, about himself." After completing his four-year ordeal in 1914 he acceded to his father's demand that he enter the business world. He joined the staff of *Publisher's Weekly* in New York as an assistant editor, and spent the next six years —except for five months as an army private at the end of 1918—in a variety of publishing jobs in New York, including a year as advertising manager of Scribner's trade-book department. "Lunching in the correct gray dining room on the twentieth floor of the Yale Club and discussing sales campaigns and advertising contracts," as he put it in an autobiographical article in 1922, made him feel secure. By his father's lights— still his standard of self-judgment—he had arrived.[3]

But at the end of the war he had a drastic change of heart. While recovering in an army hospital from an unidentified illness, perhaps the widespread influenza of 1918 (he never saw action as a Field Artilleryman during the war), he "fell into helping the other men in one way or another," by teaching English or arithmetic, reading stories, providing counseling. The experience " 'sold' me completely—in the lingo of business—on the satisfactoriness, so far as I am personally concerned, of service directly among people and in touch with their personal problems." Lynd came out of the war with "a strong faith that through creative service among people lies my surest path to this 'happiness stuff'!"[4]

To the "dismay" of his friends he resolved to renounce his "good business connection" to study for the ministry, a calling with a venerable tradition in his family. He did not believe in the traditional Christian God, he freely acknowledged, but he did assent to "the creative faith of man in man that makes men whole—the realest sort of 'salvation.' " His faith was in religion, not in God. On the personal level religion was "the encourager and nourisher of every aspiration in the individual"; as a social institution it "gathered into a single powerful current the scattered spiritual forces in society." In Lynd's view—an amalgam of liberal Protestantism and therapeutic positive thinking—religion was a "method" for "increasing to the utmost limit the frequency of the occurrence of life's creative spiritual moods." His "imagination [was] aflame with the potentialities of the religion of free men working and aspiring together and believing one another upward into the very presence of God." "Why not," he queried in another business metaphor, "go out and sell that idea to more people?" Lynd had renounced business, but not salesmanship. "I kept returning to the question: *could* this sort of religion be sold?"[5]

In the fall of 1920 he entered Manhattan's Union Theological Seminary—a liberal, interdenominational, but heavily Presbyterian institution—declaring himself on admission to be a Unitarian and member of John Haynes Holmes's Community Church, an independent, liberal pacifist congregation. His seminary transcript reveals that he excelled in all his courses—he had a three-year course grade average of 88. He took practical theology from the greatest preacher of his day, liberal Baptist Harry Emerson Fosdick; Christian ethics from the left-wing Methodist Harry F. Ward; religious education from the seminary's primary advocate of social science, George A. Coe; and (by arrangement with Columbia's Teachers' College) philosophy of education from William Heard Kilpatrick, self-proclaimed disciple and popularizer of John Dewey. In the fall of 1922, his last year at Union, he enrolled in one of John Dewey's graduate lecture courses in philosophy—either Philosophy 121, "Psychological Ethics" or Philosophy 191, "Types of Philosophic Thought"—a course that had a profound impact on his thinking and ultimately on his choice of career.[6]

But despite his success in the classroom, Lynd yearned for service in the field. In March 1921, near the end of his first year at Union, he presented himself to the Presbyterian Board of Home Missions to request a summer job. He confessed that he "did not believe in God," but expressed his strong desire to "get into the field for the summer to 'kill or cure' my question of what a personal ministry could do." Apparently undisturbed by his agnosticism, the board offered him his choice of a rural church in Indiana or "a Wyoming oil camp where there was no church and I would have to make my own way." He quickly "grabbed the second, wide open chance" and was on his way to Elk Basin.[7]

"I got here," the twenty-eight-year-old Lynd wrote in late May 1921, a week after his arrival, "to find this place a raw assortment of tar-paper shacks, tents, and two-room frame houses, thermometer down to 40, and a general attitude of 'what the hell does a minister expect to do in a place like this?' I got a job the next day as the best available way to show them I'm not a 'dude' preacher." His letter was addressed to Edward S. Martin, editor of *Harper's*, in which Lynd's anonymous "But Why Preach?" was about to appear. Martin published parts of the letter in August in his personal column along with the tantalizing gloss that in this "obscure corner of Wyoming" Lynd's "resolve to preach rather than to remain in business will be subjected to the severest test." The test might be severe, but Martin assured his readers that full details on the ordeal would appear at a later date. What Lynd was proposing and what Martin was accepting was that Lynd simultaneously test himself for the Biblical forty days in the desert and provide dramatic coverage of the test for a genteel national audience. The danger of such a self-consciously commercial venture was that Lynd would be tempted to substitute drama for experience from the outset, to see himself as a protagonist in a predetermined script. The published piece, entitled "Crude-Oil Religion," is indeed so breathlessly dramatic that it is difficult to know to what degree the account was fictionalized. But even if the article does not document Lynd's actual experience in every instance, it provides vital glimpses of his character and social perspective.[8]

His first task was to prove himself a man's man. The chief threat to the success of his mission—which was to see if "the idea of religion could be 'sold' to people just like anything else worthwhile"—was that he would be dismissed as a soft, effeminate "dude preacher," a spiritual resource for the women of the Basin. He took a grueling job as a pick-and-shovel roustabout, and had his "chance to breathe, smell, wear, handle, eat, dream crude oil six-and-one-half days a week." The initial "suspicion" of the men gave way to "friendly curiosity." Lynd was now confident, in another of his pecuniary metaphors, that "they were at least going to give me a run for my money." He proved himself a devoted ditchdigger in "a quaint crew of oil field misfits: nine of us, all American-born and all known and addressed solely by our first names." Here was a tiny, face-to-face, homogeneous community of equals, sharing their burdens, their canteens of alkaline well water, their secrets of how to get away with "soldiering on the job." But in spite of Lynd's expressed feeling of immersion in this working-class male culture, he was surely aware that he was not really one of the boys. He was the voluntary participant who for that reason remained essentially an observer. He was cultivating an image of participation for the ulterior purpose of promoting religion.

Little by little the men showed a flickering interest in the real purpose of Lynd's adventure. A respectable crowd turned out for his first Sunday-evening sermon. "I haven't come here to preach theology to you all," he told the packed assembly. "You and I have problems that look as big as a barn to us, and the thing we've a right to expect religion to do for us is to show how to meet these practical problems." After the service he put down his gleeful reaction in his journal: "Got away with it!—despite the fact that a baby in front row tried to outtalk me. 55 on deck, every seat full, 21 men, including my foreman, the surveyor, 5 of the 9 men from the ditch, and a lot of hard-boiled birds in shirt-sleeves." For the fifteen weeks that followed the sermon he was, according to this published account, a revered community leader. He launched a series of community "sings," attracted visiting "artists" from a town twenty miles away, started troops for both Boy and Girl Scouts, taught adult Sunday School, led a Wednesday-night study group on the value of prayer, took boys on camping and fishing trips. "The friendliness of the West," he decided, "is apparently without limit toward those who qualify as its own." At Elk Basin Lynd had a vision of the *Gemeinschaft* —the supportive integrated community—for which he would always yearn. "The West," he rhapsodized, had "opened its arms to the preacher."

109

The central meaning of Elk Basin for Robert Lynd, to judge by "Crude-Oil Religion," was that he had succeeded in creating community out of fragmentation, solidarity out of apathy; he had given form to the void. Since the people commonly set their sights too low, they needed an energetic organizer, a skilled community planner, to provide "spiritual and social leadership." In Elk Basin he provided that leadership for three months, and "the latent religion in this community of five hundred souls had responded." But he had created a community in which, as a relentlessly self-conscious outsider, he could never fully belong. His consolation was that he alone had understood what the people needed and had brought it into being.[9]

"Crude-Oil Religion," however, was not Robert Lynd's only published reflection upon Elk Basin. Two months later, in November 1922, "Done in Oil" appeared in *The Survey*, Paul Kellogg's reform journal. It was a muckraking piece in the best prewar progressive tradition. It was in particular an attack on philanthropist John D. Rockefeller, Jr., whose Standard Oil of Indiana controlled the companies in Elk Basin, for permitting inhumane living and working conditions at the camp. The article caused a significant stir because it drew from Rockefeller a lengthy response in the form of a rejoinder appended to Lynd's piece. The Lynd-Rockefeller episode was widely publicized, as *The Survey* gloated the following month in a full-page promotional splash; "287 papers in 185 towns and cities" reprinted parts of the articles. "The aggregate circulation of the papers from which these clippings came is 16,676,623."[10]

"Done in Oil" remarkably made no mention at all of Lynd's personal religious mission, or of the vibrant community fellowship he had sparked. To judge by this article, he had signed on as a roustabout for the sole purpose of investigating conditions at the camp—conditions that he was now able to report were unsatisfactory in the extreme. He now dwelt on "the wear and tear of the hardship of the life in the Basin": the well water that "was so poorly condensed as to turn a white man's stomach"; the absence of bathing facilities; the dreadful lack of activities for the women; the shoddy tents and tar-paper shacks; and worst of all, the twelve-hour day and the half day of work on Sunday. The picture was one of nearly unrelieved misery—quite a different portrait than that painted by "Crude-Oil Religion," in which with Lynd's aid the people organized a wholesome, fulfilling social life. Lynd now stressed that the people were being systematically defrauded, "done in," by Standard Oil "interests," which "controlled Elk Basin well nigh lock, stock and barrel." Against forces like those, the residents of Elk Basin were powerless; they could take refuge only in their "victrolas" and "battered Fords." Community life had atrophied in "the dead calm of 'all work and no play.' " Too frightened to buck the callous corporate interests, the people picked up the only crumbs they were permitted: leisure commodities with which, either at home or on the road, they passed their few hours of repose in private, cut off from their fellows. The people of Elk Basin, Lynd insisted, deserved better than this. For these were American-born Westerners—warm, generous, dependable. "One had only to look at them to mark the difference between them and the workers to whom one is accustomed in our larger cities. There was none of the heavy detachment so characteristic of the foreign born workers of the Eastern city. With one exception they were all American born, mostly the substantial type from the Middle West, and their easy raillery bespoke an open air life." [11]

What is most striking about "Crude-Oil Religion" and "Done in Oil" for the reader of *Middletown* is that the two starkly different accounts of Elk Basin correspond so closely, respectively, to the Muncie of the 1890s and the Muncie of the 1920s. What the articles suggest is that *Middletown* itself is not so much a comparative treatment of two distinct periods in the evolution of a midwestern town as it is a description of two conflicting tendencies in its current life. Middletowners displayed both active and passive impulses. They showed signs both of possessing the capacity to organize their own lives and of succumbing to the emergent national agencies of "pecuniary" culture. Like the workers of Elk Basin, the residents of Muncie were native-born Americans "of the substantial type"; Lynd explicitly chose the city for its small proportion of blacks, immigrants, Catholics, and Jews. For Lynd the resilient folk of the heartland were America's best hope. If they could not, with their long tradition of democratic participation, move toward a new communal society, then certainly the "heavy," acquiescent, foreign-born workers could not be expected to do so. For Lynd Muncie represented democracy's last stand. It is ironic that *Middletown* itself may be seen in retrospect as the last stand of the democratic idea in Robert Lynd's own thought. When he concluded in the 1930s that Muncie had indeed succumbed to colonization by pecuniary values, that popular democracy was dead, he issued a biting epitaph for both Muncie and for his own book *Middletown* in the euphemistically titled *Middletown in Transition*. He might just as well have called it *Middletown Interred*.

III

The Elk Basin articles led directly to the *Middletown* project, through the mediation, ironically, of John D. Rockefeller, Jr., himself. While he was still at Elk Basin in 1921, Lynd wrote to one of his seminary professors, William Adams Brown, an elite Presbyterian clergyman with social ties to Rockefeller. He asked Brown to bring living and working conditions at the camp to the philanthropist's attention, which Brown proceeded to do. ("Done in Oil" asserted that Lynd wrote directly to Rockefeller, but Lynd's later reminiscences name Brown as an intermediary.) Rockefeller, a deeply religious, liberal Baptist whose social and political views by the 1920s were surprisingly pro-labor, was according to Lynd genuinely disturbed by the information. But after convincing himself of the veracity of Lynd's report he nevertheless, in Lynd's recollection, dispatched his lawyers both to Lynd and to *The Survey* to try to stop publication of "Done in Oil"; he even implied that he would build a library at Elk Basin if the story was scrubbed. But one of Rockefeller's lawyers, Raymond Fosdick (brother of Harry Emerson Fosdick, Rockefeller's favorite preacher and one of Lynd's teachers at Union), confided to Lynd that since no one disputed his facts he ought not to retreat. As a compromise *The Survey* agreed to let Rockefeller respond in the same issue. His piece "A Promise of Better Days" expressed his real regret about Elk Basin, but insisted it was not representative of oil camp conditions in general or even in the West—a claim that both Lynd and editor Paul Kellogg demolished in separate rebuttals.[12]

Rockefeller and Fosdick, meanwhile, had established in January 1921 the Committee on Social and Religious Surveys. It was by Rockefeller's standards a small agency, one designed to produce "scientific" religious surveys that he believed would help both strengthen and unify the American Protestant churches. It was part of Rockefeller's general effort to Christianize the American social order—in his case not a narrowly sectarian project, but a class-conscious attempt to legitimize corporate capitalism by placing it under the guidance of a morally concerned and scientifically trained elite. Rockefeller brought in world-renowned evangelist John R. Mott to serve as titular head of the committee, and appointed his trusted lieutenant Raymond Fosdick as its treasurer.[13]

In December 1921—at precisely the moment that Rockefeller and Fosdick were trying to decide what to do with the embarrassing information that Lynd had gathered at Elk Basin—the committee decided to expand its operations. It proposed to Rockefeller that he finance in 1922 ten new projects, including "a survey of a small industrial city." It reported to him that "in the opinion of experts not only on our own staff but in the Russell Sage Foundation [which had in 1907 sponsored the famous Pittsburgh Survey, directed by Paul Kellogg] and the Federal Council of Churches, there is great need of a model survey of a city of medium size." The purpose of the study, as of all the committee's work, was not just academic. It was seeking not only to understand

"Christian social and religious activities and interests" with "the tested methods and principles of social science," but also "to foster the spirit and practice of cooperation in the moral and religious sphere." Sociology was to be a modern means of religious endeavor. It was a pursuit both scientific and moral—and therefore a key guarantor of both the efficiency and the legitimacy of American social order. It alone could both comprehend and propose morally informed solutions for complex social problems.[14]

Rockefeller accepted the idea of the Small City Study, and in early 1923 preliminary research began under the direction of sociologist William Louis Bailey of Northwestern University. Bailey set about the task of canvassing possible cities, and by springtime he had narrowed the field to five: South Bend, Indiana; Rockford, Illinois; Steubenville, Ohio; Kenosha, Wisconsin; and Jackson, Michigan. But in May the committee voted unexpectedly to terminate Bailey on the grounds that while he was a diligent soul he did not have the makings of a personable, insightful participant observer. The meeting came to the consensus that the study "should ascertain the religious and ethical attitudes and capacities of the people, and the adjustment or maladjustment of the agencies to them. It should stress the intangible psychological factors more, and the external, tabulable factors less than city surveys have generally done." The committee, advised by several Union Theological Seminary professors (including William Adams Brown) who served as consultants and attended the meeting, decided that "Mr. Robert S. Lynd would be better fitted [than Bailey] for this particular study in which the psychological viewpoint is to be stressed." This graduating seminarian, who only a few months before had been locked in acrimonious battle with Rockefeller, was committed to both of the committee's expressed goals: social cooperation and scientific fact-finding. As an added bonus, he knew how to write and how to mix with people. His diversified background in business, the ministry, journalism, and fieldwork was difficult to match. For the next three years Lynd received a $4,500 annual salary plus travel expenses and a research budget from the committee—which later in 1923 changed its name to the Institute of Social and Religious Research.[15]

Lynd never acknowledged the irony that *Middletown* was produced through the philanthropy of the very corporate leader whose outrageous neglect of oil workers Lynd had graphically detailed only a few months before. On Rockefeller's and Fosdick's part the decision to hire Lynd to head the Small City Study was a brilliant stroke. What better way to signal the objectivity of the institute's work, its independence from overt control by its benefactor? Lynd's credentials as a zealous researcher immune to Rockefeller influence had been proven and widely publicized in *The Survey* exchange. Lynd thus played an

113

important role in legitimizing the scientific status of the institute's work. But while it is clear what Lynd had to offer the institute, it is not so obvious what the Small City Study had to offer Lynd, still ostensibly bound for the ministry.

"Crude-Oil Religion," published at the start of his third and final year at the seminary, concluded with the somewhat tentative judgment that there was a place for a nondenominational Christian community church and a place for Robert Lynd personally at the head of such a congregation. At least there was room for them in a western locale isolated from urban, immigrant, "eastern" culture. Lynd already suspected that vital religion might flourish only where spontaneous social solidarity already existed, or at least where its seeds were ready to shoot forth, as at Elk Basin. In a heterogeneous city like New York, in which "the friction of life" already did and would always oppress him, religion might not be able to promote solidarity; the environment might be lethal for spiritual growth, either personal or social.

In a note Lynd wrote to himself in 1922, just before or just after the publication of "Crude-Oil Religion," he was definitely inclining toward the ministry. "The whole job of the preacher as I grope it out is to remind people of the ways in which men have found that they can give off [spiritual] energy. Note in this connection that men are not 'self-starters' in doing the things that give off the positive type of energy —or at least not to their maximum potentiality." But in spite of his ruminations on spiritual energy—and on the role of the preacher as spark plug—Lynd was actually on the verge of renouncing both the ministry and the Christian faith. If he were to come to the conclusion that religion could not contribute to both personal health and social progress—east and west—he would be compelled as a conscientious liberal Protestant to throw religion overboard.[16]

For liberal Protestantism was premised on the belief that Christianity was a force for the improvement of society, not just or even primarily a means of salvation for the individual. Lynd, Rockefeller, and most other college-educated Christians agreed about that in the 1920s. Having tied Christianity to the notion of social salvation, liberal Protestantism in fact paved the way for the further secularization of the native-born middle class, a process it was supposedly struggling to resist. For if social progress were to appear to be blocked, many reform-minded Christians like Lynd would naturally desert the church. By the end of his final year at Union—the same time that he agreed to take on the Small City Study—Lynd took the decisive step beyond religion and toward social science. It is indeed quite possible that the offer of the *Middletown* project itself precipitated his final rejection of religion in general and of preaching in particular.

A term paper Lynd wrote in his final semester for Professor Kilpatrick's Philosophy of Education course gave an account of how his mind had changed. The paper was entitled "A Critique of Preaching from the Standpoint of Modern Educational Method." He noted at the outset that in a paper written the previous term he had upheld preaching as an effective instrument for re-educating adults, of "breaking down habits and setting up new habits," since "the mood of the church service . . . affords the preacher a valuable means for producing the shock or emotional explosion requisite for the more abrupt kind of reconditioning." But he now believed that the preacher was "flying in the face of our best modern educational practice." Modern educational theory—namely, the theories of John Dewey, whose lecture course Lynd had just taken in the fall semester—stressed experimentation, tentativeness, skepticism about received dogma. The Christian preacher, by contrast, is an "enthusiastic over-believer. . . . He prefers to run the risk of believing too much and being wrong rather than believing too little." He seeks to lead people to a predetermined point, rather than inviting them to adapt themselves freely to whatever end they in good conscience choose.[17]

Dewey's faith in open inquiry, in the value of a multiplicity of freely adopted viewpoints, was a revelation to Lynd. At the age of thirty he was having his first insight into the relativity of knowledge and the pluralist value system of the pragmatists. He was simultaneously overwhelmed by the whole vast realm of social reality of which he was ignorant. It was now impossible for him to preach, not only because preaching as he conceived it was an essentially manipulative activity, but also because he did not yet know how society worked. "It has taken me three years of studying [at Union] . . . to realize that there literally is no place in the pulpit of the Christian church in this country for a man who is an experimental thinker interested in unearthing the facts and seeing them in *all* their relations." He now proposed to devote himself to "a calm weighing of all the facts." Once he had the facts, he could try "helping people to face the facts and think through their problems"—a task he previously thought belonged to the preacher, but which he now assigned to the social scientist.[18]

The danger of his new fact-finding perspective—a danger he did not yet grasp—was that he could never master the infinity of facts and relations among facts available to be learned. As he would himself argue fifteen years later in *Knowledge for What?*, empiricism divorced from provisional conclusions might lead to impotence, a freezing of the will to act. But now he was galvanized by his heady discovery of the experimental method. It promised to permit him to continue his quest for the moral society, for social solidarity, while allowing him to renounce the manipulative model of preaching with which he had gone to Elk Basin—and which was the outgrowth of his earlier career as a salesman and advertiser. Imagining himself to be a sociologist, a detached student of society, was for Lynd a means of delivering himself from the temptation to which he had succumbed at the oil camp—that of steering people toward an end he had chosen for them. In the mid-1930s he would come once again to embrace the manipulative ideal. His ideal type sociologist would then resemble the kind of preacher he rejected in 1923: the expert in "reconditioning." But through the 1920s he held that ideal in check. In that decade, when with Helen's help he was creating *Middletown*, his goal for the sociologist was more modest: to understand modern society and through his writing to help people "face the facts and think through their problems." If there was to be democratic progress it would have to arise out of the democratic, intelligent activity of people themselves.

IV

Robert Lynd's relationship with the staff of the Institute of Social and Religious Research between 1923 and 1928 was marked by a series of stormy eruptions. He was forced again and again to summon up his salesman's skills, developed during years in publishing and advertising, to keep the Small City Study afloat. Without his diplomatic maneuverings *Middletown* would probably not have seen the light of day. It was with tongue firmly in cheek that he thanked the ISRR in the book's preface for having been "generous in criticism and suggestion." The course of Lynd's conflicts with the ISRR is instructive because it helps illuminate both the distinctive form and content of the book and the dispute over the role of values in social research, which racked the ISRR and the broader social science community during these years.

Like Lynd and the members of the ISRR, many other social scientists were struggling to reconcile their religious and moral concerns with their scientific scruples. Indeed, throughout the northern Protestant intelligentsia between the 1880s and the 1930s thinkers were engaged in an often troubling shift from predominantly religious to predominantly secular, scientific modes of thought. For many of them, as for Lynd and the others at the ISRR, this transition meant not a simple displacement of the religious by the scientific, but an unsettled mix between the two. Just as the new ideology of consumption combined religious and secular motifs and impulses—as in the work of Bruce Barton—so the analysts of the new consumer society invoked religious and secular ideals and norms. Lynd himself was determined to address in *Middletown* the fundamental question of the moral legitimacy of the emerging American consumer society. But at the same time he had to satisfy his own scientific standards, and those of the institute, which barred straightforward advocacy or polemics. It was only after three years of debate and conflict at the ISRR that Lynd managed to formulate a standpoint that persuasively linked moral critique with scientific analysis—the standpoint that gave *Middletown* its originality and power.[19]

There were two basic factions within the ISRR, each representing a different conception of the institute's mission. One group pushed for a series of social surveys in the well-established tradition of Paul Kellogg's Pittsburgh Survey (6 volumes, 1909–1914) and Shelby Harrison's Springfield [Illinois] Survey (3 volumes, 1918–1920). These studies, themselves based on the model of Charles Booth's painstaking late nineteenth-century survey of the London working class, sought to identify the most pressing social problems and propose practical, "efficient" solutions. They were at bottom problem-solving enterprises, the pride of the new generation of professional social workers. The clergymen and missionaries who sat on the Board of Trustees of the institute, the Federal Council officials active in ISRR deliberations, and influential outside experts like Shelby Harrison were strong advocates of this policy-oriented approach. These mostly clerical reformers considered their perspective "scientific" in the general sense that it was based on the collection of data. They called for the ISRR to survey the religious scene—an area overlooked on the whole by earlier social surveys—and propose specific recommendations for strengthening and unifying Protestant America. They also called for direct participation in the Small City Study by the religious leaders of the chosen town.

The other group believed that the institute's primary goal ought to be "objective fact-finding," not problem-solving. Staff members in the New York office like Executive Secretary Galen Fisher; his assistant, Trevor Bowen; and research specialists C. Luther Fry and Stanley Went—supported by influential outside consultants like Wesley Mitchell, Robert Park, Leon Marshall, and Lawrence Frank—were suspicious of special pleading on the part of clerical reformers and stressed the scientific objectives of the ISRR with considerably more single-mindedness. Certain members of the scientific faction, especially Fry and Went, tended to restrict the meaning of "scientific" to "statistical," while others, like Fisher, remained open to more impressionistic methods. But they all agreed that it was premature to propose policies when the empirical groundwork had not been laid. In the case of the Small City Study they were determined to keep it from falling captive to the denominational leaders of the selected city.[20]

After being appointed director of the study on May 11, 1923, Robert Lynd wasted no time trying to establish his control of the project.

117

On May 17 he sent Fisher the first in a long series of memoranda on how he would go about studying the city he had chosen: South Bend, Indiana. The point of the project, in Fisher's summary of Lynd's words, was "to study the life of South Bend in order to discover the origin and nature of its spiritual energies." His preliminary research would include "one month working as a laborer in at least two key industries of South Bend." At the end of June he stressed that "the purpose of the survey is to produce not an efficiency survey of the churches of South Bend, but rather a new type of survey: an inquiry first and foremost into precisely what is the spiritual life of the community, with a special reference to its dynamic aspects, i.e., how do new spiritual impulses arise? What agencies evoke and nourish them, etc.?" Lynd lined up solidly with Fisher's scientific faction by rejecting the old-fashioned "efficiency survey." He also underlined the "spiritual" focus of the study —a point on which all members of the institute agreed. What he did not reveal was that his conception of the "spiritual" was already a good deal less "religious" than that of either faction of the ISRR. Over the next few years he would come to realize that by "spiritual" he really meant "cultural," a shift that would initially disturb the institute and almost lead to the cancellation of the project.[21]

For the time being Lynd wrote memo after memo telling the staff and trustees what they wanted to hear. As he put it in April 1924, his goal was "to define and measure the changes in the life (i.e., habits or behavior) of a small city over the critical period since 1890 as those changes affect the problem of the small city church," and to conduct "a straight fact-finding study." This formulation had something for each group at the institute—the measurement of change in strict, fact-finding fashion for the scientific group, and attention to the problems of the small-city church for the clerical reformers. But there is no doubt that his real intentions already went well beyond this masterfully diplomatic statement. He knew perfectly well that the problems of the small-city church would receive little emphasis. He also understood that his interest was not just in fact-finding but in criticism based on fact-finding, a position that would later ironically put him in implicit alliance with the reformers' faction. At this point, however, he willingly submerged his true intentions in order to secure a renewed contract for the expensive research phase of the study.[22]

As late as November 1923, Lynd still intended to study South Bend, but with the proviso that his work be limited "to the white-American stock" of the city. "The reason for this," he explained in another memo to Fisher, "is obvious. Since we are attempting a difficult new technique in a highly complicated field, it is desirable to simplify our situation as far as possible. The interaction of the material and cultural trends in the city with our native psychology is problem enough without introducing into this initial study the complicating factor of a psychology molded by a foreign environment." The November meeting of the ISRR accepted his reasoning but suggested an alternative: find a smaller "white-American" city that could be studied as a whole. Lynd found the idea compelling, and in early December journeyed to Decatur, Illinois, and Kokomo and Muncie, Indiana. He picked Muncie, a large town of 38,000 (of which 92 percent were native-born whites; of that group another 92 percent were the children of native-born whites). In January 1924 Helen joined him there for two months of initial spadework. When Fisher passed through town in mid-March he noted that Robert had already made a surprising number of contacts. "Lynd has been working like a beaver at Muncie," he informed Raymond Fosdick. In early April Fosdick approved the funding for the major phase of the Lynds' research, which lasted fifteen months and required the full-time services of a statistician, a stenographer, and an interviewer—in addition to Helen's own half-time position.[23]

The choice of homogeneous Muncie was not simply, as *Middletown* would later assert explicitly, the result of Robert Lynd's desire to investigate industrialization ("cultural change") unencumbered by the variable of ethnicity ("racial change"). It was also, as the Elk Basin articles of the previous year suggest, the product of his belief that the hope for social progress lay uniquely in the spirit and vision of the "substantial type" of American, the native-born Protestant of the Middle West. Muncie would offer the full drama of a proud, resilient people buffeted by consumer capitalism yet capable of grasping the nature of the forces arrayed against them and working to shape their own future. By rejecting the ISRR's original plan for a study of an ethnically diversified city like Springfield he was also rejecting the example of Robert Park's Chicago research group, with various members of which he conferred several times in December and January. The Chicago sociologists studied the ethnically mixed city because it was typical of modern society. Lynd agreed that it was typical and self-consciously selected the atypical, traditional, vanishing Protestant town—for him the locus of inherited virtue and "spiritual energy."

The Lynds' reception in Muncie, Helen Lynd later recalled, "was very friendly. We didn't meet any opposition. Early on we were invited to dinner, first by Mrs. Stevens, who was a social leader, and then by the Balls [the dominant family in Muncie]." Robert Lynd eagerly leapt into the life of the business class. He quickly befriended "a doctor, a banker, and a real estate man in the city," and the four assembled once a week for dinner and discussion. "We called them," Helen remembered, "the Sewing Circle." Lynd certainly made an effort to cultivate the Muncie elite, but he literally sought out whoever crossed his path. He made friends easily, and unlike Helen felt completely at home. (He later told her that he could happily have spent the rest of his life there, a thought that appalled her.) Three ordinary Middletowners in particular became key sources: John Dragoo, his loquacious landlord; Rosa Burmaster, a radical schoolteacher; and Max Mathews, one of the three socialists in town, who went so far as to steal unidentified documents from his employer for the Lynds' use. Robert himself was so eager to pierce the protective shell of the community that despite his recent rejection of religion, he volunteered to sing solos in a Muncie church. There could have been no more effective way of enlisting the cooperation of the natives, even if it meant—as at Elk Basin—posing as something he was not, in this case a Christian believer. Once again he was the self-conscious observer as participant. "Bob's particular contribution was everything," Helen concluded. "Planning it, thinking up things, imaginatively saying, 'Well, if this, then that.' He made friends with everybody. Any situation, whether it was Rotary Club or singing in church or meeting with the Sewing Circle, it all worked into the study. Then he would take those things and organize them." During the research it was clear to both of them that "it was his study." Only when Robert had finished the first draft of the manuscript was it decided "that we were sharing the book"; even at that, "the writing was much more his than mine."[24]

What the institute staff discovered as the Lynds' chapters rapidly accumulated in the spring of 1926 was that the "spiritual" focus of the study had been completely supplanted by what Robert Lynd now termed a "cultural" approach to Muncie. No one on the staff appreciated this strong infusion of anthropology into a sociological project, for it diverted the study not only from religious problems, but from strict, empirical fact-finding as well. Even Fisher, who had consistently supported Lynd against his adversaries, thought this was going too far. Now Lynd was in effect building criticism and even satire right into the framework of his book, much as Veblen had done in *The Theory of the Leisure Class*. He was now posing as a "naive observer" who had happened upon Muncie the way Margaret Mead had just come upon Samoa. He had made his personal detachment from Muncie the cornerstone of his perspective. He had suddenly relativized, and therefore challenged, Muncie's entire mode of life even while refraining from outright fault-finding. At first it appeared that the Lynds' anthropological turn might once again endanger the continuation of the project. But it turned out instead to be a brilliant strategic switch that ensured the book's publication.

Certainly the Lynds had good intellectual reasons for framing *Middletown*, in the words of the subtitle, as a "study in modern American culture." To study culture meant in their view to study in holistic fashion the technology, social institutions, patterns of behavior, and underlying value system of a people—although in keeping with the latest trend in American social science, they put heavy stress on the latter. In the 1920s a number of sociologists, notably William F. Ogburn, W. I. Thomas, and Charles A. Ellwood, were promoting the holistic view of culture; by the late twenties a modest movement had been mounted to challenge the standard sociological perspective—which, whether still outwardly reformist or militantly empiricist, remained wedded to "commonsense" analysis of discrete behavioral or institutional patterns. For one like Robert Lynd who had recently rejected religion but still harbored strong spiritual impulses, the anthropological approach offered an attractive compromise, one that was midway between religion and scientific sociology. Like religion (and early "reform" sociology), it considered values and beliefs to be crucial, but like scientific sociology it regarded no single value system as normative. While the dominant trend in sociology was toward ever finer, statistical measurement of narrow institutional or behavioral patterns, those sociologists like Lynd who craved a more global viewpoint—one within which questions of value could still be raised—found their inspiration in anthropology.

But whatever the intellectual appeal of anthropology, the Lynds' choice served an institutional purpose too. It may indeed have been their need for a more persuasive standpoint in their difficult negotiations with the ISRR that led them to appreciate the utility of cultural anthropology. The cultural approach fit the bill because it offered a "scientific" justification for going beyond fact-finding. This led members of the reform faction like Shelby Harrison to take a new interest in the manuscript, since it weakened the case the scientific group had always made against nonempirical work. Cultural anthropology appeared to provide a much needed boost to all those concerned not just with collecting facts, but with examining (and ultimately advocating) values. The data gatherers on the New York staff—Luther Fry and Stanley Went—found themselves outflanked. Lynd sealed his strategy by cultivating the goodwill of the cultural anthropologist Clark Wissler, head curator of the American Museum of Natural History, who vouched for the scientific character of the Lynds' approach. The renowned Wissler was a formidable feather in Lynd's cap not only because of his stature as a social scientist but also because of his small-town midwestern roots. Having grown up thirty-five miles from Muncie, in Richmond, Indiana, he spoke with firsthand knowledge of Muncie itself. His "actual knowledge" of Muncie, he wrote Fisher on July 7, persuaded him of Lynd's "objectivity." That was enough for Fisher, who now voiced his "dissent from the trend of opinion of the technical staff." "Of course it will not be a model," he wrote of the manuscript, "but it is a pioneer effort."[25]

Revising and condensing the manuscript consumed the following year and a half; the Lynds' work was slowed by Robert's acceptance in 1927 of the job of Wesley Mitchell's assistant (later converted to Permanent Secretary) at the Social Science Research Council. On March 7, 1928, Fisher wrote Lynd of the institute's "definite and final" decision to publish *Middletown*. When *Middletown* appeared in January 1929— five years after the Lynds had gone to Muncie—Harcourt promoted it zealously. Over the next eight years of depression it sold 32,000 copies at five dollars each. "Nobody was as surprised as we," Helen later remembered, "when it came out with front page reviews in the *Times* and *Herald Tribune*. Brentano's window was filled with nothing but *Middletown*."[26]

V

Middletown was one of the first, if not the very first, functionalist works in American sociology. Following the recent lead of Malinowski (*The Argonauts of the Western Pacific*, 1922) and Radcliffe-Brown (*The Andaman Islanders*, 1922), who in their turn expressed a heavy debt to Durkheim, the Lynds described a cultural system in which all aspects of life functioned as parts of a coherent whole. Muncie, they held, was a pecuniary culture: The natives' belief and behavior in each sphere of life contributed to the maintenance of "a culture in which everything hinges on money." That central focus itself conditioned future ideas and actions in a closed cycle of causation. The pecuniary culture that Veblen had detected thirty years before in the "leisure class" had now spread throughout the entire society. All of Muncie's primary rituals helped to buttress the reigning system of values.

But *Middletown* was not just a functionalist analysis. Malinowski and Radcliffe-Brown prided themselves on their rejection of the historical and distributional perspectives that governed earlier anthropological work. They abstracted from history and even geography to uncover the essential inner workings of a cultural system. The Lynds by contrast insisted that the Muncie of 1924 could only be understood in terms of the Muncie of 1890. Middletowners who in 1924 were in their fifties had according to the Lynds grown to adulthood in an entirely different culture, a traditional world characterized by participatory democracy and spontaneous fellowship in work and play.[27]

What the Lynds had done was to employ the functionalist framework for a moral purpose, much as Veblen in *The Theory of the Leisure Class* or Gilman in *Women and Economics* had invoked the scheme of evolutionary stages of an earlier generation of anthropologists. The Lynds quite consciously exaggerated the coherence and uniformity of Muncie's culture in both 1924 and 1890 in order to make a moral—and by implication political—point: Americans were in the process of abandoning their democratic cultural heritage. The concrete Muncie of 1924 was an unsettled town in transition between two cultural value systems. A severe conflict was taking place, one that the Lynds could not contain within functionalist assumptions. Pecuniary culture was a dominant tendency, an ascendant ideology, but it was not unopposed. "More and more of the activities of living" were, they wrote, "coming to be strained through the bars of the dollar sign" in an age in which for more and more people of all classes a job was a means of obtaining money, not of performing an intrinsically useful or pleasurable task. Middletowners were "tending increasingly to delegate their interests" to self-appointed authorities and experts not only in the public realm of politics but in personal areas like child-raising. Yet the memory of an alternative value system—of community-centered self-reliance—was so immediate and so intense, according to the Lynds, that Muncie's townspeople were bothered by their own emergent form of behavior. They sensed they were not living up to their own democratic ideals; they were perplexed about how to realize them in the industrial era that had overtaken them with such dizzying suddenness.[28]

Here the advantage for the Lynds' purposes of focusing on small, homogeneous, Protestant Muncie was apparent. It allowed them to dramatize the underlying clash of cultural value systems that was obscured by the racial and ethnic conflicts, by the fragmentation and anomie of larger cities. Robert Lynd was in fact consciously challenging the "ecological" perspective of Robert Park of the Chicago School, which tended both to regard urbanization as a more fundamental process than industrialization and to conceive of human society as a "natural" as opposed to a "cultural" reality. Park was impressed by the ways in which the metropolis resembled both a natural organism with a life of its own and an ecological system of interacting subgroups. Despite his insistence that sociology examine the "moral order" as well as the "ecological order," his perspective and that of the Chicago School was essentially naturalistic and determinist. Urbanization was an impersonal process in which individuals played no determining role. They were fish in the stream of social change. For Park the typical modern man was a being acted upon, not acting: the stranger, the member of the crowd, the deviant.[29]

By keeping social change analytically contained within the realm of culture as opposed to nature, the Lynds were able to preserve the possibility of resistance. Their own account does at times veer toward technological determinism; they sometimes imply that new inventions like automobiles and moving pictures are autonomous agents that not only condition future cultural development but also insinuate themselves automatically—without need of human agency—into a commanding cultural position. But the determinism of their stress on technology is counterbalanced by their lingering faith in the moral traditions of Protestant American culture. The Protestant democracy of 1890 had been displaced by industrial development, but it was still present in a latent form. Thanks to their cultural inheritance, Middletowners still possessed the capacity to recognize the futility of consumer culture and to work, in the last words of the book, toward "a re-examination" of "institutions themselves."

The Lynds knew that it was out of the question to imagine or advocate a return to the agrarian democracy of the 1890s—which they probably realized was more ideal than reality in Muncie even then—although in their personal lives they cultivated the "spontaneous," nonpecuniary leisure they associated with the nineties: family singing and reading aloud, bicycling, hiking, camping. *Middletown* reports that "few people today walk for pleasure . . . and the small boys of the city are wont to call out in a disgusted tone to a stray bicycler, 'Aw, why don't you buy a machine!' " That cyclist was Lynd, who preferred not to use a car in Muncie itself. But neither he nor Helen were purists. While in Muncie they took frequent weekend trips to Brown County State Park in the Hoosier National Forest, 120 miles away—a spontaneous activity made possible by the automobile.[30]

It was impossible to envision a return to the 1890s for the obvious reason that the industrial transformation had destroyed its social basis. High-speed machine production had not only largely erased the distinction between skilled and semiskilled labor, it had also undermined the apprenticeship system that had guaranteed continuity within the family from father to son. The home was no longer a center of economic production or even family social life but a base from which each family member set out for leisure-time consumption with his own peer group. Government and politics, which formerly attracted widespread and heated participation, now met either "apathy or repugnance." "In a civilization in which the health of the community is gauged by its financial pulse," the Lynds observed, "preoccupation with private rather than public business on the part of its ablest citizens is increasingly regarded . . . as not only a normal but a desirable state of affairs."

In 1924 Middletowners no longer assembled to debate ideas, values, or goals in their churches, clubs, and union halls. The men and women of the 1890s—business-class men and women and working-class men—gathered regularly to discuss philosophical, ethical, and political questions. The men got together on their day of rest, the Sabbath; by 1924 the Sabbath had become the Sunday holiday, a day of recreation that for two-thirds of Muncie's residents usually meant a ride in an automobile. A number of women's clubs did preserve a pale reflection of the earlier tradition in 1924, but far fewer Middletowners—and almost no men, even among the ministers—now read serious books at all. These had given way to popular magazines and moving pictures, just as public meetings had fallen victim to the private car. Newspapers, no longer controlled by their reader-subscribers, or directed by their owner-editors, were now in the Lynds' view bland mouthpieces of the advertisers. Public education had vastly expanded, especially at the high school level, but it was designed not to train the mind for inquiry but to infuse accepted values. Religion, previously a "spontaneous and pervasive part of the life of the city," was now an institution struggling to regain some semblance of its earlier power through the latest techniques of advertising publicity.[31]

In the face of these precipitous, monumental changes, Muncie was confused, and the confusion ran all the way up and down the social scale. "Both businessmen and workingmen seem to be running for dear life in this business of making the money they earn keep pace with the even more rapid growth of their subjective wants." *Middletown* posits no selfish elite manipulating the masses through seductive promises of material satisfaction. True, "large-scale advertising," which Robert knew at first hand, together with "popular magazines, movies, radio, and other channels of increased cultural diffusion from without [were] rapidly changing habits of thought as to what things are essential to living." But these potent agents of change, which "hammered," "rammed," and "pounded away" at Muncie, were ironically welcomed by the very consumers they sought to overwhelm. Since work and community life now provided fewer genuine satisfactions, Middletowners looked hungrily to the consumer marketplace for compensatory fulfillment. Advertisers did not simply impose their wills on or create new needs in innocent, unwilling victims. It would be just as true to say that their products were called into being by the active demand of consumers in search of release, of health in an age that put worldly satisfaction increasingly on a par with or even ahead of otherworldly salvation.[32]

According to the Lynds, social change in Middletown originated "from without"; within Muncie itself there was no conflict of any magnitude between social groups. Hence it was impossible for the Lynds to put any store in class struggle as a means of progressive change. Even if the laboring population in Muncie had been organized in 1924, as it had been in 1890, workers would not have constituted a force for progress. With the erosion of their skills, workers had abandoned their self-image as the sinew of society, as a class capable of moral and political leadership. Like the businessmen, they were bewildered by the cultural contradictions of their time. During 1924, the Lynds wrote, Muncie's "leading paper offered the following prescriptions for local prosperity: 'The first duty of a citizen is to produce'; and later, 'The American citizen's first importance to his country is no longer that of citizen but that of consumer. Consumption is a new necessity.'" Everyone in Muncie was "fumbling earnestly" to make sense of the abrupt invasion of new necessities from the outside world.[33]

For the Lynds the problem with Muncie's emergent consumer culture was not that people had more goods, more labor-saving devices, more leisure—they were not in a state of surfeit for which abstention or asceticism could be proposed as an antidote. Nor was the problem one of political oppression, for which political organization could be prescribed as a solution. Nor was it a breakdown of social or economic order, for which a remedy might be sought in novel forms of social or economic organization. At bottom the crisis in Muncie lay not in the realm of power but in the realm of culture. A consumer culture was dangerous because it furthered the people's view of themselves as agents only in the arena of consumption, not in the arenas of production and politics. The people were coming to embrace a role in which their activity consisted of receiving, not creating—receiving mass-produced goods and images, purchasing vicarious experience. They were not totally passive, but their autonomy was increasingly confined to the consumer sphere.

At bottom Middletowners were suffering from "new forms of social illiteracy" created by the combined effects of "the massed weight of advertising and professional publicity" and "the muzzling of self-criticism" enforced by the schools and civic clubs. Since the problem was fundamentally one of illiteracy—not, it must be underlined, of "irrationality"—the solution was a process of re-education. In the immediate, Middletowners needed to educate themselves in "effective consumption." "As more of the things utilized as food, clothing, and shelter are being shifted from home production to purchase for a price," they needed to learn to "distinguish among various grades of milk, bread, vacuum cleaners, and fireless cookers . . . and so on through hundreds of items." Over the long run they had to acquire the habit of "self-appraisal and self-criticism," which it had once been the task of religion to promote, and which alone might spark an ultimate rejection and transcending of consumer culture.[34]

Some reviewers of *Middletown*, like H. L. Mencken, predictably misread it as a put-down of the "Babbitts," "jackasses," and "ignoramuses" that people the small American city. Indeed, books like Sinclair Lewis's *Main Street* (1920) and *Babbitt* (1922) probably predisposed many Americans to take the Lynds simply as two more satirists of small-town parochialism. Mencken, who found the book "as exhilarating as even the dirtiest of the new novels" (a commendation that Harcourt saw fit to use in promoting the volume), believed that it confirmed his view of every one of the 143 towns in the 25,000 to 50,000 population bracket. "They are all Middletowns—dull, stupid, complacent, and forlorn." That this was a pernicious interpretation of both small-town America and the Lynds' book was pointed out by John Dewey, who was deeply affected by *Middletown* and was in the spring of 1929, according to a friend of Robert Lynd, "quoting [it] on every possible occasion." The confusions in Middletown's culture stemmed in Dewey's view not from the irrationality of the people but from the abruptness of the transformation it had undergone. "There are those, of course, who attribute it to the fact that people being, generally speaking, morons and boobs, must be expected to act out the parts to which they are assigned . . . [but] the more one knows of history the more one comes to believe that traditions and institutions count more than native capacity or incapacity in explaining things." [35]

Like Dewey, the Lynds believed that people had the capacity to grasp the cultural configuration of their day and to mobilize themselves to work for democratic change. But in *Middletown* they did not indicate what political form if any that work might take. The Institute of Social and Religious Research would not have permitted programmatic advocacy in the manuscript, but even if it had, it seems unlikely that the Lynds would have been more specific. For one thing, at this stage of his life Robert Lynd was extremely anxious to establish himself as a social scientist. When he objected to Harcourt's use of Mencken's "dirty novel" remark, he did so not on moral grounds but because "such publicity does not help me professionally." He had realized for several years that *Middletown* was crucial for his advancement. "In view of my great professional stake in the study," he wrote to Fosdick in June 1926, "no one can be more concerned than I that the manuscript be . . . an objective, scientific piece of work." In fact *Middletown* did lead directly to two offers of tenured professorships: Charles Horton Cooley's chair at the University of Michigan, which Lynd turned down (in part because Helen had in 1929 begun teaching at Sarah Lawrence), and a position at Columbia, which he accepted for 1931–1932. *Middletown*, minus most of the sections Helen had written, was accepted as his dissertation by Columbia, which granted him a Ph.D. in 1931. It was only after professional security had been bestowed upon him that Robert Lynd took an active interest in the political implications of his work. [36]

But there is another reason for *Middletown*'s silence on the proper course of political action. Like most social critics in the 1920s—a decade of general disillusionment with political idealism—the Lynds were confused about the proper course of action. The reader of *Middletown* might at least have expected them, however, to argue that since Muncie's cultural crisis originated from without, the solution would also have to come from without. Furthermore, given the strong influence on Robert Lynd of Veblen and Veblen's student Wesley Mitchell, one might have expected *Middletown* to call in some appropriately muted fashion for reform by an engineering or social science elite. One of Mitchell's writings that Lynd especially liked was in fact "The Backward Art of Spending Money" (1912), in which Mitchell had called for the creation of "a professional class of Doctors of Domestic Science, who will be employed in organizing households, giving expert counsel to the newly wed . . . and the like." "The mass of women," he dreamed, could be induced "to employ these elect as freely as they now employ physicians."

But the Lynds, far from suggesting the need for a new class of experts, stressed on the contrary that Muncie's "prevalent mood of bewilderment" was in part the product of the rise of that very class. "Life was simpler for my mother," one "thoughtful mother" informed the Lynds. "In those days one did not realize that there was so much to be known about the care of children. I realize that I ought to be half a dozen experts, but I am afraid of making mistakes and usually do not know where to go for advice." Middletowners' "difficulties outrun their best efforts to cope with them," the Lynds concluded, because of the cacophony of conflicting demands issued by tradition on the one hand and by modern experts and advertisers on the other.[37]

Middletown did show signs of the social-engineering mentality to which Robert Lynd would give free rein in the late thirties. The Lynds placed themselves among "those [who were] desirous of applying more effective planning and control to Middletown's living." They were disturbed by the "casualness" with which important decisions both public and private (including the choice of a job or a spouse) were made in Muncie. They yearned for a more methodical, more organized social life, for greater collective solidarity. But at the same time they craved what they never tired of calling "spontaneity"—unprescribed, nonpecuniary activity—and distrusted the spurious new forms of organization that consumer culture was imposing upon leisure, information-gathering, religion, politics, and other spheres of life. In *Middletown* they seemed at times to have trouble deciding which they feared most —casualness or method, spontaneity or organization.[38]

The Lynds held back from Veblen's and Mitchell's progressive vision of reform by elites because the alternative progressive vision of John Dewey was still central to Robert's thinking: Re-education was a process of individual growth that took place through a person's efforts to solve problems or, in Deweyan parlance, to adjust to the environment. The reform of culture was intimately connected to the process by which individuals themselves grew. Individual growth in Dewey's view occurred as a person deepened his participation in a community or set of communities; individual fulfillment was of necessity communal as well. This position was in fact not far from the view of antebellum reformers, for whom spiritual conversion was a precondition (and for some an efficient cause) of institutional reform. It was also not very far from the young Robert Lynd, who imagined spiritual energy to be a source of social reformation. The Institute of Social and Religious Research ought to have taken some solace from the fact that despite his apparent rejection of the "spiritual" for the "cultural," Lynd still viewed the latter in terms strongly reminiscent of the former.

Middletown was on one level a secular jeremiad that lashed its readers with a relentless chronicle of their faults while calling them to repentance and conversion. Still speaking in part as a Christian preacher, Lynd was pleading not only for education in new habits, but for conversion to a new, nonpecuniary culture. The establishment of that culture depended upon the combined weight of individual conversions. It also called for the voluntary adoption of a new ethic of self-sacrifice, of putting the community welfare ahead of individual gain. Individuals ought to seek self-fulfillment, Lynd believed, but not by maximizing their own advantage in the marketplace. Genuine self-fulfillment came to a person as a by-product of cooperative participation in the life of a community. Like Dewey, Lynd refused to countenance any reform that was an imposition from above, that did not flow out of the conscious growth of people themselves. But his democratic faith could not withstand the shock of the social and economic breakdown that followed hard upon his and Helen's rise to celebrity.[39]

VI

When Robert Lynd returned to Muncie with five research assistants (not including Helen) in June 1935, he had no intention of writing a second volume of *Middletown*. Asked by the Muncie *Evening Press* "if his present visit means that he is writing another book about Muncie, Dr. Lynd exclaimed, 'Heavens, no! There are limits to the patience and generosity of the people of any single community.' " He envisioned only a new appendix to *Middletown* that would trace "the main lines of social change in Muncie since 1925, including of course the major readjustments" stemming from the Depression. He was seeking not only new information, he claimed, but "frank criticism" of the earlier book. "No one is more conscious than I of the impossibility of avoiding some errors, at least of emphasis, in the difficult task of catching the complicated life of a city as dynamic as Muncie between the covers of a book. As a Hoosier born and bred, I was in a very real sense writing in *Middletown* about my own culture, and I am accordingly eager to get suggestions and criticisms."[40]

The criticisms that Lynd did receive from Muncie readers concerned the allegedly "cold," "mechanical" character of the text, its tone of near brutal detachment, its failure to feel and highlight the underlying warmth of Middletown's spirit. Robert Lynd was not impressed with this argument. He responded to it icily in his eighty-five-page dismissal of "The Middletown Spirit" that forms the penultimate chapter of *Middletown in Transition* (a chapter that he wrote without Helen's assistance). The primary change of emphasis in the second volume was in fact not suggested either by Muncie readers or even by Lynd's two weeks of research in June 1935. The overriding theme of the book, written mostly in the summer of 1936, was the irrationality of Middletowners, their inability to comprehend the course of either social change or their own lives. *Middletown* had erred, Robert Lynd announced in the preface, because it tended "to regard human nature as 'rational,' 'free,' and 'responsible,' and there is large precedent for so doing. On the other hand, the emphasis of recent psychology is that actions of human beings are only to a limited extent rational, while to a far greater extent they are colored by individual emotional needs and responsive to previous culture conditioning."[41]

There was nothing original about Robert Lynd's application of "recent psychology" to the study of society. It was a commonplace, even an emerging orthodoxy, among social scientists to doubt the moral and mental capacity and potential of ordinary people. It was Lynd's erstwhile Deweyan faith in the common man that was now considered a sentimental anachronism. Walter Lippmann had given the new view widespread currency as early as 1913 in his first book, *A Preface to Politics*—a popularization of, among other things, his teacher and friend Graham Wallas's *Human Nature and Politics* (1908), which focused on the allegedly irrational character of political action and belief. In the wake of the World War—during which psychologists "proved" that half of all white draftees were "morons" (mental age below thirteen years), and intellectuals like Captain Walter Lippmann enjoyed the heady experience of composing propaganda for domestic and foreign consumption—it seemed increasingly evident that commoners lacked the ability even to comprehend, much less shape, the world around them. Lippmann in his *Public Opinion* (1922), Harold Lasswell in his *Propaganda Techniques in the World War* (1927) and *Psychopathology and Politics* (1930), and many others took for granted that the political arena was in essence—not just in practice—a cauldron of irrational impulse, not a battleground of rational conviction.[42]

Lynd's change of heart stemmed from his thinking not about government propaganda or psychological testing during wartime, but about advertising propaganda during the Depression. Wesley Mitchell and William F. Ogburn selected him in the summer of 1930 to contribute the chapter on consumption patterns in a magisterial volume projected by President Hoover's Research Committee on Social Trends. He investigated the question for more than a year and produced his report during the severely depressed winter of 1931–1932 (while teaching his graduate course "Social Aspects of Consumption in Contemporary Society" as a first-year professor at Columbia). Lynd noted that the number of national advertisers had grown from 5,000 in 1925 to 8,500 in 1930, and that their strategies had taken increasingly pernicious forms in recent years. "The tendency of contemporary merchandising is to elevate more and more commodities to the class of personality buffers"—to make them appear to be tools for overcoming "job insecurity, social insecurity, monotony, loneliness, failure to marry, and other situations of tension." Moreover, "There is a ceaseless quest for what advertising men call 'million dollar merchandising ideas' (e.g., 'halitosis' as applied to Listerine) to disguise commodities still further by identifying them with cryptic characteristics." Advertisers first hid the true merits (if any) of their products by promoting them as means to personal fulfillment, then concealed them further by fabricating confusing, pseudoscientific labels and "driving goods under their real names off the retail market."

Lynd's essay "The People as Consumers" went a long way toward documenting new patterns in both advertising and consumption, but it offered no evidence at all for its pivotal claim that "we can no longer be content with the attempt to understand consumption habits by viewing the consumer simply as the rational, soberly constant being. . . . It is probably nearer the truth to regard human beings as only partially rational bundles of impulses and habits shaped in response to an unsynchronized environment, with resulting tensions." Of course few observers would have defended the proposition that consumers were "simply" rational, soberly constant beings, just as few would have disputed the view that men were only partially rational; Lynd was setting up a straw man. His real point—one that marked an important shift in his thinking—was that the power of advertisers was irresistible, that consumers were impotent in the face of "the increasing organization of business," "the massed pressures of industry." *Middletown* had argued that while average Americans were no longer significant forces in the realm of production or politics, they were to a large degree active, purposeful agents in the realm of consumption. Now Lynd believed them to be passive even as consumers. They were no longer capable of making rational, discriminating decisions among products, or, more broadly, of either rejecting advertising propaganda altogether or using the consumer marketplace for rationally chosen ends—including the desire (however offensive to Lynd) to be pretty, stylish, or up-to-date. It was one thing to argue that the consumer marketplace was "administered" by producers seeking profits, but it was another to claim that consumers were inert, incapable of using even a rigged environment for ends of their own. Certain ends might be ignoble or immoral from Lynd's viewpoint, but that did not make those who chose them "irrational." Given the culture in which they lived, such behavior might be eminently rational.[43]

Nowhere in "The People as Consumers" or in his other articles of the early and mid-thirties did Lynd explain how or why his mind had changed on the matter of consumer rationality. But a reading of those pieces strongly suggests that the shift was closely related to his growing political activism. The articles typically begin with a graphic depiction of advertising power—"the long and adroit fingers of the producer tampering with what the consumer 'wants' "—and end with a call for a new federal role, perhaps a Department of the Consumer, to protect people from business manipulation. As an activist lobbying for expanded government control in consumer affairs, it was natural for Lynd to want to portray the individual consumer as passive, cornered, unable to help himself. "Once take the assumed high degree of rationality out of consumer choices," he wrote in early 1932, "and recognize the consumer as a hard-beset mariner willing to make for almost any likely port in a storm, it becomes largely a question of whose signal lights can beckon to him alluringly." The only hope for the mariner was government intervention to regulate the signal lights in the collective interest.[44]

It is highly ironic that as soon as Lynd obtained his tenured professorship at Columbia—in recognition of the "scientific" work he had undertaken in the twenties—he turned decisively toward problem-solving, the pursuit represented at the ISRR by men like Shelby Harrison and against which Lynd had sometimes inveighed with great force. Lynd was brought to Columbia in 1931 at the urging of Robert MacIver (strongly supported by Wesley Mitchell, a member of the same Graduate Faculty of Political Science, which comprised history, economics, public law, and social science). MacIver recommended Lynd to the faculty as the author of "perhaps the most noteworthy single volume in the field of American sociology which has appeared in the last decade," and as the man who would promote at Columbia the empirical study of communities in which Chicago excelled. But although he began two major research projects in his first three years at Columbia—one a study of the impact of the Depression on 150 native-born white Manhattan families, the other a study of several hundred business-class families in Montclair, New Jersey, during the Depression—neither came close to completion. "He was appointed here," his friend and colleague Paul Lazarsfeld later reminisced, "with the expectation that he would develop a tradition of empirical research. He didn't do it. . . . During the Depression he got extremely politically conscious. He grew up completely without any political interest. . . . You have the feeling he has to atone for not having seen the light earlier."[45]

In July 1933 Lynd's political awareness took organizational shape when he was appointed to the Consumers' Advisory Board of the National Recovery Administration. In May 1934 he became chairman of its Committee on Standards, and in December 1934 he joined its Executive Committee. He had become a part-time New Dealer, traveling regularly to Washington at government expense, pushing for consumer interests in an agency much more concerned about the needs of business and even of organized labor than of consumers. At a time when many intellectuals were turning to socialism and even the Communist Party, Lynd was joining the administrative elite. While many radical intellectuals romantically extolled the virtues of the proletariat, Lynd embraced the liberal elitism of the managerial class. He even took to the public microphone to defend the C.A.B. against radical detractors. In a radio debate on "The New Deal and the Consumer" over N.B.C., John T. Flynn called the C.A.B. symbolic window-dressing; Lynd responded with the administrator's timeless lament that "being lambasted by people like you on the outside" made it harder for him to represent the consumer.[46]

Perhaps Lynd was right in his belief that a federal agency to shield consumers against corporate advertisers was a necessity. But he made a heavy intellectual sacrifice in the course of justifying and drumming up support for federal intervention. Lynd now believed that common people lacked not only the special virtue that many radicals found in them; they also lacked the capacity to function rationally in a pecuniary culture. He had jettisoned Dewey and embraced Lippmann, but without seeking intellectual justification for the switch. He merely asserted that the consumer was essentially irrational. In defense of his belief he noted only that advertising men had known the truth all along. "Business in its public guise insists that the consumer is rational, that he knows what he wants and what is best for him. . . . But business on the job, in its shirtsleeves, knows better. . . . The advertising agency and the university school of business were manipulating a realistic theory of human nature at a time when economic theory was still talking about consumer 'choice.' Great consumer-habit fabricating plants like the J. Walter Thompson Co. and Batten, Barton, Durstine and Osborn do not proceed on the assumption that the consumer is coldly rational."[47]

Armed with his "realistic theory," Lynd traveled to Muncie in June 1935. It is unclear how the projected new appendix became a second 500-page volume, especially since in early 1935 Lynd was apparently working again on his study of Manhattan families. What is clear is that Alfred Harcourt was strongly pushing for another big-seller. Harcourt in fact later suggested even a third volume, to which the Lynds replied that two were already enough exploitation for one city. But it is possible that his plea for a second volume fell on receptive ears because Lynd saw a chance to issue the kind of frank, polemical statement that his own scientific scruples, career anxieties, and ISRR regulations had prevented in *Middletown*.[48]

Where *Middletown* focused on the question of culture, assumed the irrationality of a pecuniary value system, and called upon Middletowners to resist it through education and personal conversion, *Middletown in Transition* stressed the role of power, asserted the irrationality and impotence of the people, and called for professional managers— including federally financed planners—to mold social institutions in the public interest. The shift in focus is evident at once in the lengths of chapters devoted to key topics. One-fifth of *Middletown*'s text dealt with religion, and another fifth with leisure, against one-twentieth of the second volume on religion and one-tenth on leisure. By contrast, one-fifth of *Middletown in Transition* dealt with government (the chapters on "Caring for the Unable" and "The Machinery of Government") compared to one-fifteenth of the first book. And volume two added entirely novel sections on Muncie's all-powerful elite ("The 'X' Family") and on the inanities of "The Middletown Spirit."

Muncie, according to *Middletown in Transition*, was a city "tightly controlled" from above by its business class; and at the apex of that class stood the "X" family, the Balls. They were in effect "a reigning royal family," in command of Muncie's economic, political, and cultural life. Even their generous philanthropy "operates as part of the local business-class control system." The Lynds stressed that there was no "personal malevolence" in the Balls' domination of their fellows: "It cannot be too often reiterated that the X control of Middletown is for the most part unconscious rather than deliberate." They granted too that "X control in Middletown is informal and a great deal of it unplanned in any central coordinated sense." But the diffuseness of Ball power in Muncie made it seem to the Lynds all the more irresistible. Why, then, one is forced to ask, did the Lynds not mention the Balls in *Middletown*? Robert deliberately omitted any reference to the "reigning royal family," of whose existence he became rapidly aware in 1924, because he felt it interfered with the argument he wanted to make about "modern American culture." He did later tell Helen that if he had known about the Balls before setting up camp in Muncie, he would have selected a different city on the grounds that the Balls made Muncie untypical. But by the time he had grasped their commanding role in town, he claimed, the research team was already in place. *Middletown* and *Middletown in Transition* therefore have a great deal in common, respectively, with "Crude-Oil Religion" and "Done in Oil." The first in each pair abstracts from concrete power relationships and stresses the democratic potential of the people's culture; the second in each pair stresses the elite domination that renders popular awareness and action problematic or impossible. Of course the Lynds ought to have admitted in *Middletown* that they were leaving a tremendously powerful family out of their account, and explained why they were doing so; simply to suppress the information was scarcely defensible. Better yet, they might have attempted to deal simultaneously with cultural forces and power relationships.[49]

In *Middletown in Transition* Muncie's masses were caught in a double vise. National advertisers continued to pound away at their habits, while the Balls, supported by the rest of the local business class, acted decisively (even if "unconsciously") to keep them contentedly subordinate. Snagged in this double web, the average Middletowner was from Robert Lynd's standpoint thoroughly, contemptibly passive. "The willingness of these individual working-class atoms to dance to any tune that will give them an automobile and 'show them a good time' " he found disgusting. His chapter "The Middletown Spirit," which at eighty-five pages occupies one-sixth of the text, is pocked with abrupt put-downs. "Like most other people, Middletown folk don't want to have to think too much"; they were satisfied to remain in "the thick blubber of custom that envelops the city's life," and to think what they were instructed to think. The business elite, no longer bewildered, "skim the cream from the economy" and then—through their "control [of] the press, the radio, the movies, and the other formal media of diffusion of attitudes and opinions"—"tell the cityful of people largely living off the skimmed milk of the economy what to believe." Rather than turn to some form of radicalism, Middletowners of the working class—"inarticulate and not pondering causes"—were growing fearful and sullen. Twice in *Middletown in Transition* the Lynds expressed their own fear that Muncie's middling elements, workers and small businessmen, were ripe for fascism. "The way may be paved," they noted at the conclusion of the book, "for an acceptance of a type of control that will manhandle life deliberately and coercively at certain points to the end of rescuing a semblance of control."[50]

The only hopeful sign the Lynds detected in the Muncie of 1935 was the recent arrival of federal assistance and with it the first fledgling effort to plan institutions in the public interest. Just as an earlier generation of intellectuals had found "social possibilities" (John Dewey's phrase) in the carnage of the First World War, the Lynds found in the Depression a unique opportunity to teach Middletown "that some problems cannot be coped with on a basis of self-sufficient local autonomy." As Middletown "grasped eagerly" at federal relief funds, "it has unconsciously been breaching the psychological walls that mark off *its* life, *its* adminstrative boundaries, and *its* fiscal problems from those of the wider culture." The Lynds were cautiously hopeful that "with the interjection of Federal planning into the local scene . . . precedents have been established and bench marks set, to which the culture may return more and more familiarly in the future."[51]

Many commentators have pointed out that in comparison to the Lynds' first volume, *Middletown in Transition* is a disappointing book. It was rapidly thrown together, with much less conceptual, stylistic, and organizational care. While it improved on *Middletown* by raising the issue of power in Muncie, it seriously exaggerated the omnipotence of the Ball family in particular and the business elite in general. Their judgment on business dominance fails to take account of evidence in the text itself—for example, in the unsuccessful elite effort to procure a sewage treatment plant for the murky White River that flowed past their elegant homes—that the well-to-do did not always get their way. But the deeper flaw in *Middletown in Transition* lies in its assumptions about, and portrayal of, the ordinary people of Muncie. Like the "consumers" in Robert Lynd's articles of the early thirties, Middletowners were now irrational, governed by impulse, "hypnotized by the gorged stream of new things to buy." While in 1929 culture was still to some degree a resource, a tradition of independence and reason on which Muncie could draw, culture in 1935 was simply a process of conditioning, in which symbols like "independence" were real only in the sense that they could deceive and manipulate. They were part of the "folklore" that, as Thurman Arnold noted in his simultaneously released *Folklore of Capitalism*, skilled leaders knew how to utilize for their own advantage.[52]

Robert Lynd agreed with Thurman Arnold's diagnosis of American folklore as a potent set of manipulable symbols, but was outraged by Arnold's bemused, detached acquiescence in the situation. "Mr. Arnold's analysis of current folkways is so good and so importantly true as far as it goes," Lynd wrote in the spring of 1938, "that it is a pity he leaves it at the stage that will make it a devastatingly useful handbook for fascists." Lynd noted that "like Mr. Arnold, the rest of us have few illusions as to the 'rationality' of human behavior," but urged that we "use our knowledge of 'how things work' to change institutional behavior so that men's fleeting moments of rationality will be maximized." Lynd spent the year 1938 trying to work out a set of principles for transcending capitalism while taking account of the essential limits of human reason. At the end of that time he made it publicly clear that he had little faith in lengthening the "moments of rationality" of average Americans. He hoped rather to do the reverse: to shorten, to circumscribe their moments of irrationality by planning a society that took their moral and intellectual weakness into account.[53]

In March he returned to his alma mater to deliver his four Stafford Little Lectures on "American Culture and the Social Sciences," the last of which confronted his Princeton audience with what he called "some outrageous hypotheses." Since private capitalism could not be made to operate for the maximum welfare of the whole population, he argued, and since human beings were primarily "emotional" rather than rational, it was the general responsibility of planners to determine the course of social change. And it was their specific role "to place people where they can be most useful." Now Lynd had gone beyond even the perspective of *Middletown in Transition*, which had itself warned against "a type of control that will manhandle life deliberately and coercively."[54]

Before revising his lectures for publication, Robert Lynd went with Helen to the Soviet Union for three weeks in August. "We thought it would be interesting to try to do a 'Middletown' in Russia," Lynd later recalled. Unlike Stuart Chase and Ruth Benedict, who compared Muncie to primitive societies in *Mexico* and *Patterns of Culture*, Lynd hoped to juxtapose Middletown and a culture that was from his standpoint more advanced, more committed to stating social problems "positively" and planning solutions in the collective interest. The Soviets were apparently not overly enthusiastic about the idea; the secret police even rounded the Lynds up and "grilled" them "for about two hours" after they drove off without permission into the countryside. But the experience failed to dim Lynd's ardor for centralized planning.[55]

Knowledge for What?, Robert Lynd's last book (though he continued teaching at Columbia until 1960), appeared in April 1939—two years after *Middletown in Transition*, a decade after *Middletown*. The early chapters constituted a passionate brief for an activist social science, for a return to the reformist roots of American sociology. "The essence of science is to analyze, to draw inferences, *and then to implement action*," Lynd exhorted. He thus eliminated the long-standing and for him personally troubling dichotomy between scientific understanding and social problem-solving by the simple expedient of including the latter in his definition of the former. This was the thesis of *Knowledge for What?* that the book's reviewers tended to stress, and for the most part—as in Robert MacIver's lengthy dismissal—to reject.

Curiously the reviews on the whole neglected the final chapter, which reiterated the "outrageous hypotheses" from the Princeton lectures.[56]

Thanks to recent advances in biology and psychology, Lynd argued, social science understood that "the stout assertions of the 'equality' of human beings" of the Enlightenment were passé. It was now the responsibility of social science to "show the way to restructure the culture so as to care for these inequalities." Many individuals were unable to "cope intelligently" with the "complexities of daily living." The Deweyan solution to that problem, to which Lynd had subscribed in the twenties, was the process of education, of learning to cope with complexity, which was the motor of cultural reform. Now Lynd dismissed the notion of "educating the individual up to most of these problems, for many of the problems are of a complexity that baffles even the specialist. The need is rather to rebuild the culture so as to adjust the situation to the individual." That was the path, in Lynd's view, already adopted by the Soviets: not individual education, but "positive" social planning.[57]

During the 1930s most American intellectuals on the left came to hold an increasingly negative opinion of the Soviet experiment and an increasingly positive attitude toward the New Deal. Robert Lynd reversed the usual progression by moving from New Deal administrator in the early thirties to frequent defender of the Soviet cause at the end of the decade. In *Knowledge for What?* he did caution against painting "too glowing" a portrait of Soviet culture, and against wooden applications of Russian solutions to American problems. But he was greatly impressed with what he had seen in Russia in 1938 and on the level of general principle found it highly relevant to America. "The Soviet Union's experiment represents a genuine effort to avoid the two extremes of Nazi over-control from the top and of our own American unorganized confusion at the grass-roots of local living." He reported approvingly the remark of a Soviet official in Moscow that "something over half the entire adult population of the city [was] . . . actively engaged in some form of . . . socially integrative work." Soviet culture refused "to allow its human participants to become socially lost in the shuffle." Everyone was included, was guaranteed—and if necessary, assigned—a fitting place in the social whole. Hence, Lynd concluded, "time may prove that despite our present greater freedoms, only the Soviet Union among contemporary great nations is building for basic liberties." He was certainly aware of the Moscow trials, which beginning in 1936 had convinced many American intellectuals on the left that the Soviet regime had little interest in basic liberties. But when Lynd spoke of liberty he meant something else: the liberty to have an appropriate function in the cultural whole, to engage in "socially directed participation." That liberty was too basic to be left to the caprice of individual free choice; some would use that freedom unwisely and be lost in the shuffle.

What Lynd was proposing, although he failed to formulate a specific program of action, was a therapeutic priesthood of social scientists akin to but with considerably broader powers than Wesley Mitchell's Doctors of Domestic Science. These benevolent "intermediary experts" would excuse the individual from "the necessity of coping with certain issues in their raw complexities." They would plan a culture in which "citizens from birth to death had as little chance as possible to invest their savings ignorantly, to purchase sub-standard commodities, to marry disastrously, to have unwanted children 'accidentally,' to postpone needed operations, to go into blind-alley jobs, and so on." This was neither fascism, communism, nor socialism, and Lynd gave it no political label. It was instead Bellamy's Utopia, fifty years after *Looking Backward*. It was a vision of a culture free of conflict and deceit, with no wasted energy, no moral failures, in perfect equilibrium—and a society administered by a disciplined band of selfless planners.[58]

Robert Lynd had arrived at the logical end point of his social analysis. *Middletown* had been a forceful attack upon the values of consumer culture, an eloquent condemnation of the passivity that the institutions of that culture increasingly imposed on Americans. *Middletown in Transition* broke sharply with that perspective and embraced one of the main ideological underpinnings of consumer society itself: The people were themselves irrational, subject to direct manipulation by whichever organized power got to them first. *Knowledge for What?* took the final step by calling for social scientists to beat the corporate advertisers at their own game—the forthright takeover by trained experts of much of the personal decision-making of everyday life. Lynd was embracing the principle of elite rule, but he was passing beyond the notion of a professional or managerial elite that, however influential, remained subordinate to a propertied ruling class. He was calling for a new ruling class, one that legitimated itself not just through the production of goods but through the production of knowledge and of communal solidarity based upon that knowledge. In a sense his dream was continuous with John D. Rockefeller, Jr.'s own effort to harmonize class relationships in advanced capitalist society by creating a morally responsible, spiritually enlightened ruling class. They agreed that only a ruling class committed to a moral vision—a vision based upon social scientific wisdom—could discipline the anarchic impulses of consumer capitalism and create a new society that was "caring."

What was distinctive about Lynd's managerial vision, aside from his assumption that such a society would socialize large-scale property rather than leave it in the hands of men like Rockefeller, was his utter honesty in admitting that the organization of a caring social order would require a starkly novel form of coercion. While the moral concerns that he shared with Rockefeller and many in the older generation of sociologists marked him as an anachronism in the post-Depression social scientific elite, he gave unusually clear expression to the manipulative ideal that the new generation inherited and maintained. What was often concealed or camouflaged in the work of other social scientists, Lynd shouted from the rooftops. He was an embittered critic of the relativistic hedonism of consumer culture, but the very completeness of his alienation brought him fervently, vociferously into line with one of that culture's main supports—the theory of benevolent management by trained professionals. Like Henry James, Robert Lynd provides a clue to the awesome pervasiveness of consumer culture in twentieth-century America. Its central assumptions turn up where one would least expect them: in the lives and work of those commonly thought to have held them in the deepest contempt.

Lynd never did give up his distaste for the consumer ethic; in that respect he remained a strong, indeed bitter critic of consumer culture. Like his idol Thorstein Veblen he detested the notion that living could be conceived as the art of consuming, and he bewailed the invasion of academia by business values. He could not stomach those who had in his view devoted themselves to mastering the rules of the social marketplace, to augmenting the value of their personal stock in the exchange of selves. He yearned for a more moral, rigorous, productive life, as had so many other men and women in Protestant America since the late nineteenth century. Like many of them Lynd had had to confront the insurmountable problem that his search for the moral life lacked a transcendent referent; he could find no ideal, in the absence of the God he had renounced, for which he could sacrifice himself. What he refused to do was to trivialize his quest for real life by converting it into a hunt for novel experience, for "health," for professional aggrandizement, or for any of the forms of purchased fulfillment. Lynd resigned himself to the fact that for him there could be no fulfillment. He possessed the conscience, but not the faith, of the classic Calvinist. His father's earnestness remained, but not his father's conviction.

During the 1930s Lynd had become increasingly intimidated by the quantitative prowess of the younger generation of sociologists, of whom one of the leaders was his friend Paul Lazarsfeld. By 1940, when Lazarsfeld joined the Columbia faculty at Lynd's urging, Lynd was feeling painfully inadequate among his professional peers. He was never able to complete either the two Depression surveys he began in the thirties or a project on power in America on which he worked erratically in the fifties—and which both Lazarsfeld and another colleague, Robert Merton, tried repeatedly but without success to persuade him to finish. Lynd had lost faith in his own work. He was frequently depressed, and though he occasionally wrote and spoke for radical causes in the forties and fifties, he gradually withdrew from the intellectual arena.[59]

Convinced that he lacked the respect of his colleagues, Lynd felt cut adrift. He despaired of what he termed, in a 1940 letter to his old Union Seminary professor and radical pro-Soviet activist Harry F. Ward, "this world of loneliness." In the mid-1950s, as he passed his sixtieth birthday, he did take some solace in the image of the with-drawn, solitary man of reason—an image cultivated simultaneously, though in a much more enraged manner, by his Columbia colleague C. Wright Mills. "I find this a dismaying world," he wrote in a private memo, "in which to try to be myself and a person I can live with because I respect myself." He continued:

I have said over and over again to students something like this: "We live in a difficult world in which the prognosis is bad. The single decent man was never so impotent as today in America. . . . But the victory a single human being can achieve—particularly an intellectual—is to try to know the score in his lifetime; for what is needed is scratches of decency on the windowpane of our time; and the one ultimate indignity of life is to go over the hill into oblivion without at least understanding what it is that is wrong with our time and why it is wrong." This may sound quixotic and soppy. . . . But it is also important—to me—to be trying to do what is decent, rather than simply drifting or cashing in on the times in which one happens to live.

To the very end he held out for the old-fashioned value of decency, but he could do little to mitigate his overwhelming feeling of isolation. The story of *Middletown*, whose old-fashioned values were condemned by the eminent domain of the consumer culture, was mirrored in the life of Robert Lynd, who found himself homeless in mid-twentieth-century America.[60]

POLITICS AS CONSUMPTION:
MANAGING THE MODERN AMERICAN ELECTION

ROBERT B. WESTBROOK

Surveying the development of "propaganda" in 1928, Edward Bernays, the father of the public relations industry, lamented the limited impact of modern marketing practice on American electoral politics. "Politics," he observed, "was the first big business in America. Therefore there is a good deal of irony in the fact that business has learned everything that politics has had to teach, but that politics has failed to learn very much from business methods of mass distribution of ideas and products." Businessmen had incorporated the pageantry and spectacle of politics into their sales campaigns, but politicians had failed to see the pertinence to elections of the "real work and campaign of business," which consisted of "intensive study of the public, the manufacture of products based on this study, and exhaustive use of every means of reaching the public." As one observer commented, it was "amazing that the very men who make their millions out of cleverly devised drives for soap and bonds and cars will turn around and give large contributions to be expended for vote-getting in an utterly inefficient and antiquated fashion."[1]

One hears few such complaints today. The intervening half-century has seen the rapid assimilation of "the real work and campaign of business" to American electoral politics. Critics now lament the all-too-successful efforts of Bernays and his progeny to transform elections into marketing campaigns. "For too long a time," one journalist wrote recently, the relationship between citizens and their leaders "has been the relationship of persons to packages . . . packages with human face and form—and, somewhere within the wrappings, no doubt, a winning but fallible human personality—but a package put together by pollsters, image-makers, pulsetakers, and speech writers. Voting under such conditions is not making a choice. It is buying a product."[2]

This essay examines the "commodification" of modern American electoral politics. It places this development within the context of the lingering death of the "pre-market" politics of the nineteenth-century party system and the emergence of a managerial ethos based on the application of the wisdom of advertising, public relations, and behavioral science to problems of social control. It argues that the most visible manifestation of the commodity form in modern elections—the packaging and sale of candidates to voter-consumers—is but a part of a greater pattern of commodification in which the skills of those who manage elections and the attributes of voters themselves are also packaged and sold. The electoral relationship, it suggests, has become not one of persons to packages but of packages to packages, a relationship shaped by managers who are themselves for sale.

I have tried to view this transformation of electoral politics as part of the larger history of American consumer culture, a culture in which, as Raymond Williams has said, "the dominant mode of human perception and interaction is very generally mediated by commodities." To embed twentieth-century politics in this context is to expand the study of consumer culture beyond its conventional boundaries, but I believe that exploring the full meaning of this culture demands a broad understanding of the cultural constitution of commodities and of the realm of commodity exchange. We are, after all, dealing with a culture that presents even "human beings and their detachable characteristics as commodities, either for purchase, or, more generally and more discreetly, for window shopping." The essays in this collection underscore the need to continue exploring the ways that commodity forms have remolded our society across a wide spectrum of experience. We must ask, with Bernays' contemporary Georg Lukacs, "How far is commodity exchange together with its structural consequences able to influence the *total* outer and inner life of society?"[3]

This essay is a modest contribution to this larger project. In focusing on elections, I have limited myself to one major aspect of the transformation of twentieth-century American political culture. But the study of campaigning is a good place to begin because it clearly reveals the evolution of that culture between 1880 and 1980. And it is here that the thinness of American democracy is often most painfully apparent.

Elections are also a good place to observe the connections between the development of an American consumer culture and the expansion of managerial power. Although consumer culture imprisons us all, there is little equality among the inmates. The transformation of electioneering is part of the wider effort by managers and professionals to "rationalize" the whole of twentieth-century American society through strategies of surveillance, commodification, and information management. The rise of the professional campaign consultant traced here is bound up with what Christopher Lasch has termed "the shift from an authoritative to a manipulative style of social control—a shift that has transformed not only industry but politics, the school, and finally even the family." Modern political consultants are cousins to industrial relations experts, ad executives, and the various helping professionals; and they, like Henry James, Edward Bok, Bruce Barton, Robert Lynd, and Werner von Braun, have dreamed the managerial dream of a well-ordered society propelled by the predictable desires of apparently autonomous consumers.[4]

I

The emergence of a new managerial elite in twentieth-century American elections was rooted in the steady transformation of the nation's political system that began in the 1890s. It was connected most especially to the slow decline of the political party as a major institution in American political life. The strategies of managerial control based on the commodification of politics arose amidst the decay of partisan culture and the eclipse of the quite different electoral strategies that were a central feature of that culture.

The style of nineteenth-century elections was shaped by three related conditions: Elections were highly competitive, voting turnout was very high, and voters were deeply partisan. Only one national election between 1836 and 1896 qualifies as a landslide (1872), while ten of the twenty-one presidential elections in the twentieth century have been landslides. Mean turnout for presidential elections between 1876 and 1896 was nearly 80 percent, and off-year elections in this same period showed a mean turnout of 63 percent. Mean turnout for twentieth-century presidential elections have not risen above 65 percent in any election, and, in the 1920s and 1970s, the figure has hovered around the 50 percent mark. Off-year elections in this century have rarely produced turnouts of 50 percent and have dipped as low as 33 percent (in 1926). Nineteenth-century voters were also much more partisan than contemporary voters. For men of all classes party affiliation was an important aspect of personal identity. Two-thirds of the voters habitually voted a straight ticket, and another 10 percent voted on most occasions for the candidates of one party. This compares with an estimated 62 percent of the electorate who split their tickets in 1980. The independent voter was a rare bird in nineteenth-century politics. They were confined to a small elite of wealthy, well-educated men who denounced the partisan culture of the vast majority of the nation from the pages of genteel magazines. Partisans returned the favor by questioning the manhood of those who would set themselves apart from such an important aspect of nineteenth-century male identity as the party label. John J. Ingalls, a Republican senator from Kansas, characterized independents as a "third sex." Nonpartisans were "the neuter gender not popular either in nature or society."[5]

Close elections, high turnouts, and deeply partisan voters reinforced the "military" style nineteenth-century politicians adopted for their campaigns. Elections hinged on the question of which party could most fully mobilize its army of highly partisan voters. There was very little question of how voters would vote when they got to the polls; the task was to get them there in great enough numbers to defeat the opposing "army." The central concern of the campaign was to raise the morale and enthusiasm of a party's troops and demoralize those of the opposition. The principal device for building morale was huge rallies at which the party's soldiers would be exhorted by their leaders to advance upon the polls on election day, and the rank and file would display their party colors in massive parades led by military bands. The symbols of party loyalty and tradition would be trotted out by party orators, and the whole campaign took on the character of a ritual of solidarity. But the parties were not above employing less savory tactics, like intimidating enemy voters, voting "repeaters," stuffing ballot boxes, falsifying returns, or importing voters from out of town to stand in for imaginary voters on the rolls.[6]

The slow "decomposition" of the partisan political culture of the late nineteenth century began with the "critical elections" of the early 1890s, which brought the era of highly competitive campaigns to an end. In 1896 the decisive victory of the Republicans and their standard-bearer, William McKinley, over the Democrats and William Jennings Bryan signaled a dramatic political realignment. Southern Republicans and, in many areas, Northern Democrats became virtually extinct. While party competition survived in a few states, in most states voters had no real choice at the polls. A large percentage of eligible voters dropped out of the electorate, joining Southern blacks who were pushed out by systematic disenfranchisement campaigns. Voter turn-out plummeted, partisanship declined, and the campaign organizations of the political parties atrophied. By the 1920s, voter turnout in presidential elections had dipped to around 50 percent, and off-year elections attracted but a third of the electorate.[7]

The political party was also severely weakened in this period by the attacks launched on it by "progressive" anti-party reformers, who sought to put an end to the corruption of machine politics. Ballot reforms and a direct primary system in many states weakened party control over voting, nominating, and political recruitment. In many cities a coalition of businessmen and reformers led an offensive against urban bosses and their immigrant clientele. Reforms such as at-large elections for city council positions, nonpartisan local elections, and the introduction of city-manager government eroded party authority in many cities and were symptomatic of the broader effort of progressive reformers to replace politics with administration and wrest power away from partisan elites and invest it in "expert" authorities. The principal victim of the successes of this reform movement was the patronage system that was the backbone of partisan organization. Only in those states and cities where the parties were able to slow the erosion of their patronage resources did strong partisan organization survive.[8]

As party organization atrophied amid noncompetitive elections and anti-party reform, many of the political and social functions exercised by nineteenth-century parties began to pass to other organizations and institutions. By the early twentieth century most Americans had abandoned political parties as a vehicle for the prosecution of their social and economic interests in favor of bureaucratic functional interest groups like trade associations, labor unions, and professional associations. Parties lost much of the already limited "distributive" policymaking functions they had exercised in the nineteenth century and became purely "constituent" parties that continued to play an important role in the electoral process but performed few policy functions. The parties also lost their entertainment functions to the blossoming mass culture industry, and lost their near monopoly on political information with the displacement of the party press by the "objective" media of modern mass journalism.[9]

The process of party decomposition was slowed temporarily by the creation of the New Deal party system. Under the impact of the New Deal realignment, the party system began a slow process of nationalization, which over a forty-year period restored two-party competition in most states. For a time the decline in participation and partisanship was reversed, but they were not restored to the levels that had prevailed in the nineteenth century. The proportion of the population that identified itself as independent grew from 12 to 23 percent between 1936 and 1952, and the largest "party" in the electorate remained the party of non-voters.[10]

The last twenty years have seen the process of party decomposition move forward rapidly, and developments in this period have rivaled those of the early 1900s in their corrosive impact on the parties. During the 1950s and early 1960s the pattern of party identification in the American electorate remained stable and reflected the partisan loyalties established by the New Deal realignment. A little more than a third of the population strongly identified with one of the political parties; about 40 percent were weak party identifiers; and the remaining fourth of the populace identified itself as independent. After 1964 this pattern changed substantially. By 1974 the number of strong party identifiers had declined to about a fourth of the population, while the number of independents had increased to 38 percent. Split-ticket voting also increased markedly in this period, and public opinion polls have shown a steady decline in support for the party system and in favorable attitudes toward both parties.[11]

The important thing about these developments is that they reflect not a shift in partisan loyalties—a realignment—but the disaffection of voters with parties per se—what Everett Ladd has called "dealignment," a movement "away from parties altogether." By the 1960s and 1970s the issues that divided the electorate—race, the war in Vietnam, "life-style" (drugs, abortion, women's rights), Watergate, inflation—were not issues on which the positions of the two parties were clearly differentiated. Their effect was not to realign partisan commitments, as the issues of the 1930s had done, but to produce a widespread disaffection with political institutions as such. This was reflected by rising levels of political alienation as well as the decline of electoral participation to levels approaching those of the 1920s.[12]

The declining partisanship of the electorate in the last two decades has been accompanied by and has contributed to the erosion of the parties' control of the electoral process, particularly at the presidential level. Recruitment for the presidency and other offices no longer proceeds through party channels but is now more a matter of candidate self-selection and the development of a personal organization. These organizations are, moreover, increasingly based less on personal loyalties (like that of the Kennedys) than on purely contractual arrangements between candidates and the experts they need to run their campaigns. Many candidates have been successful without party support, and several of these have run on an explicitly anti-party platform. State parties have now become largely irrelevant to presidential nominations, which are determined in direct state primaries. The mandating of convention delegates through state primaries has also substantially reduced the role of the national convention, for, barring a closely divided party electorate, the nominating decision will be made not at the convention but in the primaries. The convention has become a ritual endorsement of a decision that has been made before it begins. The post-Watergate reforms in campaign spending have also adversely affected the parties, for the effect of these reforms, which limit individual contributions as well as overall spending by the parties, has been to curb the influence of party money on elections without significantly reducing the influence of money from other sources (such as "independent" political action committees). The fact that the law distinguishes the overall spending permitted to presidential candidates from that permitted to national parties promotes the further separation of the personal candidate organizations of the presidential candidates from party organizations. The effect of these developments has been substantially to deprive the American political parties of the one important function they continued to exercise for the first half of the twentieth century: control of the electoral process.[13]

The decline of American political parties has been viewed by many of its chroniclers as a decline of democracy, and, as a consequence, a whiff of nostalgia for a lost golden age often creeps into their analysis. Walter Dean Burnham, for example, has characterized the nineteenth-century American political system as "incomparably the most thoroughly democratized of any in the world," and has viewed the decomposition of this system in the twentieth century as a democratic declension.[14] There are two principal problems with this argument. First, it identifies democracy with broad voter participation in competitive two-party elections without inquiring into the question of whether such participation provided voters with an effective means of shaping public policy. Second, it equates the exercise of democratic citizenship with participation in the life of political parties without asking whether the parties themselves were democratic institutions.

It is difficult to claim that nineteenth-century American politics met either of these tests for democracy. The policymaking role of the nineteenth-century parties was limited, and policy mandates were as difficult to discern in elections then as they are now. Nineteenth-century parties, like their twentieth-century successors, served primarily a "constituent" function, legitimating the constitutional order by overseeing the peaceful succession of power. Nineteenth-century parties were, moreover, no more democratic in structure than in function. They were hierarchical, if not highly centralized, institutions ("armies") that did little to foster the growth of participatory decision-making within their ranks. Partisan politics in the nineteenth century was as much an obstacle to as a vehicle for democratic politics; high turnout and party competition do not of themselves make for democracy.

It is true, as Burnham says, that the nineteenth-century American electoral system was relatively the most democratic in the world at the time and that this can no longer be said to be the case in the twentieth century, yet this says more about the advance of democracy in Europe than about its decline in the United States. It is hard to sustain the judgment that nineteenth-century American politics was more democratic than twentieth-century American politics if we use as our criterion the opportunity each provided for the ordinary citizen to participate in the public decisions affecting his life. The differences between the two systems lie in the different ways this opportunity was circumscribed. Nineteenth-century politics was, to be sure, an important part of the expressive lives of those (mostly white, uniformly male) citizens who took part in its rituals, as twentieth-century politics is not for those who still bother to vote. Nineteenth-century partisan culture fostered an active, rich symbolic experience of community, ethno-religious, and class solidarity, while for the modern American voter electoral politics has, by virtue of its transformation into an exercise in mass marketing, come to share with other spheres of experience the peculiar features of the culture of consumption: passivity, atomization, and spectatorship. Nevertheless, however troubled we may be by this fact, we do ourselves a disservice if we weave a democratic romance around the partisan armies of the nineteenth century. The watershed of the 1890s was not that between democracy and oligarchy but between two different oligarchic systems, neither of which, as historian Lawrence Goodwyn has said, provided citizens with much of a chance to "see themselves experimenting in democratic forms."[15]

This is not, however, to say that the possibilities of democracy in

America have not been adversely affected by the decline of the party. The political party was the one broadly participatory institution in American political life, and, for this reason, it was the one institution that held within it the promise of a more expansive democracy. It was the genius of the Populists to see this and to attempt to reconstruct and radicalize the participatory practices of the third-party system in order to democratize control of the political economy. Their defeat and the subsequent decay of these practices and the partisan culture that fostered them cut most Americans off from the active role in organized public life that might have been theirs and set the stage for a redefinition of politics as consumption.

II

With the decline of partisanship and the atrophy of party organization, a new style emerged in American election campaigns, a style that historian Richard Jensen has termed "merchandising." Merchandising campaigns relied not on the mobilizing efforts of a semipermanent army of party workers but on appeals directed at voters through the communications media by experts skilled in the techniques of mass persuasion. The military-style campaigns of the late nineteenth century were inappropriate to elections marked by low turnout and weakening partisanship, and without an extensive patronage system, parties lacked the resources with which to build and sustain an army of loyal workers.[16]

This is not to say that these political armies died overnight. In some large cities like Chicago, Philadelphia, Pittsburgh, Jersey City, and St. Louis, where the parties were able to retain control over city governments and patronage rewards, military campaigns and metaphors remained very much alive.[17] In most of the country, however, winning elections became less a matter of mobilizing the faithful and more a matter of attracting the undecided.

This reconceptualization of the voter as a consumer rather than a soldier was part of the effort of parties to maintain control over the electoral process in the face of the deterioration of partisan culture and organization. Experts in merchandising were called upon because party politicians lacked the skills to run a commercialized campaign. Such experts were not perceived initially as a threat to a party power but as a means for securing that power through the adaptation to new circumstances. The ultimate effect of this new style of campaigning was not, however, to stay the process of party decomposition but to accelerate its progress and to vest control of election campaigns in the experts in mass merchandising to whom the parties had turned for help. Up until the 1960s, the parties remained in control of campaigning throughout most of the country, sustained by their mild and short-lived comeback during the New Deal. The signs of their obsolescence were, nonetheless, clearly marked, as were those of the growing independence of political consultants. By the sixties, it was apparent that merchandising experts were functionally indispensable to political campaigns, but parties were not.

The first signs of a shift of campaign styles were discernible in the early 1890s. Party professionals were already turning from the partisan spectacles of the military style to issue-oriented "educational" campaigns that relied less on rallies and parades than on lectures and the mass distribution of pamphlets, leaflets, and other literature. The most impressive of these campaigns was Mark Hanna's 1896 feat: distributing 200 million pieces of Republican Party literature to the nation's 15 million voters. Prominent businessmen-politicians like John Wanamaker and Chauncey Depew urged the parties to put campaigns on a "business basis" and called upon their colleagues to utilize the new techniques of mass advertising. "Every enterprise, every business, and I might add every institution must be advertised to be a success," Depew declared. "To talk in any other strain would be madness."[18]

However, despite the presence in early merchandising campaigns of such prominent advertising executives as Albert Lasker and Hill Blackett, the principal experts that parties called upon prior to World War II were newspapermen who served as press agents during elections. Pioneering PR men like Ivy Lee, George F. Parker, and George Creel were all ex-reporters who began their careers in public relations as publicity men for political candidates, and by the second decade of the century a publicity agent was considered an element essential to a successful campaign. In 1929 the Democratic Party established the first full-time partisan publicity bureau under the direction of newspaperman Charles Michelson. The Republicans were quick to follow suit, establishing their own permanent publicity bureau shortly after Michelson began to operate, and they joined the Democrats in expanding the role of public relations experts in the elections of the 1930s and early 1940s. But even in the 1940s political propaganda was undeveloped. Politicians had yet to master, as political scientist Pendleton Herring observed in 1940, "the more subtle ways of manipulating public opinion."[19]

The most notable exception to this was in California, where in

1933 two public relations experts, Clem Whittaker and Leone Baxter, had founded Campaigns Inc., the first company devoted exclusively to the management of political campaigns. California provided a particularly hospitable environment for the growth of professional campaign management. In no state were political parties hit harder by progressive reforms. Under the leadership of Hiram Johnson, California progressives launched a vigorous anti-party crusade that instituted the initiative, referendum, and recall; nonpartisan elections for city, county, school district, and judicial elections; cross-filing for statewide elections; and a drastic reduction in the patronage resources available to elected officials. California was also fruitful soil for the growth of professional media politics in the 1930s and 1940s because of its tremendous suburban population, which made permanent party organization very difficult. As a consequence, California politicians anticipated later national developments by thinking in terms of personal organizations that reached the voters through media campaigns managed by professional consultants.[20]

Whittaker and Baxter managed seventy-five campaigns in California between 1933 and 1955, winning seventy of them. Campaigns Inc. *supplanted* rather than merely supplemented the campaign management functions of the political party. Indeed, perhaps no campaign management firm has ever been able to attain the level of control over all aspects of a campaign that Whittaker and Baxter achieved in their heyday. They demanded complete authority over virtually all aspects of a campaign—from the drawing up of a campaign blueprint and budget, to the selection of the themes and issues upon which the campaign would focus, to the implementation of their strategy. The chief responsibility of the candidate, from Whittaker and Baxter's point of view, was to raise the money necessary to pay their "prideful" fee. Whittaker complained that there was a big difference between the marketing of commodities and the marketing of candidates in that the latter were resistant to complete managerial control.

An automobile is an inanimate object; it can't object to your sales talk, and if you step on the starter, it usually runs. A candidate, on the other hand, can and does talk back—and can sometimes talk you out of an election. . . . We have the problem of human relations; the relation of the candidate to his manager or managers, his willingness or unwillingness to hew to the line on the plan of strategy which has been worked out . . . his ability or inability to measure up to the character you give him by your carefully-prepared build up.[21]

Nationally, the most important developments in political campaigning in the period between the late forties and late sixties were the establishment of commercial advertising agencies in a prominent role in major political campaigns and of television as a principal campaign weapon. These developments were related, for candidates sought out the ad agencies in part because of their expertise in the use of the new medium. By the mid-fifties, major advertising agencies had become important actors in presidential politics, and campaign strategy and metaphors had become fully commercialized. In the 1956 campaign, *Nation's Business* happily predicted, "Both parties will merchandise their candidates and issues by the same methods that business has developed to sell goods." No one was blunter about the commercialization of politics than G.O.P. ad man Rosser Reeves, who remarked that he thought of "a man in a voting booth who hesitates between two levers as if he were pausing between competing tubes of toothpaste in a drugstore. The brand that has made the highest penetration on his brain will win his choice." [22]

The presidential election of 1952 was the first time that television played a major role in a national campaign. Both parties recognized the importance of TV, and together they spent $3 million for the purchase of broadcast time. The Democrats proved unimaginative, devoting most of their TV time to the coverage of traditional speeches. The Republicans, on the other hand, realized that TV was not simply radio with pictures but a means of communication opening new possibilities and requiring a new approach. Set speeches, Eisenhower-Nixon strategists argued, "cannot impart the real warmth of personality with which both candidates are endowed. Therefore, informal, intimate television productions addressed directly to the individual American and his family, their problems and their hopes, are necessary to make the most of the ticket's human assets." The key task, according to one Republican ad man, was that of "merchandising Eisenhower's frankness, honesty, and integrity, his sincere and wholesome approach," a task to which television was thought to be particularly well suited. [23]

In 1952 the Republicans were much more heavily loaded with experienced commercial public relations and advertising talent than the Democrats. The Republican ad agencies—Batten, Barton, Durstine, and Osborne and Ted Bates and Company—deemphasized speeches and "talking heads" in favor of fast-moving documentary films and a blitz of thirty-second spot commercials such as those entitled "Eisenhower Answers the Nation!" in which Ike offered penetrating answers to probing questions asked him by an offstage voice. For example:

VOICE: Mr. Eisenhower, what about the high cost of living?
EISENHOWER: My wife, Mamie, worries about the same thing. I tell her it's our job to change that on November 4. [24]

155

The Democrats were caught off guard by the spot campaign. George Ball protested that the Republicans had "conceived not an election campaign in the usual sense, but a super-colossal multimillion dollar production designed to sell an inadequate ticket to the American people precisely in the way they sell soap, ammoniated toothpaste, hair tonic, or bubble gum." Adlai Stevenson offered the first of many obligatory complaints by merchandised candidates about merchandising campaigns, declaring that "the idea that you can merchandise candidates for high office like breakfast cereal . . . is the ultimate indignity to the democratic process." Nonetheless, in 1956 the Democrats tried to catch up. The director of publicity for the Democratic National Committee, Samuel Brightman, affirmed that "our whole operation is an exercise in PR. We're now more aware of PR and the potentialities of new techniques and channels of communication." In 1956 the party engaged the services of the advertising agency Norman, Craig and Kummel, a firm already famous for its "I Dreamed I Went Walking in My Maidenform Bra" campaign.[25]

The high point of the marriage of politician and ad agency was reached in the mid-1960s. Major agencies joined with candidates sensitive to image politics like John Kennedy and Ronald Reagan to produce campaigns as sophisticated as those launched for any other commodity. In the 1964 presidential race Lyndon Johnson and Barry Goldwater saturated the nation's major media markets with 10,000 spot announcements. In 1966 candidates in state races followed suit. Nelson Rockefeller bought air time for over 3,000 spots produced by Jack Tinker and Partners. The agency, which had never worked on a political campaign, but was noted for its Alka-Seltzer commercials, produced a series of imaginative ads noteworthy for the fact that Rockefeller himself (who was personally unpopular at the time) appeared in none of them. He defeated his opponent by a wide margin.[26]

Although many major American advertising agencies played an important role in political campaigns in the 1950s and 1960s, it was not a role that they always relished. Political campaigns were short-lived, pressure-filled, and, compared to regular accounts, not very profitable propositions.[27] For the ad agencies, politics was a sideline, and, by the late sixties, they had been displaced at the center of merchandising political campaigns by managers and consultants who, like Whittaker and Baxter, specialized in political campaigns and offered candidates a broad range of services. The conditions that had provided a favorable environment for the growth of professional campaign management in California—rapid population growth, spatial mobility, suburbanization, weak party organizations, and declining partisanship—had by the sixties spread to most of the nation, and, at all electoral levels, candidates abandoned party organization and established personal, ad hoc, contractual organizations managed by experts in media campaigning.

The increase in full-service campaign management firms was rapid in the sixties and early seventies. In 1960 professional campaign managers were at work regularly in less than ten states. By 1970 there were a hundred firms offering complete campaign management (sixty of which did most of their work in political campaigns), and another two hundred companies offering some professional management service to political candidates. The growth in narrower and more specialized campaign services has been no less dramatic, and today it is a rare campaign that does not make use of some sort of political consultant. These consultants make their services available to management firms as well as to candidates who prefer to put together their own package of experts. In today's electoral marketplace, a candidate can buy anything from complete campaign management to a single speech.[28]

Most campaign consultants regard themselves as professionals and businessmen above all else. As a consequence, they subordinate personal ideological and political commitments to a concern for turning a profit and building a professional reputation. Many scrupulously observe party lines, but most do so because working for both parties is considered to be bad for business. As consultant Michael Kaye observes: "I work only for Democrats. I don't work for just Democrats because I think they are the only good pure people on this planet. It is the same reason that in the [product] advertising business I didn't work for two clients in the same business." There are, of course, exceptions to the rule of ideological flexibility. The most important of these are the ideologues of the New Right like direct mail king Richard Viguerie, who sets strict ideological standards for his clients (and employees). On the other hand, there are a growing number of consultants who are quite cavalier about party distinctions as well as ideology. One firm, Decision Making Information, even took polls for both sides in a congressional race in 1966.[29]

In the 1970s political consultants ceased to be behind-the-scenes operators and emerged as public figures in their own right. By the end of the decade, prominent consultants like Patrick Caddell, David Garth, Tony Schwartz, Richard Viguerie, and Richard Wirthlin were the subject of as nearly as much news coverage during elections as the candidates they managed. Consultants had become status symbols for candidates; association with a big-name consultant insured that the candidate would be taken seriously by other politicians, journalists, and financial contributors. So important had the symbolic importance of consultants become that many candidates held press conferences at the beginning of a campaign to show off "their" expert. Simply put, as one ad man said, "the consultants are *the* political scene now."[30]

III

Modern political consultants have finally answered the call to put American electoral politics fully on a "business basis." They have established a political market in which voters are bought and sold as part of the most significant commodity form of the mass communications industries, the audience. Like other important managers of these industries, political consultants are marketing commodities to "audiences which they are also producing and exchanging, as commodities."[31] They package candidates for sale to voters they have previously packaged for sale (as audiences) to candidates. Some consultants specialize in the sale of audiences, others specialize in the sale of candidates, and some do both. If I devote more attention to the first of these skills here, it is because it is the least recognized aspect of commercialized electioneering.

Indeed, as Dallas Smythe has argued, the central position of the audience commodity in twentieth-century capitalism as a whole is often overlooked. Audiences are the commodities produced by the owners and managers of the institutions of the mass media and sold by them to advertisers. The managers of the mass media produce these audiences by attracting the attention and sustaining the loyalty of consumers with the inducements of entertainment and news, the "free lunch" sandwiched in between the advertisers' messages. It is this attention, this time, this "labor" that advertisers purchase; the audience commodity is "a non-durable producers' good which is bought and used in the marketing of the advertiser's product."[32]

Advertisers seek to reach those audiences that will be most attentive to their particular messages. Thus audience commodities and the markets in which they are exchanged are specialized by the demographic and attitudinal specifications that they bear. It is the task of experts in market research to provide the specifications of particular audiences and to assess the impact of advertising on the behavior of the members of such audiences. Marketing experts hence play an important mediating role between the producers and buyers of the audience commodity.

Political consultants buy voter audiences for candidates from the managers of the mass media, and, in some instances, produce these commodities themselves (most notably in the case of direct mail entrepreneurs like Richard Viguerie). More importantly, they conduct the kind of market research or polling appropriate to this type of audience. This research produces the audience specifications used to shape a campaign's media strategy. Follow-up research determines the effectiveness of this strategy over the course of a campaign. The principal feature distinguishing political campaigning of the recent past from earlier merchandising campaigning is the leading role played by the pollster, who has supplanted the advertising man as the dominant figure in modern campaign management.

The extensive use of polls has joined the practice of the political consultants to the theoretical ambitions of behavioral science. The relatively small number of academic social scientists who have become directly involved in campaign consulting is no indication of the importance of social science to the development of modern election management, for it is from the theory and research of major American social psychologists, sociologists, and political scientists that professional campaign consultants have drawn much of their "esoteric" knowledge and techniques. The power of the political consultant rests on his ability to convince his clients that the application of this knowledge is a necessary, if not sufficient, condition of electoral victory.

The conjunction of managerial power and applied social science is not, of course, a phenomenon peculiar to electoral politics. Indeed, electoral politics was one of the last arenas of American life to be colonized by experts armed with social scientific knowledge. Like managers in factories, advertising agencies, schools, hospitals, and other institutions, political consultants have sought to develop techniques that will enable them to effectively predict and control the behavior of large numbers of people involved in complex social systems. They have naturally found mainstream American social science a useful ally. The dominant position of managerial experts in modern American society results, as Alasdair MacIntyre has said, from the translation of the prophecy of positivistic social science into a social performance. Managers "justify themselves and their claims to authority, power, and money by invoking their competence as scientific managers of social change," legitimating their rule by an appeal to "a body of scientific and above all social scientific knowledge . . . understood as comprising a set of universal law-like generalizations."[33]

The claim to be able to provide universal law-like generalizations about social life, modeled on those of the natural sciences, is, of course, the central claim of positivistic social science. Such generalizations, positivists argue, enable the scientist to establish causal relationships between social phenomena and to predict the consequences of the interaction of these phenomena. This basic science of social life opens the door to an effective science of social engineering in which the interaction of social variables is controlled and manipulated to produce desired consequences. The fact that social scientists have been unable to establish such law-like generalizations has not deterred managers from successfully laying claim to power on the basis of the presumed existence of such laws and their own ability to utilize them in the engineering of social life. The prophecies of social science have, as MacIntyre concludes, produced *"not* scientifically managed social control, but a successful dramatic imitation of such control."[34]

In the United States, one significant irony of the alliance of social science and managerial power is the fact that the dream of a science of social engineering was, until the 1940s, principally a dream of radical and reform-minded social scientists. Its most prominent exponents were critics of capitalist society, ranging from technocratic progressives like Stuart Chase and Robert Lynd who envisioned a society guided by radical experts to radical democrats like John Dewey who called for a society in which social scientific knowledge was integrated into the activities of an egalitarian political community.[35] By the forties, however, American social science was dominated by those who simultaneously proclaimed their value neutrality and sought the support of managerial power through intimations of an ever more effective apparatus of social control. As Todd Gitlin has observed, the forties were "a time when administered politics, administered markets, administered culture, administered education were each coming into its own, each becoming legitimate, each developing tight interlocks with the others. . . . Universities, corporations, and foundations were finding themselves in sometimes uneasy but mutually indispensable partnerships; and they were meeting under the sign of behaviorism."[36]

The professional campaign manager relies heavily on two of the cornerstones of behavioral science: "attitude" psychology, which has provided him with the social-psychological theory upon which his efforts at social engineering have been built, and survey research, which has given him a tool with which to keep the attitudes of large populations of voters under ready surveillance. Survey research on public attitudes emerged in the 1930s and 1940s as a focal point of the collaboration between commercial marketing specialists and social scientists, and it was part of the baggage that each subsequently brought to the study of the American voter.

Social psychologists define an attitude as "an enduring evaluative disposition" toward some object or class of objects, a disposition comprised of cognitive, affective, and behavioral components.[37] In the late nineteenth century, "attitude" was a concept rooted in Darwinian biology, and, until the early twentieth century, it combined physiological as well as psychological dimensions; it referred to a disposition of the body as well as the mind. However, under the leadership of Chicago sociologist William I. Thomas the concept was in the United States stripped of its physiological component and interpreted as a purely psychological "tendency to action," a kind of "template" that predisposed people to respond in certain ways to particular objects or situations. These templates were neither purely intellectual nor purely emotional but a compound of thoughts and feelings. As historian Donald Fleming has shown, the concept of attitude met a historical need of twentieth-century intellectuals for a conception of man that took account of what was seen to be the incapacity of most individuals for sustained rationality without denying the rational component of the behavior of even the most impulsive of men and women. The concept of attitude was an alternative to the simple characterization of mankind as basically irrational.[38]

The need for such a concept grew out of the effort of the bourgeois white Euro-American male to understand and control people he saw as very much unlike himself—children, mental patients, primitive people, peasants, immigrants, Negroes, and women. The minds of such people had to be understood, if only for manipulative purposes, and the dream of a science of attitudinal management was never far from the surface of the thinking of those American social scientists who developed the concept. Attitude psychology was seen as the key to a predictive science of human behavior that would provide the basis for social control through intervention in the processes of attitude formation and change.

Attitudes were regarded as deep-seated tendencies in the human psyche that were not readily apparent to the scientific observer but had to be inferred from overt behaviors, including the expression of "opinions." A key problem was, therefore, to find reliable techniques for measuring and interpreting attitudes on the basis of an analysis of the medium of opinions through which they were expressed. The foundation for such techniques was laid in 1928 by Chicago psychologist L. L. Thurstone, and over the course of the next two decades psychologists and sociologists led by Louis Guttman, Paul Lazarsfeld, and Rensis Likert developed increasingly sophisticated techniques of attitude measurement that enabled researchers to infer individual attitudes and measure their intensity through the analysis of responses to carefully constructed questionnaires.[39]

In the 1930s these techniques of attitude measurement were yoked to the newly developed sampling techniques of survey research, a marriage that enabled social scientists to guarantee the statistical significance of the attitudes their studies uncovered. Scientific sampling of public opinion grew principally out of research in marketing and advertising, and was a manifestation of the larger drive for efficiency and rationalization that altered the face of American capitalism after the turn of the century. After World War I, survey research became an important part of marketing and advertising practices, and in 1936 market researchers achieved a major triumph in the political arena when their sampling techniques, wielded by marketing experts like George Gallup, yielded an accurate prediction of a Roosevelt victory and made a laughingstock of the *Literary Digest*, which had forecast a Landon triumph on the basis of a huge straw poll innocent of even the most basic sampling controls. The conjoining of attitude research and scientific survey research formed the intellectual foundation for much of the collaboration of managerial power and social science after 1935. One of the principal manifestations of this collaboration was the founding and rapid growth of the two great American institutes of applied social research—the Bureau of Applied Social Research at Columbia organized by Paul Lazarsfeld in 1940 and the Survey Research Center at the University of Michigan put together by Rensis Likert and Angus Campbell in 1946. Much of the research on American voting behavior from which political consultants derived their operational theory of electoral engineering was produced by scholars at these two institutions.[40]

Paul Lazarsfeld was the single most important social scientist in bringing attitude measurement to bear on both business marketing and voting research. His early American career is an important example of the interaction of the prophecy of positivistic social science and the social performance of managers. The central preoccupation of Lazarsfeld's work was to develop a general theory of human action (*Handlung*), a science of human choice. His research on particular kinds of human choices such as voting or buying soap was directed toward this larger end. As a theorist, he showed little interest in the substance of a particular choice; he was after that Holy Grail of positivism, a predictive science of human behavior. Thus, for example, an important article written by Lazarsfeld and some of his BASR colleagues on the "psychology of voting" argued:

The act of voting can well be used as a paradigm for many other activities. The decisions that a modern Western man makes every few years in the political arena are similar to those he makes every day as a consumer of goods and services . . . systematic analysis of the factors affecting one decision, such as voting, for which a considerable body of empirical data is available, should therefore contribute to the understanding of behavior in many other sectors of modern life.[41]

There were those like CBS Radio and McFadden Publications, however, who were very interested in particular choices, and Lazarsfeld built his career on the coincidence of his abstract and largely methodological interests with the marketing interests of such clients. From his point of view, his relationship with these clients was a kind of mutual exploitation built on the happy intersection of the needs of giant corporations and the ambitions of social science.[42]

Following his emigration to the United States from Austria in

1933, Lazarsfeld survived on the strength of his ability to sell attitude research to American business. The purpose of market research, he told the American Management Association, was to generate "knowledge by means of which to forecast and control consumer behavior," and successful market research was thus "a matter of gaining detailed understanding of specific human reactions":

Our actual buying behavior is largely an expression of *specific attitudes*, that is action-tendencies toward particular objects, reflecting the varied directions of motivation as these have been molded in the courses of experience. . . . The attitudes that lead to buying hence lie at the very heart of market research problems.[43]

Such arguments were met with enthusiasm by businessmen, who were more than eager to join in the search for a science of consumption. As one ad man declared, "The separate bits and pieces of knowledge of human behavior have clearly begun to fall into place, and it is clear that this knowledge is of great practical value to the 'mind makers' . . . those privileged groups who control the mass media of communication and persuasion." However, despite an abundance of good will on both sides, social scientists have yet to provide market researchers with the sort of knowledge they need effectively to forecast and control consumer behavior. The more social scientists have studied consumer behavior, the more complex has the analysis of the buying decision become. The marketer's dream of a theory that would direct him to a limited number of manipulable variables has not been realized.[44]

In the early 1940s Lazarsfeld and the BASR launched the first major study employing attitude research to examine American voting behavior. Lazarsfeld saw *The People's Choice* as a further investigation of the psychology of choice and of the effects of advertising on consumer buying decisions. Indeed, Lazarsfeld originally intended to study consumer purchases; a sample of housewives would be surveyed over time to establish a link between changes in buying decisions and exposure to advertising. Lazarsfeld could not get funding, however, so he turned to voting instead and received a grant from the Rockefeller Foundation. *The People's Choice* initiated a social science tradition that applied the theory and techniques of market research to voting behavior. As the authors of the SRC's classic study of *The American Voter* declared, "We want to predict whether a given individual is going to vote, and which candidate he will choose." For the scholars, voting studies would provide the basis of a predictive theory of human choice. Political consultants watched attentively; they hoped such a theory would undergird a science of electoral engineering that would enable them not only to predict but to control human choice.[45]

Lazarsfeld's belief in the commensurability of buying and voting and the importance of attitude research for the understanding of each percolated slowly into American politics in the 1940s. In 1950 the Committee on Political Parties of the American Political Science Association noted that "relatively little use has been made by the parties of social survey techniques as a basis for political campaigns. Nor have the parties shown much interest in the study of the social, economic, and psychological factors that influence the results of the election contests." This situation changed rapidly, however, with the integration into campaigning of consultants trained in market research. The Republicans predictably took the lead. In 1956 G.O.P. public relations man L. Richard Guylay explained that "scientific methods take the guesswork out of politics." The extensive use of polling in presidential campaigns began in 1960 when Louis Harris conducted polls in key primary states for John Kennedy. In 1962 two-thirds of the candidates for the Senate used polls, and by 1966 pollsters were employed by 85 percent of the winning candidates for the Senate, virtually all gubernatorial candidates, and half of all victorious congressmen. By 1970 survey research had become the heart of political campaigning.[46]

But the hope of the political consultants for a science of "attitude engineering" has proven as difficult to realize as the similar dream of their colleagues in commercial marketing. Social science has been unable to deliver law-like generalizations that could lead to the predictive control of voting. Ironically, one "law" it has developed—the "law of minimal effects"—holds that the capacity of a political campaign to induce attitude change in voters is extremely limited. Research has revealed that the political attitudes of voters are hardened dispositions in large measure impervious to efforts to transform them through mass-mediated persuasion. Those attitudes that are intensely held, such as strong partisan identification or ideological commitments, even work to set up strong perceptual barriers that filter out or distort messages that challenge these attitudes. But most importantly, "undecided" voters, whose attitudes are held with less intensity and who do not set up strong perceptual barriers to the messages of a campaign, are no less resistant to planned conversions."[47]

This "law" has exercised an enormous influence on campaign strategy, for it means that a short-term campaign designed to change public attitudes is unlikely to succeed. The strategy of the campaign manager has not been to try to change voter attitudes but to take them into account as givens in the situation in which he must operate. He attempts to use existing attitudes and make them work for him: first, by reinforcing the intensely held attitudes of those voters favorably disposed toward his candidate, and, second, by creating a perceptual environment that will make it appear to the undecided voter that a vote for a particular candidate (or against a particular candidate) is the best way to express his attitudes at the polls. This second strategy is the most important, because it is usually the undecided voters who determine the outcome of an election.[48]

Thus, whatever success a professional campaign consultant has in determining the outcome of an election comes not through his ability to control voter attitudes (which he cannot do) but through his ability to best his opponents in a competitive contest of information and image management, which manipulates voter choice in only the most indirect and imprecise fashion. Despite the proliferation of technological paraphernalia in modern campaigns, contemporary electioneering is less a science than an art—a "dramatic imitation" of scientific management. The more candid consultants, like Robert Goodman, admit as much:

We are still artists, trying to develop a dramatic way of capturing the attention and then inspiring resolve. The new technology is in its infant stage for those who practice the media arts. . . . We're becoming a little more error free. But we really don't know a great deal. If we knew more we would be dangerous.[49]

The failure of social science to provide campaign managers with the operational theory of their dreams has not, however, diminished the importance of attitude research in the merchandising campaign. The crucial importance of such research for the manager trying to shape the voters' perceptions (rather than change their attitudes) is that it enables his candidate to tell those voters that are of decisive importance to his victory exactly what they want to hear. Consultants in firms like Voter Perspectives are in the business of selling "domestic intelligence" on important audiences. They promise to help the candidate achieve "EMPATHY and RAPPORT with the voter" by providing him with information on how the key sectors of the electorate feel about him and his stands on the election issues. He can then use this intelligence to "decide which issues or voting blocks require an *emotional* or *angry* presentation and which issues or blocks to treat logically or rationally."[50]

Pollsters in modern campaigns rely on several different kinds of polls to accumulate critical data on the voter audiences that they sell to candidates. The first is the pre-campaign or "benchmark" poll taken a year or more before election day which tests the relative strength of a candidate's support, the quality of his or her image, and the nature of the issues that are uppermost in the voters' minds. Sometimes the pre-campaign poll even antedates the selection of a candidate. In Niagara, New York, in 1980, the local Republican Party recruited Daniel J. Bazzani as their candidate for the state assembly on the basis of a poll that indicated that the voters "wanted an Italian, someone from Niagara Falls, college-educated with some government experience, and young."[51]

During the heat of the campaign, consultants run daily "tracking polls" on small samples of likely voters that attempt to assess voter perceptions of the latest issues and images and establish "trend lines" that will shape strategy in the last days of a race. Two other kinds of surveys, involving small samples, are "panel surveys" in which previously polled voters are re-interviewed several weeks later to measure shifts of opinion, and "focus groups," nonrandom groups of a dozen or so "representative" voter types, who are invited to discuss a campaign's candidates, issues, and media tactics by consultants who keep them under surveillance from behind a two-way mirror. The aim of all these polls is to package an audience for candidates. Once this package has been delivered, and candidates know what it is that voters know and desire, it is up to the media consultants to package the candidate so that voters will think they are getting just what they want. The consultants' goal is not to convince voters to buy their candidate but to fashion a candidate the voters want to buy.[52]

IV

The packaging of candidates to mirror previously packaged audiences is a relatively recent development. A major difference between the campaigns of the 1950s and early 1960s managed by advertising agencies and those of the late 1960s and 1970s managed by professional political consultants lies in the relationship each established between attitude research and advertising. As Joseph Napolitan commented, "Agencies often use research to *justify* what they already have done, or to test the impact of what they do. First they make the spot, then they test audience reaction to it; the campaign manager does his research first, and by the time he makes the spot he's pretty certain that it's on target."[53] In the seventies, even ad men readily acknowledged the importance of survey research:

Commercials do not sell; all they can do is create a favorable environment, and this environment can only be created through the marriage of attitudinal research and the commercial. . . . Not only are we dependent on attitudinal study for our themes but also for the very language that we must use in communicating with the voters.[54]

This is not to suggest that the job of the political media adviser is an easy one. The task of commodifying candidates remains difficult; mirror-making is a skilled craft.

In media campaigning the candidate commodity is presented to the voter audience through paid and unpaid media. In the first instance, consultants package the candidate through advertisements that draw heavily on the techniques of commercial advertising to present an image of the candidate and his stands on the issues that will resonate with voter desire. In the second instance, they stage "pseudo-events" that present this same image for those voters who are attentive to the "news" media.

Media campaigning is by definition mediated communication, communication by means of a technology that permits the consultant to control to a degree the package and the context in which it will be presented to the voter. In paid media, the consultant has maximum control over the image, limited only by the malleability of his commodity. The key to effective political advertising, as for all advertising, is to use this control to package the commodity so that it constitutes a "projective field" that will reflect back to the consumer images of well-being to be achieved in consumption.[55] This is more difficult to do with candidates than with cigarettes, but media consultants have nonetheless worked some impressive magic.

Consultants often urge candidates to modify the physical characteristics of the package they offer to voters. Product design can symbolize and implicate product performance, and makeup, hairdo, and wardrobe are crucial in this respect. In 1968 Richard Nixon vowed not to repeat the mistakes he made in 1960 in ignoring these concerns, and he went on a diet to reduce his jowls, maintained a constant suntan, and shaved several times a day. Often a candidate's credentials as well as his physical appearance must be carefully packaged. In 1962 Edward Kennedy found himself in a tough race for the Senate seat previously held by his brother John. Kennedy's biggest asset was the fact that he was a Kennedy, but he suffered from his relative lack of significant public service. His consultants came to terms with this "experience" issue in two somewhat contradictory but seemingly effective ways. First they sought to create an image of Kennedy as a candidate who was in truth experienced by providing him with extensive coaching on all major issues and by pumping up his few public achievements, like his membership in the Massachusetts Bar Association. Second, they argued that Kennedy had something more important than experience: His brother was President of the United States.[56]

Consultants will sometimes use what might be termed "selective quotation" to build up their candidates's credentials. During the Republican primaries in 1980, John Connally ran a commercial in Iowa featuring a segment of a glowing introduction that Governor Ray had given to a Connally speech, implying that the governor supported the Texan when in fact Ray had endorsed Howard Baker. In these same primaries, Baker's media men constructed a commercial that highlighted a standing ovation by a crowd of supporters in response to Baker's tough reply to the complaints of an Iranian student about American policy toward his nation. In reality, the crowd in the film was cheering at the end of Baker's speech and not following his response to the student, which drew no such applause.[57]

Issue positions are also an important attribute of the candidate commodity. Here the emphasis is on ambiguity and vagueness. Specific policy proposals are rare in campaign communications. Problems are identified and their solution is promised, but, as Benjamin Page has shown, "policy stands are infrequent, inconspicuous, and unspecific." Winning candidates are often those who are most skilled at "appearing to say much while actually saying little." Because candidates are aiming for what Garry Wills has termed "the broadest common denominator in voter manipulability," they play upon the concerns of the electorate without taking the detailed policy positions that might cost them an important constituency, for "the more detailed a candidate's stance, the harder it becomes for voters to put favorable interpretations on that stand."[58]

Like commercial advertisers, political consultants attempt to build an image for their product by the manner in which it is contextualized in advertisements, and in contextualizing candidates they employ many of the same formats and much of the same "grammar of representation" as their colleagues in the business world. An image of warmth and sincerity is conveyed by the abstract qualities of the roaring fire in the fireplace behind the candidates, wisdom by the book-lined shelves that surround them, youthful vigor by the young people with whom they speak on the beach, and patriotism and commitment to the public interest by the ubiquitous flag at their side.[59]

One of the most oft-used imports from the contextualization formats of commercial advertising is the "man-in-the-street" interview or endorsement, which enables the candidates to identify themselves with particular groups of voters. If, for example, the polls show that ticket-splitting, blue-collar workers are a critical segment of the electorate that is leaning toward a candidate, his consultants will devise a commercial featuring endorsements by such people, who are identified by the symbols of their group identity: hard hats, factory gates, heavy equipment, etc. Or perhaps it is the votes of the elderly that are crucial. Endorsements will be forthcoming in this case from retired people, and withered visage, cardigan sweater, and easy chair will be prominently displayed.[60]

168

Political advertising will also draw on the conventions of its media to make a point. The conventions of photographic portraiture, for example, are, as Roland Barthes observed, "replete with signs":

A full-face photograph underlines the realistic outlook of the candidate, especially if he is provided with scrutinizing glasses. Everything there expresses penetration, gravity, frankness: the future deputy is looking squarely at the enemy, the obstacle, the "problem." A three-quarter face photograph, which is more common, suggests the tyranny of an ideal: the gaze is lost nobly in the future . . . the face is lifted towards a supernatural light which draws it up and elevates it to the realm of a higher humanity; the candidate reaches the Olympus of elevated feelings, where all political contradictions are solved.[61]

Political advertising has with time developed its own particular clichés. Numerous ads, for example, feature a photograph of the candidate in shirt-sleeves with his sport coat or jacket slung over his shoulder, an image of white-collar diligence, informality, and accessibility. Another oft-used image is that of the candidate busy at his desk with a telephone in hand, signs of a "can-do" representative capable of wielding the powers of persuasion on behalf of his or her constituency. Another tactic of commercial advertising that has become increasingly popular in political campaigns is "positioning," a form of negative advertising in which candidates not only announce their own virtues but imply that these virtues are lacking in the competition. An excellent example of positioning was the ads used by Jimmy Carter in his fight with Edward Kennedy for the Democratic presidential nomination in 1980. Building on the advantage that surveys indicated he had in "personal qualities" over Kennedy, who was plagued by family problems and the memory of Chappaquiddick, Carter ran ads that announced he had performed the jobs of husband, father, and President with distinction and lauded his honesty:

You may not always agree with President Carter, but you'll never wonder whether he's telling the truth. It's hard to think of a more useful quality in a president than telling the simple truth. President Carter—for the truth.

The implication of these advertisements, of course, was: "Senator Kennedy, poor husband and father and suspected liar—for something less than the truth."[62]

The principal advantage of paid media is that it vests control of image and context in the candidate's consultants. This very fact, however, detracts from the credibility of political advertising. For this reason, consultants also rely heavily on unpaid media, which, at the cost of a measure of control, provide a greater degree of credibility. In order

169

to gain this added credibility without an undue loss of control, consultants attempt to confine unpaid media coverage of their candidate's campaign to "pseudo-events," that is, to speeches, interviews, and "debates" that they have set up, events that are established for no other purpose than to be covered by the news media. The aim is to transform "news" into unpaid advertising, disguising the candidate's message as part of the "free lunch" of mass communication. In the United States, consultants have benefited from compliant news media, particularly television, which has confined most of its reporting on election campaigns to pseudo-events.[63]

There are, of course, limits to the ability of consultants to package candidates, limits much greater than those facing commercial ad men. As Clem Whittaker complained, candidates, unlike other commodities, have a capacity and a propensity to depart from the script and talk themselves out of an election. Moreover, a political candidate, unlike a bar of soap, has a history that clings like dandruff despite the best efforts of the consultants to "recontextualize" the past and make "historical untruth" a "political reality."[64] But professional political consultants have still done a remarkable job of reifying elections into a relationship between packaged voters and packaged candidates. They have created a politics consonant with the "marketing orientation" that suffuses social relationships throughout twentieth-century American society. The integration of survey research with the techniques of advertising and public relations has made American political campaigns a kind of institutional reflection of the "other-directed" personality that haunts consumer culture. Attitude research is the candidate's "radar," providing him with the kind of surveillance and detailed information on significant others for which David Riesman's other-directed individual would sell his soul (if he had one). The candidate's image is the face that every other-directed person would present to the world if he could only get a scientific sample of his friends and associates to periodically fill out a questionnaire. The polity has become a caricature of the social world of the lonely crowd, a world in which success rests on "a good set of data and an eye for the possibilities."[65]

V

The manipulative power of the political consultants rests on their capacity to control the information that is disseminated in an election campaign. They do not change the wants and desires of voters but rather attempt to create a perceptual universe in which these wants and desires will lead the voter to choose their candidate. The ability of the consultants effectively to pursue this strategy stems less from their professional skills than from the structural characteristics of the political market. Because voting has become for most Americans little more than one of a myriad of consumption choices in a high-intensity market in commodities, voter consumers tend to assimilate their political choices to the "rationale of irrationality" that generally governs consumer behavior. In a society in which consumers are compelled continually to reinterpret their needs in the context of a rapidly changing array of goods and services, it is irrational to accrue the "information costs" that would enable them to make a well-informed decision about the purchase of any single commodity. As a consequence, as Staffan Linder, William Leiss, and others have argued, consumers "must be content to become acquainted with the claims advanced on behalf of commodities (by advertisers and consumers) and to decide to accept—provisionally and arbitrarily—one set of claims rather than another." Advertisers know this, and they take advantage of it by providing "quasi-information for people who lack time to acquire the genuine insights." The advertiser, Linder shows, "helps to close the information gap, at the same time exploiting the information gap that is bound to remain."[66]

In the political market, these effects are lessened somewhat by the limited number of political commodities confronting the voter at any one time. However, the special character of this market offers additional difficulties. Elections are markets in "collective goods" in which it does not pay the voter consumers to invest the resources (time, energy, money) necessary to acquire the information that would enable them to cast a well-informed vote. The instrumental benefits to be gained by casting one vote in an election in which thousands or millions of votes are cast are extremely uncertain and most likely extremely limited. Hence it is rational for the voter (who has already made a decision of dubious instrumental rationality in deciding to vote) to try to cut the costs of voting by relying on whatever "free" or inexpensive information can be picked up in everyday life. The consultants recognize this logic, and they do everything they can to gain access to the channels of information upon which voters are likely to rely: the six o'clock news, a commercial before or after a favorite TV show, a "personal" phone call. Insofar as voters act as rational consumers, they render themselves susceptible to the manipulation of candidates and their consultants.[67]

Consumers recognize that they are burdened with a rationale of irrationality and that it leaves them open to manipulative managerial power. As Robert Merton noted in one of the earliest and best studies of mass persuasion:

They see themselves as the target for ingenious methods of control, through advertising which cajoles, promises, terrorizes; through propagandas that, utilizing available techniques, guide the unwitting audience into opinions which may or may not coincide with the best interests of themselves or their affiliates; through cumulatively subtle methods of salesmanship which may simulate values common to both salesman and client for private and self-interested motives.

A climate of "reciprocal distrust," Merton argued, was intrinsic to a consumer culture in which "men will tend to look at every relationship through a tradesman's eyes" and "society is experienced as an arena for rival frauds." [68]

Voters, too, are aware of the dilemmas and powerlessness that the structure of the political market imposes on them. They have responded by manifesting the symptoms (e.g., non-voting) of what social scientists have termed "political alienation." The expressions of such alienation are varied. They include the despair of the Philadelphia social worker who said in the midst of the 1980 elections, "I'm afraid of the responsibility of voting. I feel like I've been lied to so much and I don't feel I'm knowledgeable enough to know if I'm being lied to. It's kind of scary, choosing somebody. I feel rotten being one of those apathetic voters, but you feel so helpless in an election like this." They include as well the cynicism of the inside-dopester at The New Yorker who noted the emergence of an "operational aesthetic" in merchandising campaigns in which consultants offered sophisticated voters an invitation to "admire the elaborate device with which we are trying to befuddle your judgment." [69]

An end to this alienation presupposes an end to politics as consumption and a revival of republican conceptions of citizenship. Politics must be defined and constituted as a realm of experience in which men and women act not as consumers but together as participants in the common life of their community. It means the construction of public space in which citizens may debate the public good and accrue the expressive benefits of civic action. This does not, as some have recently claimed, require the revival of political parties dominated by elites, but it may well entail a revival of Martin Van Buren's notion of parties as institutions of civic education. Long ago, Alexis de Tocqueville celebrated the "wise conduct" of American lawmakers who, he said, gave "each part of the land its own political life so that there should be an infinite number of occasions for the citizens to act together and so that every day they should feel that they depended on one another." [70] Historians, no doubt, would contest the accuracy of Tocqueville's description of early nineteenth-century American politics, but, right or wrong, the political life he celebrated is not to be found in the United States today. If such a politics is to be fashioned, it will require a cultural transformation of the most radical sort, for republican democracy poses a challenge not only to the power of a new breed of political managers but also to the power of consumer culture itself.

VII

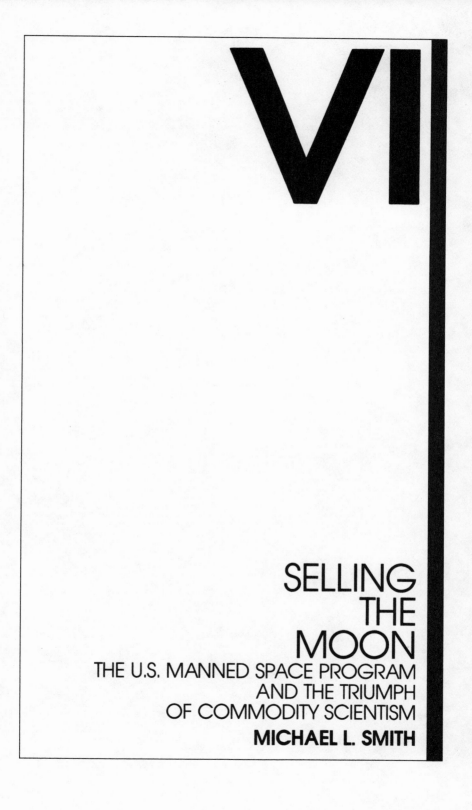

SELLING
THE
MOON
THE U.S. MANNED SPACE PROGRAM
AND THE TRIUMPH
OF COMMODITY SCIENTISM

MICHAEL L. SMITH

"**B**y golly, we've done it!" were the first words millions of television spectators heard when the Apollo 11 lunar module touched down on the surface of the moon. They were spoken, not by the astronauts, or even by the Mission Control technicians in Houston, but by CBS newscaster Walter Cronkite. The ambiguous scope of his pronoun was apt. Spokespersons for the lunar mission defined that "we" with varying degrees of inclusiveness: the astronauts and technical crew, the nation, humankind. But Cronkite could have meant any of these, including the inner circle of direct participants, for he and the mass media "space coverage" he personified were an indispensable aspect of the event. Arguably, in what Guy Debord has called "the society of the spectacle," media coverage of Apollo *was* the event. Never before had so ambitious an undertaking depended so thoroughly on its public presentation for significance.[1]

The U.S. manned space program of the 1960s provided a salient chapter in the evolution of consumer culture—not just through its technical accomplishments, but by the forms of display its designers and publicists adopted. The project's social function and presentation techniques approximated those of the most highly developed communication medium in American culture: advertising. In a sense, the twelve-year effort to put Americans on the moon constituted the most elaborate advertising campaign ever devised. Its audience was truly global. Eight hundred million people saw or heard the first men on the moon.

The product of this spectacular "advertisement" was not the hardware of space exploration. Missiles, astronauts, and lunar footprints simply provided a visually dramatic new iconography through which the real product could be conveyed: an image of national purpose that equated technological preeminence with military, ideological, and cultural supremacy.

Conceived in the wake of the Sputnik scare, the project's desired effect appeared to be straightforward enough—a Cold War assertion of superiority over the Soviet Union. The merchants of space emerged from two institutions familiar with that goal: the "military-industrial complex," as President Eisenhower called it, and the news media. The first group included Pentagon strategists, scientists, and engineers involved with defense-related research and development; defense and aerospace contractors; and their allies in government—civilian and military agencies, congressmen, and even Presidents—who found support of an aggressive manned space program politically useful. The second group consisted of publishers, editors, and reporters for newspapers, magazines, and the newly developing national television newscasts. The needs and powers of these two groups differed, and dissension between and within them emerged repeatedly.[2] Their shared interest in the manned space program centered on its capacity to generate publicity: The first group sought it, and the second made an industry of supplying it. Their roles seemed simple: The defense establishment would deliver the "payload" for the public depiction of Americans in space, while the news media provided the vehicle.

The enterprise, however, quickly expanded in scope as its designers recognized that the project's success depended more on the impression it created than on the engineering feats it accomplished. To differentiate U.S. efforts in space from those of the Soviets, Apollo had to convey more than an extraterrestrial show of force; it must portray American use of technology as benign, elegant, beyond the earthbound concerns of military and diplomatic strategy. To succeed fully, the manned space program had to project an image directly contradicting its origins.

Such a task required compelling methods of presentation—methods previously developed by advertisers. The emblematic application of technology surrounding projects Mercury, Gemini, and Apollo embodied the government's increasing postwar reliance on the image-making techniques of the marketplace. Like the marketing of automobiles, the selling of the moon involved not just the problem-solving capacities of science and engineering, but above all the manufacture of a reassuring social image of technology and expertise.

Mission Control, of course, was not merely a Sunbelt efflorescence of Madison Avenue. To be sure, advertisers appropriated images, rituals, and eventually even astronauts from the manned space program. Conversely, NASA occasionally borrowed directly from the pantheon of names, images, and associations stockpiled by advertising. (As John Noble Wilford notes, the space agency named its first manned project Mercury "because a Greek god had a heroic ring and Mercury was considered to be the most familiar of the Olympians to Americans —thanks more to Detroit than to the god or the planet.")[3]

NASA and the news media, however, did not have to enlist the services of an ad agency in order to apply the techniques of advertising to space. By the 1960s any depiction of a man in a shiny new vehicle dealt with images and techniques already made familiar by advertising. It is in this capacity—as a principal source of public attitudes toward science and technology—that advertising influenced the state's depiction of the space race. The underlying relationship of the manned space program to the advertising industry resembled that of a guest conductor to a resident orchestra. NASA waved an impressive baton, but it was primarily because of advertising's ensemble of instruments and performers that the audience knew the score.

Long before Apollo, merchants and generals had discovered the social impact of parading new and exotic products. But in post–World

War II America the display value of technology had attained a new preeminence, often overshadowing the technical specifications for a given product, the managerial decisions leading to its development, and even its actual performance. This elevation of technological display marked the emergence of commodity scientism as the prevailing social idiom of science and technology.

The term "scientism" generally connotes a belief in the power and universal applicability of the scientific method. It represents an apparent fusion of opposites: a superstitious belief in the power of science and technology. One of its key assumptions is that science and technology (often referred to interchangeably) proceed in an inevitable sequence of events. Traditionally, the term has applied to those who equate this sequence with progress. The belief in technological determinism, however, is shared by many who consider the proliferation of science and technology to be as destructive as it is irreversible. Technophiles and technophobes alike tend to discern innovations of science and technology as not only inevitable but incomprehensible, and therefore magical. They simply disagree on whether it is white or black magic.

As the previous essays in this collection have noted, the emergence of a consumer culture in the United States has been marked by the transformation of social and personal attributes into detached, salable commodities. Technology has served both as handmaiden and as object of this process. When science itself is commodified, the products of a market-aimed technology are mistaken for the scientific process, and those products, like science, become invested with the inexorable, magical qualities of an unseen social force. For the consumer, the rise of commodity scientism has meant the eclipse of technological literacy by an endless procession of miracle-promising experts and products. For advertisers and governments, it has meant the capacity to recontextualize technology, to assign to its products social attributes that are largely independent of the products' technical design or function.

Commodity scientism emerged, in part, as a response to the steady removal of technological process from daily life. With each passing decade most twentieth-century Americans found technology to be more vital in their lives and less comprehensible. Not only machines but the decisions to create and apply them escalated in complexity and in public inaccessibility, withdrawing behind what Herbert Marcuse called a "technological veil."[4] As public understanding of the social uses of science blurred, only the products of this mysterious realm of expertise periodically burst forth from behind the veil: a polio vaccine, permanent-press shirts, ballistic missiles. As a result, Americans increasingly identified these commodities, rather than the choices and techniques that produced them, as science itself.

179

This widening gap between process and product, however, did not develop purely as an autonomous and inevitable effect of industrialization. By the close of the First World War, the advertising industry had begun to recognize that the technological veil could serve as a projecting screen—that the half-discernible silhouettes of technological change could be manipulated into salable images. In the shadow-puppet realm of consumer culture, where images of things often appear more convincing and expressive than the things themselves, advertising has served as the principal social medium for commodity scientism. The arms race and the space race demarcate the steady progress of this manipulation of technological display from the private to the public sector.

Most interpreters of the manned space program have fallen into opposing camps—either celebrating it as a triumph (of science, of nationalism, or of our collective "sense of wonder") or denouncing it as "an extravagant feat of technological exhibitionism."[5] Celebrants point to the exuberant public response—in the U.S. and abroad—to the first moon landing, as evidence of the program's success. Detractors fault national leaders for creating the entire manned space program purely to generate and manipulate that exuberance. Neither of these characterizations tells us much about why the program evolved as it did, or what it signified.

In charting the genesis of the astronaut, historians generally point to the humble, 180-pound Sputnik as the ship that forced a thousand launches. But the social significance of the U.S. manned space program is fully discernible only when examined alongside the changing contexts for viewing technology in an advanced consumer culture: the evolution of technological display in industrializing America; the advertising industry's perfection of commodity scientism; the role of the atom bomb in extending this social definition of science into national defense policy; and the U.S. government's "crisis of national purpose" in the 1960s. Viewed in this light, the flight of Apollo 11 represents the triumph of commodity scientism as an agent of national self-definition.

TECHNOLOGY AS DISPLAY

Products of technology and science hasve always been assigned social meanings well beyond their apparent design or function. Americans were not the first to discover this tendency, nor did they have to wait until the twentieth century to do so. By the late nineteenth century, the United States had come to excel in two particularly revealing arenas of display: scientific survey expeditions and the great fairs. Both enterprises familiarized the nation with certain display rituals and associations that remained long after the Grand Canyon or the White City had receded from public attention.

From Lewis and Clark's reconnaissance of 1804–1806 to the geological expeditions of Powell, Hayden, and King in the post–Civil War decades, explorer-scientists mapped and inventoried the continent, while—often unintentionally—abetting the acquisition and development of land and natural resources. At the same time they were amassing a collection of artifacts and images that contributed to the expanding nation's public image. Their geological and biological specimens filled the country's multiplying natural history museums. And as written accounts, illustrations, and stereoscopic viewcards of their expeditions drifted from the western mountains and plains into Victorian parlors, Americans learned to identify their growing country—and their scientists—with intrepid explorers, acting as advance scouts along an ever receding horizon of amazing curiosities and unimagined opportunities.[6]

As the nation reached the end of both the continent and the century, however, the need for such expeditions diminished. But the display value of the national explorer-scientist seemed to increase as his opportunities dwindled. The polar expeditions of the early twentieth century did not lead to startling new discoveries, annexations, or gold rushes; they did permit the planting of the flag in new territory, and a symbolic conquest in the names of science and national greatness. By mid-century, the "frontiers" of scientific exploration were no longer geographic; planting a flag on the moon created not the substance but a self-conscious simulation of territorial and scientific conquest.

Fairs, too, performed an emblematic as well as a practical function. The proliferation of industrial exhibits, from local mechanics' fairs to the great expositions, often presented fairgoers with their first glimpse of some recent innovation—electric lights, the telephone, new agricultural or industrial equipment. The dramatic display settings created by the fairs also provided symbols of technological prowess for the manufacturer, the consumer, and the nation. At the 1876 Centennial Exposition in Philadelphia, George Corliss's forty-foot-high steam engine supplied the power for all of Machinery Hall; but it generated much more energy among its spectators, who viewed the Corliss engine as a triumph of man over nature, and as an embodiment of "the national genius." The technical and emblematic functions, though distinct, coexisted in the same double towers of pistons, rods, and cylinders.[7]

In the decades to follow, manufacturers recognized and elaborated upon Corliss's insight: that the display value of a product can be as important as its function. At the 1939 New York World's Fair, the

most dramatic technological innovation on exhibit—the television—
exemplified a growing emphasis on hidden function, projected image.
Technological changes—particularly in electricity and electronics—
abetted the disappearance of process from the consumer's view. But
the general shift from process to product had less to do with technological change itself than with corporate marketing strategies. The 1939
fair's "theme center," unlike the Corliss engine, was a purely symbolic
contrivance: "the Trylon, a slender, graceful spire, taller than the
Washington Monument, and the Perisphere, a giant globe as high as
an 18-story building."[8] Inside the Perisphere, visitors glided on automated ramps past "Democracity"—a scale-model depiction of the thoroughly engineered city of the future. Everything they saw—Trylon,
Perisphere, Democracity—bore the exotic futuristic names and precise
white streamlined surfaces of an engineered utopia. Yet unlike the
Corliss engine, these splendid new symbols of technocracy completed
no tasks, presented no innovations; they embodied the elevation of
display value over technical function. Their only industrial use came at
the close of the fair, when the government reclaimed the steel girders
of the Trylon and Perisphere for the production of bombs and
tanks.[9]

The Corliss engine and the Trylon and Perisphere were only brief
and unusually self-conscious artifacts in the history of American technological display. But they suggest an important pattern of change in
the needs and techniques of display-makers. Fairgoers in 1939 were far
more familiar with the products of technological change than their
grandparents had been in 1876, but less sure of how or why these
products had come into being. By 1939 technological display revealed
less about the design of a new device than about its sponsor. The
Machinery Hall of earlier fairs had diversified into a shopping center of
separate structures, many of them (like the cash register–shaped National Cash Register building) serving as a corporate logos for the products on display. As products overshadowed process, the marketplace
was overtaking the workplace as the major source of popular attitudes
toward science and technology. The 1939 World's Fair, as one of its
designers lamented, did not resemble the engineered society of the
future so much as a "huge department store."[10]

The changing fairs reflected not just new technology but a fundamental shift in the culture's ways of seeing technology. By 1939 the
principal function of technological display was to teach consumers to
equate personal and social progress with technology, and technology
with new products. The World's Fair attempted to do just that. Since
1876, however, another institution had evolved to replace the fairs:
national advertising. What fairs and expositions did sporadically and on

specific sites, advertisers learned to do every day, in every community. More than any other institution, advertising by the mid-twentieth century had assembled and reshaped the images through which all mass depictions of technology gained public recognition.

In postwar America, only the federal government possessed the communications resources capable of matching national advertising in scale and sustained impact. Its two most ambitious campaigns of technological display—the nuclear arms race and the space race—applied presentation strategies that advertisers had perfected into a kind of dance of the technological veils. To trace commodity scientism's path to the moon, we must follow the variations on that dance—from Madison Avenue to Los Alamos to Houston.

ADVERTISING AND THE RISE OF COMMODITY SCIENTISM

Reflecting transformations in the commercial culture it served, advertising since the 1920s gradually redefined technology as a social force engaging consumers rather than producers. Henry Ford's assembly lines might reveal almost nothing to his workers about the automobiles they were constructing, but advertising taught them—and everyone else—what social and economic benefits to expect from a new car. Galvanized by the burst of production following World War II, advertising firms entered a new phase of impression management and market research; they repackaged popular images of technology into a consumers' hall of mirrors, where reflections reversed reality, and a product designed to create needs could appear to satisfy them. Thus modern advertising, as Raymond Williams has indicated, learned to operate socially as a form of "*magic*: a highly organized and professional system of magical inducements and satisfactions, functionally very similar to magical systems in simpler societies, but rather strangely coexistent with a highly developed scientific technology."[11]

The success of the manned space program depended on a very similar kind of "magic." Advertisers and space publicists alike drew upon the culture's shared pool, or "ritual idiom," of technological display images.[12] For Cape Canaveral as well as Madison Avenue, the task was to link certain public expectations of technology with the product or event in question. And as their presentations accumulated, both gradually reshaped the public's perception of technology itself. But ad men preceded astronauts. Viewers might consider ads as trivial, and moonshots as compelling. National advertising, however, had permeated the culture with millions of images and techniques; and the conventions of technological display developed through ads provided the only nonmilitary view of technology and its social uses that remained available to a mass audience.

By the mid-fifties, national advertising firms had evolved several closely related patterns of technological display, three of which particularly influenced public presentation of the space program. Unveiling techniques dramatized the introduction of new products, often obscuring the product itself with lavish backdrops or innovative secret ingredients. Techniques of transitivity fostered the illusion of transferring the purported attributes of the product to the consumer, generally through actors with whom consumers were to identify. Among the variety of character types advertisers have evoked, one of the most pervasive figures is the helmsman, whose mastery over his environment through the products of technology provides a model for consumer aspiration. Together, the techniques of unveiling, transitivity, and helmsmanship so thoroughly permeated popular notions of science and engineering that every depiction of technology in postwar America showed signs of their influence. To understand why the manned space program emerged as it did, it is necessary to see what its audience saw —the patterns of technological display that confronted them daily through advertising.

In a culture that has traditionally associated physical mobility with individual autonomy and national destiny, the helmsman always has figured prominently. From sea captains to riverboat pilots to aviators, the appeal seemed to derive less from the helmsman or his craft than from the implied relation between them. The explosive acclaim following Lindbergh's solo transatlantic flight in 1927 celebrated both the man and the machine—as if the explorer-scientist had mounted the Corliss engine and taught it to fly. As Lindbergh himself insisted, neither he nor his plane, but rather the third entity that they formed together— "we"—had performed the feat.[13]

Advertisers soon learned the importance of this mutual legitimation. Each of the helmsman's display qualities conveyed value to the product, which in turn appeared to reinforce precisely those qualities in its owner. Foremost among them was his masculinity. In a male-dominated society in which mechanization has been perceived alternately as a source of power and a threat to independence, advertisers forged an alliance between technological and gender display that proved as inextricable as Lindbergh's "we." Technological sophistication and socially admired masculine traits were conveyed each through stylized variations of the other.

National advertising had portrayed technological literacy as a definitive male characteristic since the turn of the century. Depictions of the helmsman increased dramatically, however, in the fifties—a reflection, in part, of the changing work environment of middle-class "organization men" in the postwar years. "Bureaucratic values," Sara Evans notes, "emphasized 'female' traits of cooperation, passivity, and security," while "the older definitions of masculinity remained." As a result, "what one part of their consciousness valued, another part judged unmanly."[14] The helmsman and his obedient machine offered a comforting escape from these contradictions.

Few images captured this alignment of masculinity and helmsmanship so succinctly as Marlboro cigarette ads. In 1954, when Leo Burnett's advertising agency acquired the account, Marlboros were considered a "woman's cigarette." Reasoning that in a male-dominated culture a masculinized product affects everyone, Burnett decided to create for his client's product "an exclusively male personality." Accordingly, he fashioned the consummate helmsman: the Marlboro Man. Effortlessly steering his way through the world of goods, he was a pilot, or a race-car driver, or a sailor. Invariably, he had an anchor tattooed on his wrist. (Reinforcing the transitivity of the Marlboro Man's helmsmanship, millions of washable anchor tattoos were distributed with the cigarettes.) To insure that he conveyed more than technical competence, in 1962 the Marlboro Man acquired a geographical realm all his own: Marlboro Country, where the helmsmen were cowboys. The Marlboro Man thus combined stereotypes of masculine America past and present: suffusing frontier autonomy with machineage know-how, he was the Lone Ranger recast as Lindbergh.[15]

The helmsman proliferated throughout postwar advertising, but his most articulate portrayal came from car ads. The automobile was at once the most complex piece of machinery and the most symbolically charged social emblem the average consumer was likely ever to buy. As such, it elicited the ad industry's finest examples of technological display. And with the resumption of automobile production after World War II, advertisements developed the techniques of helmsmanship, transitivity, and unveiling to new heights of social ritual. Car ads of the fifties might seem remote from the launchpads of Apollo, but they merit close scrutiny; to a large extent, these ads perfected the images and associations through which manned space flight would reach the American public.

Advertisers' predilection for concealed design and dramatic unveiling reached fruition in auto ads of the fifties. Borrowing from the clandestine image of weapons production (and the major automakers continued to serve as defense contractors after the war), car companies leaked aerial "spy photos" of their new models. The introduction of the

185

ill-fated Edsel during "Sputnik autumn" (1957) featured elaborate un-veiling strategies. One advertisement revealed only the dashboard of the new model; another portrayed truckloads of canvas-wrapped Edsels en route to their public "debut." The following year, a two-minute television commercial for Chevrolet permitted only split-second glimpses of the car itself.[16]

Transitivity of power from car to driver was promoted through jargon and gadgetry. Through a deliberately unfamiliar configuration of initials, number, and neologisms, jargon provided what motivational researchers called "the illusion of rationality," conveying "inside-dope-ster" status to the consumer without requiring the slightest mechanical comprehension. Gadgets supplied the functionally marginal trappings that substituted for efficiency, safety, or durability as criteria for judging a product's design.

Gadgets and jargon were destined to play major roles in the pop-ularization of the manned space program. As advertising features, they flourished in auto ads of the fifties. A Chrysler Corporation ad for its 1959 Dodge—"The Newest of Everything Great! The Greatest of Everything New!"—offered a characteristic profusion of both tech-niques. Two of the new models' feature innovations were simply new terms: the "HC-HE engine—high compression and high economy"; and "Level-Flite Torsion-Aire"—a "new kind of suspension" that "in-troduces the first 'three-dimensional' driving—ride control, road con-trol, load control." Here were masterful creations of technojargon, studding the ad copy with hyphens and acronyms while revealing noth-ing about the actual engine or the suspension. In addition, the '59 Dodge offered an impressive array of gadgets. To facilitate the boarding of female passengers, it featured the "Swing-Out Swivel Seat that says 'Please Come In.' " And sitting at his "new elliptical steering wheel," the proud owner faced the "gleaming instrument panel" of "the first all-push-button car." The '56 Dodge had echoed an earlier, substantive innovation—automatic transmission—with a gratuitous one by replac-ing the commonplace gear-selection lever with pushbuttons ("The Magic Touch of Tomorrow!"). The '59 model added similar buttons for the windshield wipers and defrosters to create "pushbutton control of driving and weather." Like the elliptical steering wheel, the buttons added nothing more than the impression of innovation and control.[17]

But as "illusions of rationality," gadgets addressed the realm of wishes and fears. As long as they triggered interest in the product, their mechanical function could remain superfluous—even self-contradic-tory. Thus car gadgets often embodied two conflicting manifestations of technical power: the status conveyed by passive, effortless supervi-sion of "automatic control," and the vicarious sense of technical com-petence imparted by their manipulation. The problem was not confined to automobiles. As consumers became more removed from decisions regarding technology's social uses, all purveyors of technological display—including publicists for space flight—had to convince the public that the "labor-saving" status of increasingly automated technology (the hardware of transitivity) did not diminish the consumer's sense of control (or helmsmanship).

Perhaps the ultimate example of the gadget's conflicting illusions was the 1959 Cadillac's optional Autronic Eye. Earlier models had offered automatic light sensors to free drivers from manually switching their headlights from bright to dim. But automatic headlights tended to flicker erratically in response to minute fluctuations of light. General Motors solved that problem with a new gadget: "With a *twist of the dial* autronic-eye lets *you* control the automatic dimming of your lights."[18] Thus the American driver could manually control an automatic device designed to eliminate the need for manual control. If buttons on his gear selector and defroster gave him "pushbutton control of driving and weather," the Autronic Eye gave him control of his symbols of control.

The public might dismiss—even ridicule—these stylized conflations of technical and personal power. From the advertiser's point of view, that mattered very little. The persuasive power of the Swing-Out Swivel Seat or the Autronic Eye derived not so much from the gadget itself as from the social context in which it situated the prospective buyer. It triggered anxieties—about sexual prowess, technical competence, or mastery of the environment—while offering symbolic conquest of them.

By the late 1950s, claims for the magical directive capacities of technology permeated not only the world of goods but, increasingly, the world of nations. Government dependence on commodity scientism reached a critical juncture in 1945 with the development of the atomic bomb. With each new phase of the ensuing arms race, U.S. leaders became more concerned with technological display. To be sure, nuclear weapons represented an application of technology very different from automobiles; and Washington did not set out to mimic Detroit. Yet the government's depiction of the bomb, and of the weapons systems it spawned, required persuasion techniques much like those of the car ad designer. The Manhattan Project led to the most dramatic unveiling strategy in human history. Presidents and generals promised the nation new autonomy and global helmsmanship through the mere possession of their new "products." They warned that the country's prestige depended on the transitivity of nuclear power from the testing range to the geopolitical conference table. And like advertisers, they developed a growing reliance on the manipulation of appearances. Advertising provided the paradigm for technological display in American culture; the atomic bomb ushered it into the geopolitical arena.

TECHNOPOLITICS AND THE BOMB

World War II was not the first occasion for the state's application of marketplace patterns of commodity scientism. The First World War introduced unprecedented opportunities for technological display, as weapons production and national image-making alike reached brief but spectacular levels of productivity. Not until what John McPhee has called the "technological piñata" of World War II, however, did a permanent, modern-scale defense bureaucracy evolve, enlisting both the research capacities and the display value of science in the service of militarism. Techniques that had been developed by advertisers were among the resources that government appropriated for the wartime effort.[19] Among the factors contributing to the defense establishment's postwar policies, and its profound effect on public attitudes toward science and technology, nothing introduced so many changes so suddenly as the development of the atomic bomb.

"America stands at this moment at the summit of the world," Winston Churchill proclaimed in August 1945.[20] Churchill's remark was inspired by the deployment of two top-secret weapons, code-named "Fat Man" and "Little Boy," over two Japanese cities. The flashes that obliterated Hiroshima and Nagasaki etched permanent shadows of their victims onto the walls that remained standing. They inscribed an equally indelible message in the minds of a generation of world leaders: The nation that could claim scientific and technological superiority would dominate the globe.

What is often overlooked in dwelling on the destructive force and strategic weight of the A-bomb is the manner in which it was revealed to the world. Like nothing before it, the bomb exemplified the pattern of concealed development and dramatic unveiling that the advertising industry had perfected. The primary effect of this technique—a heightened capacity to manipulate the symbolic as well as the technical impact of a given product (or weapon)—had been glimpsed in previous wars. But the Manhattan Project constituted the most elaborate secret undertaking, and the most lavish concentration of scientific acumen, in history. As such, it created an unprecedented opportunity to stress the engineering of appearances as a vital attribute of the product itself.

Accordingly, two overriding aspects of U.S. government and military leaders' attitudes toward the atomic bomb determined the manner in which it entered the world: first, their adherence to a myth of inevitability concerning the use of the bomb once it was developed; and second, their preoccupation with the global impact of the new weapon's use in combat. In the summer of 1945, with Germany defeated, the Target Committee debated not whether use of the bomb against Japan was necessary but how many could be dropped, and where. The committee's report to Truman stressed "(1) obtaining the *greatest psychological effect* against Japan and (2) making the initial use *sufficiently spectacular* for the importance of the weapon to be internationally recognized when publicity on it was released."[21]

As the committee's second point suggests, Japan was not the bomb's only target. Secretary of State–designate James Byrnes echoed a view shared by Truman and Secretary of War Stimson when he told nuclear physicist Leo Szilard, in May of 1945, that wartime deployment of the bomb "would make Russia more manageable." He suggested a more immediate audience for its combat demonstration when he added, "How would you get Congress to appropriate money for atomic energy research if you do not show results for the money which has been spent already?" As Martin Sherwin has observed, it was not simply the bomb's tactical value in defeating Japan, but the *"impression*—the psychological impact of a single bomb dropped from a lone aircraft causing damage equal to that caused by thousands of bombs dropped from hundreds of aircraft—upon which [Truman, Stimson, and Byrnes] based their policy."[22]

The deployment of the atom bomb marked the accession of commodity scientism to the highest reaches of military and foreign policy. Like the marketplace before it, the state learned in the course of the century that each new product of technology was really two: the device itself, and the image of the device in the mind of the consumer or enemy. This second, symbolic weapon, as advertisers knew and generals had begun to suspect, was often the more powerful of the two. The bomb dramatically accelerated this reliance on the publicity value of military technology. By its unparalleled destructiveness, it forced the nation to rely for the first time on a weapon's image rather than on its use. As the first "atomic nation," the United States looked to its growing nuclear arsenal not just for the military supremacy it promised but for emblems of political and cultural supremacy as well.

Cold War diplomacy thus relied on a kind of nuclear transitivity, with the superpowers linking each new weapons breakthrough to functionally unrelated display attributes: the intelligence of its scientists, the wisdom of its leaders, the superiority of its political system. As the symbolic attributes of nuclear weapons overshadowed their technical function, the government became adept at the techniques by which advertisers invented social attributes for their products. Like the private sector before them, policymakers found themselves acting increasingly as agents of impression management.

This social triumph of engineered appearances is just beginning to be understood. Writing at the outset of the postwar era, David Riesman observed that in the age of mass media the earlier social model of a self-motivated, "inner-directed" personality has been giving way to a more self-absorbed, less confident "other-directed" type. The prevailing characteristic of this new personality, he noted, is the insatiable need for guidance from external sources—particularly from the bombardment of messages conveyed by the mass media; "[t]he goals toward which the other-directed person strives shifts with that guidance."[23]

More recent scholarship has refined Riesman's notion of an other-directed personality, tracing its origins more directly to the needs and marketing techniques of corporate capitalism. Advertising's "progressive fragmentation of commodities . . . into assortments of attributes and messages" has led, according to William Leiss, to a corresponding "fragmentation of individual needs into smaller and smaller elements." The consumer's task, then, is no longer simply to buy an endlessly expanding array of products, but rather to reassemble a coherent aggregate of needs—that is, an apparently integrated personality—and to match them up with a corresponding assemblage of commodity attributes. When a social system depends for its prosperity on an ever growing supply of such impressionable, other-directed consumers, the result is what Christopher Lasch has called a "culture of narcissism," subordinating "being to having," and "possession itself to appearance."[24]

The arms race and the space race demonstrated that the state as well as the consumer was susceptible to this fragmentation. Spurred on by the culture they governed, and by the immense display value they attached to atomic weaponry, postwar U.S. political leaders acquired a striking resemblance to the other-directed individual: repeatedly calling for recognized goals, but capable of sustaining only the appearance of relentless goal-seeking; so concerned with the "credibility" of their policies that credibility itself became the principal object of policymaking; obsessed with security, yet trapped in a spiral of arms acquisition that only increased the need for security. Just as the narcissistic personality learned to seek fulfillment through acts of consumption that diminished in satisfaction as they escalated in scale, so a "culture of procurement" arose among Cold War politicians, the military establishment, and defense contractors, providing the mass media with a shorthand equation of national purpose with multiple warheads and fallout shelters.[25]

Most nuclear weapons, of course, were intended never to be used. They were touted not for what they did but for what they promised to prevent; their primary attribute was the posture of confidence they inspired in their owners. Publicity, not megatonnage, became the true measure of a weapon's effectiveness, and American military and foreign policy depended increasingly on impressions—at home and abroad—of its unused stockpile of weapons.

The postwar arms race thus became a succession of symbolic deployments, not unlike the annual announcement of new car models.

As each new weapon or detection system rendered its still unpaid-for, equally oversophisticated predecessor obsolete, the pressure to develop its replacement redoubled. Generals and contractors clamored for the greater "push-button control" of an increasingly uncontrollable defense environment—all in an effort to recapture the brief, euphoric moment when America alone possessed the bomb. For the nation and the consumer alike, security and identity had become subject to buying and exhibiting an accelerating progression of technical innovations, each more expensive and less discernibly improved than the one before it. "Once the purpose of military spending is to create 'perception,' and weapons are procured as symbols," Richard J. Barnet warns, "there is never enough."[26] Perhaps what was required was not just new weapons but an entirely new display arena. The time for space was ripe.

OCCUPYING SPACE

From a technical standpoint, the space race began as a diversion of payloads in the arms race. In conjunction with their development of nuclear weapons, both the United States and the Soviet Union devoted considerable research to the perfection of missiles to carry them—research spearheaded in both countries by former Third Reich V-2 rocket engineers who had been "liberated" (and divided up) by the Allies at Peenemünde. By the early fifties, both superpowers had begun designing intercontinental ballistic missiles. Unlike the Soviet Union, the U.S. had allies within short-range missile or bomber range of its adversary. Consequently, high-thrust, long-range missiles were far more crucial to the Soviets than to the United States. On August 26, 1957, when the Kremlin announced its first successful ICBM test launch, complaints arose among some U.S. military strategists ("We captured the wrong Germans," one general lamented); but neither the government nor the press sounded a general alarm. The American Atlas missile was well under way; the U.S. enjoyed an undisputed advantage both in number and placement of bombers; American military superiority remained intact.[27]

On October 4 the Soviets once again fired one of their new ICBMs, this time extending its trajectory, and—by mounting a 36-inch diameter satellite in place of a dummy warhead—placed Sputnik I in orbit. The idea was not new. As early as August 1955 the United States had announced plans to launch a series of artificial satellites during International Geophysical Year (1957–1958). The Eisenhower Administration therefore expressed little concern over Sputnik. Defense Secretary Charles Wilson called the launch "a neat scientific trick." White

House aide Clarence Randall dismissed it as a "silly bauble . . . in the sky."[28]

Elsewhere in the government, however, Sputnik became the subject of agitated warnings. Congressional opponents of the Eisenhower Administration—notably Senate Majority Leader Lyndon Johnson and House Speaker John McCormack—contended that Ike's "sluggish" response to the Russian satellite jeopardized national security. "It is not very reassuring to be told that next year we will put a 'better' satellite into the air," Johnson complained. "Perhaps it will even have chrome trim and automatic windshield wipers."[29]

On December 6 Senator Johnson had just convened hearings on the inadequacy of U.S. space efforts when the first American satellite rocket—the Navy's Vanguard—exploded on the launchpad. Press coverage, featuring headlines like "Kaputnik" and "Stayputnik," interpreted the event as proof that a space race was under way, and that America was losing. On January 31, 1958, the first American satellite— the 31-pound Explorer I—rode an Army Redstone rocket into orbit. The Redstone's chief designer, former Peenemünde rocketeer Werner von Braun, became an instant media hero. Space news of every variety was guaranteed front-page status.

By the spring of 1958 opinion polls indicated that an initially unconcerned public had begun to contract "space fever" from Congress, the Pentagon, and the press. The actual threat posed by Sputnik proved difficult to identify. Strategically, the satellite was far less significant than the missile that carried it up. It was, however, the first "first" for the USSR since the arms race had begun, opening a vast new arena for emblematic display of technology. A growing number of American leaders convinced each other that nothing short of "the national purpose" would ride with the country's entry into space.[30]

Politicians, editors, and social commentators saw in Sputnik a symbol of the postwar drift in American culture. Conservatives feared that the "flabbiness" of an increasingly materialistic and complacent citizenry had slowed the nation's reflexes in confronting the pervasive "Red menace." Liberals shared that concern, adding their lament that the constricted scope of public affairs—Cold War posturing abroad, McCarthyism at home—had diminished the nation's "imaginative vision." While implementing a space program, the nation's leaders also launched an elaborate search for goals. In 1960 President Eisenhower appointed a Commission on National Goals, a Rockefeller-funded Special Studies Project undertook the same task, and Henry Luce commissioned a series of essays for *Life* on "The National Purpose." The other-directed nation had begun to diagnose its malady.

The unanimous conclusion was that America stood in grave peril of losing its "sense of mission." Walter Lippmann warned that the Soviet Union, unlike the United States, possessed "a sense of great purpose and of high destiny." George Kennan castigated Americans for the "overwhelming accent of life on personal comfort and amusement, with . . . a surfeit of privately sold gadgetry" but "no highly developed sense of national purpose." The Rockefeller study linked the "lack of purpose in Americans" with its "fear that our young people have lost youth's immemorial fondness for adventure, far horizons, and the challenge of the unpredictable." And most commentators stressed the global dimensions of this challenge. "Our goals abroad," the President's Commission concluded, "are inseparable from our goals at home." [31]

Stripped of its rhetorical flourishes, this "quest for national purpose" did not depart in substance from prevailing Cold War policies. What it called for was a new mode of presentation for these policies. If not purpose, then an *image* of purposefulness would redeem the nation —while providing banner headlines for the press, rejuvenated careers for "space" politicians, and a richly embellished network of aerospace managers, engineers, and contractors. And in 1960 preparation of that image was well under way—not in the pages of committee reports, but in the flight-simulator labs of Project Mercury. Spacesuits would provide the emperor's new clothes.

From the outset, then, the architects of the space program viewed it as a new source of national iconography. Accordingly, a durable and suggestive vocabulary had to be devised—one that could describe space exploits as well as link them, through analogy and repeated association, to familiar images of the nation's past and anticipated greatness. Foremost among the key words in this vocabulary was "science." Just as American culture had conflated science and technology, now "science" and "space" became synonyms. In the wake of Sputnik, major newspapers and mass-market magazines quickly acquired "science editors" whose columns were devoted almost exclusively to the space race. President Eisenhower appointed MIT president James R. Killian as his first Science Advisor purely in response to the furor over Sputnik. And Killian's Science Advisory Committee soon learned that its principal function would be as a public relations office for space policy. The committee's first assignment was to prepare an "Introduction to Space" for the "nontechnical reader" that could be "widely disseminated by all the news media." [32]

Released in March 1958, the Killian committee's report specified "four factors which give importance, urgency, and *inevitability*" to a vigorous national space program. These "factors" deserve careful scrutiny, for they encapsulate the justifications, tirelessly repeated over the next dozen years, for sending Americans into space: (1) "the compelling urge of man to explore and to discover, the thrust of curiosity that leads men to go where no one has gone before"; (2) "the defense objective";

193

THE CULTURE OF CONSUMPTION

(3) "national prestige"; and (4) "scientific observation and experiment which will add to our knowledge and understanding of the earth, the solar system, and the universe."[33] Like an M&M candy, this list of "reasons why" concentrated its primary ingredients—"defense" and "national prestige"—in the center, with an outer shell of science and exploration to provide a smooth, colorful appearance.

Perhaps the best way to compare these two realms of motivation is to think of the discretionary functions of government, such as the manned space program, as a legislative variety of play. Roger Caillois has identified two contrasting varieties of play: "competitive" play, which provides a structured performance environment resembling combat, and "vertiginous" play, in which the participant seeks unfettered discovery or imaginative improvisation, without reference to competitors, stopwatches, or performance evaluation. Caillois's terms provide a useful distinction between two basic varieties of social display rituals. Most forms of play—and of display—are not purely of one variety or the other, but some amalgam of the two.[34]

So it was with space policy. Some space enthusiasts emphasized its vertiginous aspects: "the compelling urge of man to explore and to discover," and disinterested "scientific observation and experiment." Others defended its competitive dimension: "the defense objective" and "national prestige." The key, however, to the public presentation of manned space policy rests in the fact that the overwhelming concern— the only substantive concern—of the political leaders, military strategists, and aerospace engineers and scientists who implemented the manned space program was its propaganda value, abroad and at home. The vertiginous "outer shell" of curiosity and scientific wonders attracted a vigorous following. Indeed, the merchants of space counted on that following. But U.S. space policy did not emerge from the sudden "compelling urge" among the country's political, military, and scientific elite to learn the origins of the solar system by 1969.

That fact was most clearly demonstrated by the decision to implement a *manned* space program in the first place. As most of the non-defense subsidized scientific community repeatedly stressed, nearly every measurable space objective—in communications, weather monitoring, exploration of the planets, even military reconnaissance— could be achieved far more effectively, and at considerably less expense, with automated satellites and probes rather than by manned expeditions. Sending men into space was preferable to unmanned projects for only one reason: It vastly enhanced the dramatic impression created by the nation's space exploits.

The question, then, is not whether the creators of American space policy acted from competitive motives; rather, why did they coat unequivocally competitive policies in elaborately vertiginous rhetoric?

194

Cynics have dismissed these accolades for curiosity and intellectual adventurousness, along with the astronauts themselves, as part of the candy coating that sweetened the nation's real objectives—greater power and prestige.

But perhaps more was at stake than that. The space race was consummately other-directed, revealing a curious mixture of unsurpassed power and deep insecurity among American leaders. In constant doubt of their global technological superiority, and unsure how to apply it, they rushed to outdistance their geopolitical rivals in every measurable contest for prestige. A vertiginous depiction of space policy—exploration, rather than a race—might contribute greatly to that prestige, lending the nation the appearance of a self-assured, mature state seeking knowledge for all humanity among the stars. The more other-directed they became, the more desperately Presidents and Congresses sought the inner-directed images by which to convince the world—and themselves—of their sense of purpose. A self-contradictory rhetoric emerged, as jeremiads on the enemy's impending "control of the universe" alternated with invocations of the "measureless wonders" of space.

Crucial to this appropriation of a vertiginous national image was the social characterization of science and technology. It is significant that Killian's committee grouped science with exploration rather than with defense, in spite of government funding's overwhelming preference for the latter.[35] The congressional hearings leading to the creation of NASA provided the first of many efforts to fashion outer space into an ultimate display context for the national identity—a task requiring a complete refurbishing of the public image of American science.

On April 2, 1958, Eisenhower asked Congress to create a civilian agency for the implementation of national space policy. On April 15 the new House Select Committee of Astronautics and Space Exploration began four weeks of hearings. On May 6 its counterpart in the Senate, the Special Committee on Space and Astronautics, convened for its own less extensive inquiry. The committees' respective chairmen, House Speaker McCormack and Senate Majority Leader Johnson, each opened their proceedings with warnings that the nation's military and international political prestige were at stake. "The Roman Empire controlled the world because it could build roads," Johnson noted; later "the British Empire was dominant because it had ships. In the air age we were powerful because we had airplanes. Now the Communists have established a foothold in outer space."[36] Nearly all of the House committee's witnesses were selected from among Defense Department officials, the armed services, defense contractors, or scientists and engineers connected with military or nuclear research. Despite the civilian status of the space agency-to-be, the hearings leading to its creation were dominated by men with professional interests in an agressive space policy—particularly in the military application of space technology.

Yet the transcripts of the hearings contain surprisingly little discussion of the defense objectives informing national space policy. Congressmen and witnesses alike mixed straightforward declarations of the space program's propaganda value with fanciful efforts to formulate a vertiginous rhetoric. "In space exploration, and the scientific breakthrough it implies," McCormack assured his committee, "we are beginning an era of discovery literally as far-reaching as the discovery of our own continent." Space, he added, would provide the country with a "new frontier"—"the greatest challenge to dynamic thought and deed that our pioneer spirit has ever received." The actual benefits of the undertaking, he explained, remained "beyond the threshold. What we will learn from the moon . . . no man can rightly say"; but surely "the advances will be literally beyond our present understanding."[37]

In his testimony, von Braun agreed that the impact of an energetic U.S. manned space program "will be comparable to the discovery of America." Like McCormack, he stressed the analogy between the role of territorial expansion in the nation's past and the primacy of scientific inquiry in its future. When asked what significance a national space program might have "from a nonmilitary angle," von Braun replied, "Sir, I think the whole idea of exploration of space began with the same motives that have always triggered scientific progress." He concluded with a glowing endorsement of unfettered curiosity: "People are just curious. . . . What follows in the wake of their discoveries is something for the next generation to worry about." In light of his pioneering work on the V-2 rocket for Hitler, von Braun might have detected flaws in such a cavalier scenario for the social application of technology. But if the nation's "superspace scientist" had any doubts, he did not air them before the congressional committee.[38]

Von Braun was merely one among a procession of distinguished experts who offered hymns to the unknown in the name of science. California Institute of Technology president Lee DuBridge had directed the MIT radiation lab during World War II; he had served for six years on the Atomic Energy Commission's advisory board, and had been a trustee of the Rand Corporation since 1948. He had witnessed firsthand the swiftly escalating role of the military in scientific research and development in the postwar years. Much of his testimony, however, did not address these pertinent areas of expertise. Instead, DuBridge dwelled on the space program's potential for uncovering "wholly unforeseen phenomena." "It is hardly fruitful to speculate as to what these unknown things might be," he explained, "but the history of science is replete with examples" of unanticipated discoveries. The scientist, like the explorer, might expect to learn as much by accident as by design. "There is no reason to suppose that the other side [of the moon] hides any great or undiscovered phenomena of nature," Du-Bridge told the committee. "Nor will it add anything to scientific knowledge when a man first travels in space. Yet we are all curious to know." Space generated not just a "pure scientific interest," but also "the explorer's interest—the interest in satisfying human curiosity and human yearning."[39]

As witness followed witness, an eloquent mystification of science emerged. The sheer presence of so many eminent scientists and engineers lent the hearings—and the very notion of a full-scale manned space program—the imprimatur of expertise. Yet by equating space, science, and the unpredictable discoveries of exploration, they advocated a national space policy based on a kind of Columbus Principle: Scientists, like the captain of the *Santa Maria*, have made some of their most startling discoveries by accident; therefore space exploration should proceed not on the basis of stated objectives but on the assumption that the equivalent of a New World will appear, justifying the undertaking in retrospect. Curiosity and purposefulness were the only prerequisites. The committee's witnesses did not conduct their own research in this wide-eyed fashion. Here they spoke not for science but for its display value. As many of them had done before on behalf of defense-related projects, they lent their expertise to the "illusion of rationality" Congress required to legitimate a vigorous manned space program.

In its final report, the House Select Committee enthusiastically embraced its witnesses' celebration of uncertainty. "The implications of man's entry into outer space," the report admitted, were "disturbingly imprecise." Yet "[d]iscovery is impartial and impersonal. It can be controlled by no blueprint. It can be contained by no laws." The nation, then, should not permit a lack of palpable justifications to deter it from "the most challenging and vital exploration feat of all time."[40]

The committee's report also revealed its low tolerance for criticism of a swift and unrestrained entry into the space race. Hugh Dryden, director of the National Advisory Committee for Aeronautics, had been considered Congress's first choice to head the new space agency. But during his testimony, Dryden was one of the few witnesses who expressed doubts about the wisdom of a "crash program" to put Americans into space. "[T]ossing a man up in the air and letting him come back," Dryden observed, was "like shooting a woman out of a cannon." When the news media highlighted this remark, committee chairman McCormack notified the White House of his disapproval of Dryden as NASA director. He also took him to task in the committee's final report: "Some of our sober scientists may talk with disdain of stunts no more useful, they allege, than shooting a woman out of a cannon. This may be so," the report conceded, "but we need not condemn 'stunting' out of hand. Such stunts, even if proved useless scientifically, can have a disturbing political impact." Policymakers thus spoke of the nation's space effort in two languages. When describing its intended effect, they could point candidly to the "political impact" of "stunting," but when they invoked the unpredictable wonders of science and exploration, they were fashioning the images with which to convey that effect.[41]

In December 1958 President Eisenhower initiated the selection process that would lead to NASA's first team of astronauts. In January 1961, when they completed their training, President Kennedy took the oath of office with much more enthusiasm for the manned space program than his predecessor. "Dramatic achievements in space . . . symbolize the technological power and organizing capacity of the nation," proclaimed a memo drafted by Vice President Lyndon Johnson, Defense Secretary Robert McNamara, and NASA's new administrator, James Webb. And only the inclusion of helmsmen could insure the effective expression of that symbol: "It is man, not merely machines, in space that captures the imagination of the world."[42]

On April 12, 1961, Soviet cosmonaut Yuri Gagarin became the first man to orbit the earth. On April 17 a clandestine U.S.-sponsored invasion of Cuba ended in a humiliating rout at the Bay of Pigs. On April 20 President Kennedy sent a memo to Vice President Johnson—now chairman of the new National Aeronautics and Space Council—inquiring about the feasibility of a manned lunar mission, and asking whether there might be "any other space program which promises dramatic results in which we could win?" On May 5 Alan Shepard's seventeen-minute ride on a Jupiter missile brought him tumultuous acclaim as the "first American in space." On May 25 Kennedy called a joint session of Congress to announce "that this nation should commit itself to achieving the goal, before this decade is out, of landing a man on the moon and returning him safely to earth. No single space project in this period will be more impressive to mankind," he proclaimed. "And none will be so difficult or expensive to accomplish."[43] For the next eight years, three Presidents embraced the astronauts as fellow helmsmen. What was the nature of these new seekers of the national grail?

INVENTING THE ASTRONAUT

From the moment plans for a manned space program were announced, newspapers, magazines, and television networks recognized it as an unparalleled media event. NASA public affairs officials quickly discovered that their image-making duties would be minimal; what Congress had begun, the media took up with alacrity. Long before the first astronaut left the launchpad, space enthusiasts experimented with the analogies and associations that might be attached to the event. The editors of *Newsweek* saw rejuvenative powers in space travel. "[T]he moral energies that drove America to true greatness lately seem diluted," they warned at the outset of "The Sixties: Decade of Man in Space." For too long no new arenas of conquest awaited at the national horizon. Now, however, "Man is embarking on the supreme adventure; he is heading into the universe."[44]

For those who stressed the restorative powers of this "supreme adventure," the presence of helmsmen in space was an essential aspect of the enterprise. Only when the first "awe-struck pilot" experienced "the giddy buoyancy of weightlessness" would man "break free of his terrestrial bonds." Projection of the national imagination into space required a human emissary so that "all mankind may ride along vicariously." The first astronaut's "epochal adventure," *Newsweek*'s "Space and the Atom" editor asserted, "will signal, as no satellite could, the dawn of the space age." "Machines alone will not suffice if men are able to follow," a columnist observed in *The Nation*. "The difference is that between admiring a woman's photograph and marrying her."[45]

Growing emphasis on manned space exploration as the great "collective adventure" of the sixties reflected a nervous evasion of the inadequacy of the project's scientific justification. Press coverage turned with apparent relief from "Why manned?" to "Which men?" as NASA began to select its astronauts. In spite of the project's purported importance to science, no scientists were to fly a U.S. spacecraft until the final Apollo moonshot in 1972. Instead, NASA began its search exclusively among the nation's five hundred active military test pilots. Candidates had to meet four requirements: an engineering degree "or its equivalent"; fifteen hundred hours of flight time; age limit forty; height limit five feet eleven inches; weight limit 180 pounds (precisely that of Sputnik I). One hundred ten men qualified; half of them volunteered. An exhaustive battery of physical, psychological, and intelligence tests eliminated all but the "Magnificent Seven." On April 9, 1959, the nation met its first astronauts: Carpenter, Cooper, Glenn, Grissom, Schirra, Shepard, Slayton.

Those who lamented the nation's atrophied "moral energies" found the ideal restorative talisman in the ethos of the astronaut. Stress-seeking, uniformly white Protestant, primarily of small-town or rural origins, they seemed to personify the legendary traits of an imagined earlier America. And the astronauts quickly learned to speak of themselves in frontier terms. Alan Shepard attributed his interest in

Project Mercury to "an urge to pioneer." Gus Grissom acknowledged a similar "spirit of pioneering and adventure," adding that "I think if I had been alive 150 years ago, I might have wanted to go out and help open up the West."[46]

In 1959, however, the "pioneer spirit" required revision. The appeal of the astronauts, like that of the Marlboro Man, rested in their capacity to combine the pioneering image of "150 years ago" with a forward-looking mastery of technological change. NASA's tendency to equate engineering with science helped to transform the astronauts into "space scientists." Their briefcases bulging with operation manuals, they were depicted as scouts on the technological as well as the physical frontier. Their contributions to engineering and design problems, however minimal, received emphasis in NASA press kits. (John Glenn, for example, suggested the addition of a window to future Mercury capsules.) "Fearless, but not reckless," they combined the youthful panache of a Lindbergh with the sobriety of the seasoned expert. "Here Are the U.S. Spacemen," U.S. News and World Report announced, "—Married, Mature, Fathers."[47]

NASA's unveiling strategy evolved with the project. Unmanned test launches were planned—and sometimes executed—in secrecy. Then in February 1961 the agency focused national attention on Alan Shepard, Gus Grissom, and John Glenn when it named them as pilots for the first Mercury flights. Torn between security precautions and a desire to maximize publicity, NASA chose not to reveal which of the three would "command" the first flight until just before lift-off. After Shepard's success as America's first man in space, press restrictions were dropped. Unlike the Manhattan Project, or the Soviet space program, the U.S. manned space project would occur before the eyes of the world. If this apparently unrestricted media coverage tended to obscure more than it revealed about the justifications and strategies of the space program, it nevertheless increased the display value of each flight dramatically.

As publicity exceeded even NASA's expectations, the personalities of the helmsmen became an obsession of the national press. Shepard's "driving urge to get into space," Time explained, grew out of a lifelong "personal flair" with fast machines. "Particularly fond of his white, high-powered Corvette sports car," Life reported, "he would love dearly to drive just as fast and hard as it would go." Through Shepard's eyes the awesome hardware of the launchpad acquired the familiarity of his Corvette: "A capsule is quite a bit like an automobile," he observed. Inspecting the Redstone rocket poised for his flight, America's first space hero "sort of wanted to kick the tires."[48]

Shepard's suborbital flight on May 5, 1961, yielded most of its anticipated prestige to cosmonaut Yuri Gagarin's orbital flight of April

12. Nevertheless, as *Time* observed, "the voluntary hero-making mechanisms of the U.S. worked at full blast." Central to the adulation Shepard received was the news media's determination to depict him as an autonomous, self-sufficient pilot—despite a wealth of facts to the contrary. Editors and television reporters effervesced over his "liberation from gravitational force" in a vast "playground of the imagination," "totally free of boundaries." *Time's* cover illustration of Shepard's flight depicted him free-floating in space. In an otherwise ground-controlled flight, Shepard briefly deflected the capsule's pitch and yaw in a manual operation experiment—not unlike the Cadillac's Autronic Eye. Press coverage seized upon this incident as the key to the flight. "He did not fly as far, fast, or high as Russia's Yuri Gagarin," *Life* conceded; but "he controlled the flight of his capsule—which Gagarin did not." Felix Morley proclaimed Shepard a new Lindbergh who had revived the nation's traditional strengths by asserting "the individual's control over his destiny."[49]

The distance between Lindbergh's "we" and the Mercury astronauts' "we seven," however, was marked by the emergence of a dizzying bureaucratic network of government agencies, committees, and aerospace contractors, with NASA personnel serving as coordinators. As Tom Wolfe has observed, the Mercury astronauts were so superfluous to the piloting of their capsules that many test pilots were unwilling to give up the likes of an X-15 to volunteer for a ride in a mere "tin can."[50] Confined to a space suit, strapped to a form-fitting chair, Shepard viewed the "measureless horizons of space" by squinting through a periscope. His functional role in the flight was not unlike that of a rather elaborate hood ornament. The imaginative leaps by which publicity freed the astronaut's image from the facts of his flight experience borrowed as much from Walter Mitty as from Lindbergh.

Coverage of Shepard's flight, and of Gus Grissom's follow-up suborbital flight, frequently implied a direct link between the astronaut's mission and "national purpose." With John Glenn's orbital flight the following year, the transitivity of achievement from the astronaut to the nation reached its zenith. In the months of preparation and delay preceding his flight, Glenn's personality became the paramount feature of the Mercury program. Raised in New Concord, Ohio, "a quiet shirt-sleeves-and-overalls town," he read Buck Rogers, studied chemical engineering at the hometown college, married a hometown dentist's daughter. Like Shepard, he followed "the bent I always had for mechanical things" to become an ace pilot. A member of his World War II combat squadron recalled how Glenn "would fly up alongside you and slip his wing right under yours, then tap it gently against your wing tip." But for Glenn, the technological sublime and national destiny were inseparable. To him, *Life* reported, the astronauts carried a mandate "not just to make the flights work out well but also to become symbols of the nation's future." "Purposeful Glenn" represented a purposeful America.[51]

And Americans welcomed the message. On February 20, 1962, 130 million television viewers watched Glenn's Friendship 7 launch into its three-orbital flight. A commemorative stamp appeared the moment he stepped on board the recovery carrier. Its jubilant crew marked Glenn's footprints with white paint "just as the touch-down spot of the Spirit of St. Louis was marked at Paris' Le Bourget Field." Hundreds of babies born on the day of the flight received Glenn's name. (One helpless infant in Ogden, Utah, was christened "Orbit.") The new hero's exclamation of wonder—"I've never seen anything like it!"—referred not to his flight but to the week of celebration marking his return. Writing in *Newsweek*, Raymond Moley cheered the flight as a reaffirmation of "the copybook maxims which in earlier years sustained [our] forefathers." *Time* portrayed him as "a latter-day Apollo, flashing through the unknown, sending his cool observations and random comments to earth in radio thunderbolts, acting as though orbiting the earth were his everyday occupation." And *America* dubbed Glenn "the Marine Magellan," "a Frank Meriwell of the cosmos."[52]

Like Shepard, Glenn encountered irrepressible adulation of his helmsmanship. Toward the end of his first orbit, the automatic pilot system in the Friendship 7 capsule began to malfunction; Mission Control considered aborting. But Glenn corrected the craft's yaw axis, prompting journals as diverse as *Aviation Week* and *The New Republic* to hail his flight as proof of "the primacy of man in space," a "human triumph over impersonal technology." However impressive the image of pathbreaking new technology, it was also vaguely threatening; the importance of "the man in command" remained. "Now we can get rid of some of that automatic equipment," Glenn exulted after splashdown, "and let man take over."[53]

As Project Mercury gave way to Gemini, and Gemini to Apollo, the lone helmsman was joined by a crewmate, then by another. Space publicists found that the simple elegance of the Lindbergh display format—one pilot, one craft—suffered from overcrowding and repetition; the public began to lose track of astronauts' names and personalities. Moreover, as the decade's civil rights and antiwar activities gained momentum, the appeal of a John Glenn, brimming with self-assured piety and patriotism, proved more difficult to evoke.

Not until the first lunar landing approached did the lionization of the astronaut return so exuberantly; and in the intervening years, the tone of presentation shifted. Publicity for Apollo 11 depicted the crew in more "professional," less all-encompassing terms. Their credentials as helmsmen remained prominent: Neil Armstrong, the nation learned, "had his pilot's license before his driver's license," and had "always wanted to do something daring and different." He had gone on to become "the hottest pilot ever to wear the wings of an astronaut"—"the kind of man virtually every father dreams his son will be—Eagle Scout, war hero, aeronautical engineer, test pilot and astronaut." Both he and Buzz Aldrin served as fighter pilots in Korea; he and Michael Collins were test pilots at Edwards Air Force Base, where Armstrong flew the X-15 to an altitude of 200,000 feet.[54]

But compared with their Mercury predecessors, they were more "cosmopolitan" (Collins was "born in Rome," the son of a military attaché to the U.S. embassy; Aldrin's father, a former Air Corps aviator, had been a close friend of Orville Wright, Charles Lindbergh, and rocket pioneer Robert Goddard). And their educational background received more emphasis (Aldrin held a doctorate in astronautics from MIT and had "the best scientific mind we have sent into space"; Armstrong had done postgraduate work in aeronautical engineering). "A new breed of cosmic explorer has emerged," one newsmagazine wrote of the Apollo generation. "Gone is the earlier image of the rocket-riding daredevil, the superman of the 'wild blue yonder.' The astronaut now is seen as a dedicated scientist concerned more with discovery than with setting orbiting records."[55]

For the most part, Apollo coverage focused less on individual astronauts and more on the gadgetry of space flight. Like car salesmen, reporters found that the size, speed, and special features of the spacecraft provided a welcome substitute for discussions of the mission's long-range value. Diagrams of each flight's itinerary covered the nation's newspapers, demonstrating the precision with which Houston could determine its direction. The Saturn 5 rocket that carried Apollo astronauts aloft was acclaimed as the "largest, most powerful machine ever built," with enough power ("150 million horsepower") to carry its payload "ten times faster than a bullet." At 363 feet, it stood "higher than a football field"—or, as the Chicago *Tribune* calculated, "equivalent [in length] to six Santa Marias or four Mayflowers," weighing as much as "four Santa Marias, five Mayflowers, and the United States frigate Constitution."[56]

It was through jargon, however, that space flight became most accessible to its audience. The Mercury flights had established "A-OK" and "lift-off" as passwords for national well-being and determination. Apollo generated an inexhaustible array of technojargon, fusing the telegraphic abruptness of bureaucratese with Pentagon-style obfuscation. If advertisers had been the first to discover the recontextualizing capacity of jargon, Vietnam-era military strategists and arms industries became, in Anthony Sampson's words, the new "masters of newsspeak," transforming weapons into "capabilities" and "systems," arms exports into "defence transfers," and the strafing of peasant villages into an agenda of "conflict configurations" wherein helicopters with high "fire growth capability" pursued "objectives" of "optimum interface." Not simply new terms but a new descriptive mode was emerging, insulating operator from technical function, and function from social impact.[57]

Apollo propelled this value-neutral, elegantly opaque language into the vacuum of space—an uncontested field in which to recite the catechism of American technological superiority. Space illiterates might still speak the archaic language of "rockets to the moon"; Houston spoke of "deploying Lem [the lunar module] on the lurain [lunar terrain]." For the uninitiated, Walter Cronkite patiently explained the meaning of "apolune" and "perilune." Like the Marlboro Man's tattoo, the language of Apollo provided an illusory transitivity of expertise. Only three men would make each flight; the rest of us could be jargonauts, vicariously participating in Mission Control's ethos of competence.

That ethos was never articulated directly. The Apollo 11 press kit issued to reporters by NASA offered 250 pages of acronyms and charts, but no mention of the project's purpose or social significance. Encoded into its elaborate terminology, however, was an ideology of "systems analysis"—a managerial vision of control, the very terms of which ("systems stabilization and control," "attitude control," "thrust vector control") implied the Marlboro Man's ability to command his social environment as well as his ship. Apollo 11 astronauts, the press kit explained, would launch into EPO (Earth Parking Orbit), from which a lengthy interval of TLC (Translunar Coast) would carry them to the critical LOI (Lunar Orbit Insertion). Having made lunar contact, they would engage in EVA (Extravehicular Activity), culminating in deployment of their SRCs (Sample Rock Collectors). Their mission completed, they could look forward to a Transearth Coast before final Re-entry and Splashdown would bring them back to earth. Once home, they would don their BIGs (Biological Isolation Garments) to insure against contamination.[58]

The detached, problem-solving specificity of NASA jargon served a further purpose. As the crew of Apollo 11 made clear at a pre-launch press conference, their mission was to convey a sense of mission. Self-contained details of the flight's agenda insulated them from awkward questions concerning substantive goals or justifications for the enterprise. "The objective of this flight," Neil Armstrong announced, "is precisely to take men to the moon, make a landing there, and return. That is the objective. There are a number of secondary objectives," he added; "[b]ut the primary objective is the ability to demonstrate that man, in fact, can do this kind of job. How we'll use that information in the centuries to come," he concluded on a familiar note, "only history will tell."[59]

As the Apollo program replicated its moon landings, their display value began to diminish. As they grew in scale, they lost immediacy. Loudon Wainwright, who had covered the manned space program for *Life* since the first Mercury launches, attributed his "growing sense of non-excitement" at the moon launch to "the attrition of 10 years," adding that "precision has a way of dehumanizing adventure." But the major difficulty with the display value of the moonshot was its sponsors' inability to keep the technology of spaceflight apace with the overriding demands of technological display. What advertising had that Apollo lacked was the fathomless resilience of the quack. The actor in the doctor's smock could—and must—change his pitch to match the moment. That was precisely how his sponsor achieved a predictable market; the product could stay the same because its image was free to change.[60]

For example, in 1958, when national space policy was first coalescing, Vought Aircraft portrayed its Crusader III carrier fighter planes ("Cru-SAD-er") streaking across a two-page ad in national newsmagazines ("Automated, missile-armed, missile-fast, it will extend the Nuclear Navy's knockout power to the edge of space"). By 1969 Vought—now Ling-Temco-Vought—was one of the nation's primary defense contractors. At the height of an unpopular war, it still placed ads in national newsmagazines. Now, however, a typical ad depicted a thoughtful young man with stars and spinning electrons in his head. "We're in the business of extending man's senses," the caption declared. ("We can turn a mission concept into sophisticated hardware faster, better, at lower cost than just about anyone." "Our mission: Extending man's senses. What's yours?") For its part, presentation of the man-in-space program proceeded as though the intervening decade had never happened.[61]

Were the merchants of space, then, simply less adept at display modification than a good advertising agency? Or was Apollo's lag in image more willful? In an earlier culture's mythology, Mercury fashioned and delivered to Apollo a harp so beautifully executed that when Apollo played it all Olympus fell into a dream. In many respects the Apollo space capsule was also a time capsule, allowing the nation's Space van Winkles to carry a vision of the fifties intact through My Lai and Watts, assassinations and campus riots, and the Tet offensive. For many commentators, both friend and foe, the social function of Apollo was to sustain a pre-Vietnam dream of conquest.

As late as October 1968 Werner von Braun warned readers of *U.S. News and World Report* that preoccupation with the Vietnam War, the "riots in the cities, and so forth" had "distracted from interest in space" to the point that the nation may have "settled for no. 2 in space." Of recent cuts in NASA's budget, he lamented, "It is like being ordered to disarm while the war is still on."[62]

The following summer *U.S. News and World Report* proclaimed the first moon landing to be above all "a symbolic 'conquest' ": By "harnessing natural resources on a wartime scale," and by designating private industry rather than the state to construct the project, America "has emerged, after a decade of self-doubt, as the most technologically and scientifically advanced of all nations." In the years to come, *U.S. News* predicted, Americans would lead the conquest of space, mining and colonizing the moon and planets. Interplanetary military bases, it conceded, seemed less likely than in the early Sputnik days; missiles from the moon, for example, would require two or three days' travel time, as opposed to fifteen minutes for earthbound missiles. "Nevertheless weapons on the moon . . . might be *psychologically intimidating.*"[63]

Both supporters and critics of Apollo agreed that the Eagle flew like a hawk. William F. Buckley declared the moon landing an "unmitigatedly glorious" "aristocratic venture." His *National Review* blasted "Flat-Earth Liberals" for "ignor[ing] realities of national competition for the sake of abstract UN-type pieties." Carey McWilliams, editor of *The Nation*, agreed that Cold War competition dominated the confusion of motives surrounding the project, but found nothing "glorious" in that fact. Asking "What Price Moondust?," McWilliams noted with trepidation that NASA director Thomas O. Paine had "defended NASA's budget by saying that the technology involved would be helpful in 'winning the next war,' a comment that somewhat tarnishes the 'Space Olympics' image of the moon race."[64]

A few of Apollo's interpreters located the object of its "conquest" closer to home. Eric Hoffer called the landing "the triumph of the squares"—a reaffirmation of traditional middle-class values that had recently endured pervasive denunciation and ridicule. Writing from a different perspective, Peter Collier agreed. "Of, by, and for middle-class America," he wrote in *Ramparts*, "the astronauts were its revenge against all the scruffy third-worlders and long-haired deviants who had stolen arrogantly onto the center stage." The first men on the moon "were to be our Aeneas, removing America's household gods—a flag and a television—to a foreign clime." No need to defoliate or tear-gas the moon; no guerrillas crouched behind those craters, no noisy demonstrators could march into the Sea of Tranquillity.[65]

Such visions of vicarious conquest often melted into dreams of escape. Some scientists and science fiction writers (who occupied nearly interchangeable positions of authority in the mass media) argued that moonflight signaled an evolutionary leap forward. Isaac Asimov exulted in the *New York Times Magazine:* "The Moon Could Answer the Riddle of Life." Apollo's objectives might be unclear at the moment, but he provided "the answer (or anyway, *an* answer) to those who ask why we are spending billions to reach the moon, when it is so much more important to cure cancer on earth. All science is one. If we push back the boundaries of the darkness in any direction, the added light illuminates all places, and not merely the immediate area uncovered." The Columbus Principle still reigned in the form of the "spin-off." Space men were hailed as deliverers of a storehouse of unanticipated wonders, from Teflon to improved electrocardiographs—as if the way to develop a better electrocardiograph were to send men to the moon.[66]

For some of Apollo's defenders, the sense of discovery and escape was more generalized. Louis J. Halle proclaimed the Apollo flights to be "man's liberation from this earthly prison"—a vicarious release from "intellectual claustrophobia." "Our position is simply that of the intelligent creatures confined to the ocean deeps," he asserted in *The New Republic.* "Now, however, that we are at last beginning to escape from our native confines, there is no telling what light we may find in the larger universe to dissipate the darkness in our minds."[67]

Several of the manned space project's more outspoken critics agreed that the lunar landing constituted an "escape," but of a less laudable variety. *Ebony* wondered what the astronauts might say to any extraterrestrials they might encounter: "Are they going to say, 'We have millions of people starving to death back home so we thought we'd drop by to see how you're faring'?" Novelist Kurt Vonnegut held a similar view. "Earth is such a pretty blue and pink and white pearl in the pictures NASA sent me," he wrote in the *New York Times Magazine.* "It looks so *clean.* You can't see all the hungry, angry earthlings down there—and the smoke and the sewage and trash and sophisticated weaponry."[68]

Mission Control, once an overarching emblem of American use of technology, appeared to many by 1969 to be an arcade of evasions. "The moon is an escape from our earthly responsibilities," Anthony Lewis concluded in the *New York Times,* "and like other escapes, it leaves a troubled conscience." Our discomfort did not stem simply from the discovery of poverty and ugliness in a nation of unprecedented wealth; these problems we had the "technical apparatus" to solve, if we so desired. "What we lack is any agreed moral basis for their solution, a common vision of the good society. Perhaps we are the twentieth century Vikings," Lewis mused, "driven, conquering without humanizing qualities. We would know the stars but we do not know ourselves."[69]

The lunar landings were a triumph of engineering. They also signified the victory of impression management over substantive policy in American government. The manned space program demonstrated that the national purpose had joined the other commodities of consumer culture as something that could be televised and sold. One widely reprinted photograph featured Apollo's Saturn 5 rocket poised alongside the rising moon, suggesting a lavish reincarnation of the Trylon and Perisphere: beautiful, richly evocative, but rather useless once the exposition was concluded.

And if Apollo proved far less disappointing and destructive than the war in Vietnam, those two campaigns of state-sponsored technological display had more in common than crater-pocked terrain. Whether in the hills of Khe Sanh or on the Sea of Tranquillity, the deployment of American technology evoked similar questions at home and abroad: How could so much power accomplish so little real improvement? Faith in appearances and the impression of "credibility" might sell millions of oversized, inefficient automobiles; but the lunar module—and the ship of state—could not be so quickly traded in. The years following "moon summer" brought the "credibility crisis" of Watergate, the "energy crisis," new awareness of the environmental and health hazards of industrial technology, an accelerated arms race, and a depressed economy. Decisions concerning the social use of technology, and the masking of those decisions through commodity scientism, were no longer—as Werner von Braun had hoped—"something for the next generation to worry about."

SPLASHDOWN

Even after the final Apollo flight in 1972, American advertisers had not forgotten the similarity between the helmsman and the astronaut. Although forbidden to endorse products during their years in the space program, several astronauts appeared in advertisements in the 1970s— almost always for automakers, airlines, or other transportation-based industries. In 1972 Buzz Aldrin, with a "Doctor of Science from MIT and a walk on the Moon under his belt," praised Volkswagen's "new computerized Self-Analysis System" for being "wired along the same principle of a space craft": "Keeping that print-out sheet after the check-up," he observed, "is like checking in with Mission Control when you're 200,000 miles out in space. It gives you a nice, secure feeling."[70]

More often than not, astronauts were called in to improve the image of some ailing corporation in the transportation industry. Wally Schirra, one of the Original Seven, commander of Apollo 7, and Cronkite's co-anchorperson for CBS coverage of Apollo 11, appeared in a commercial for the nation's railroads. Eastern Airlines moved to reverse a slump in sales by hiring Apollo 8 commander Frank Borman as its president—a position that entailed appearances in commercials for his new employer. McDonnell-Douglas, a prime contractor for NASA since the early Mercury days, received considerable criticism for its defective DC-10s—first in 1974, and again in 1979, when two disastrous accidents and a series of near-crashes touched off a national controversy. In 1980 Apollo 12 commander Pete Conrad appeared in a series of commercials to praise the safety and dependability of Mc-Donnell-Douglas products.

Chrysler Corporation, another long-term NASA contractor, producer of the "all push-button Dodge" and two generations of tanks, adhered to its faith in oversized cars throughout the skyrocketing oil price hikes and shortages of the 1970s. In 1979, on the brink of financial losses so devastating that only massive federal funds would keep the company afloat, Chrysler hired Neil Armstrong to praise its superior engineering. "Long ago I learned that all engineering is a matter of designing machines to solve problems," Armstrong announced in a full-page newspaper ad. In a commercial unveiled during the telecast of the Super Bowl, the first man on the moon advised the nation to look to Chrysler "to meet the driving needs we all have today."[71]

The hardware of manned space flight, too, remains the object of display. In the central exhibit area of the Smithsonian's Air and Space Museum, visitors can take in, with a single panoramic gaze, Kitty Hawk, the *Spirit of St. Louis*, Glenn's Friendship 7 capsule, Apollo's *Columbia*, and a moon rock. But perhaps the most revealing artifact of the first decade of American space policy is at the now deserted Mission Control headquarters in Houston. The roomful of computer terminals, already archaic in appearance, calls to mind an electronic variation on Plato's parable of the cave, in which prisoners sit immobilized, their backs to the firelight, able to see nothing "except the shadows cast from the fire on[to] the wall of the cave that fronted them"—as if the world had been devised by "exhibitors of puppet shows." On the day the Eagle landed, the *Washington Post* proclaimed that "[t]he creature who had once stood blinking at the door of his Paleolithic cave has come a long way. . . . At long last, man is on the brink of mastering the universe." "Then in every way," Plato concluded, "such prisoners would deem reality to be nothing else than the shadows of artificial objects."[72]

NOTES

INTRODUCTION

1. Edward Bellamy, *Looking Backward* [1888] (New York, 1960), p. 137.
2. Richard M. Nixon, *Six Crises* (New York, 1962), p. 280.

I
FROM SALVATION TO SELF-REALIZATION:
Advertising and the Therapeutic Roots of the Consumer Culture, 1880–1930

Note: For financial support, I am grateful to the University of Missouri Research Council and the National Endowment for the Humanities. For criticism and advice, I want to thank the other contributors to this volume, especially Richard Fox and Christopher Wilson, and my editors at Pantheon, André Schiffrin, Philip Pochoda, and Robin Stevens. As always, Karen Parker Lears has been my best critic, guide, and friend.

1. Virginia Woolf, "Mr. Bennett and Mrs. Brown," [1924] in *The Captain's Death Bed and Other Essays* (New York, 1950), p. 96.
2. Daniel Boorstin, *The Americans: The Democratic Experience* (New York, 1973), esp. Part II; Stuart Ewen, *Captains of Consciousness* (New York, 1976). By far the best treatments of advertising (though they concern England rather than the United States) are Raymond Williams, "Advertising: the Magic System" in his *Problems in Materialism and Culture* (London, 1980), pp. 170–95, and Judith Williamson's thoughtful semiological study, *Decoding Advertisements* (London, 1978).
3. On the emergence of a therapeutic ethos, see Donald Meyer, *The Positive Thinkers*, 2nd ed. (New York, 1980); Philip Rieff, *The Triumph of the Therapeutic* (New York, 1966); and Christopher Lasch, *The Culture of Narcissism* (New York, 1978). My *No Place of Grace: Antimodernism and the Transformation of American Culture, 1880–1920* (New York, 1981) attempts to refine and broaden the definition of "the therapeutic"—to present it as a way of life embraced by those sometimes only dimly aware of psychiatry.
4. Roosevelt, letter to Denis Donohue, Jr., October 22, 1886, in Elting E. Morison, ed. *The Letters of Theodore Roosevelt*, 8 vols. (Cambridge, Mass., 1951–54), 1: 114; Marcuse, *One-Dimensional Man* (Boston, 1964). Gramsci's concept of hegemony can be pieced together from his *Modern Prince*, trans. Louis Marks (New York, 1967) and his *Prison Notebooks*, trans. Quentin Hoare and Geoffrey Nowell Smith (New York, 1971).
5. Raymond Williams, "Base and Superstructure in Marxist Cultural Theory," *New Left Review* 82 (October 1973) is a thoughtful account of this process. *No Place of Grace* attempts to go beyond Gramsci and Williams by stressing the unconscious determinants of hegemony.
6. The best description of these developments is John H. Haller and Robin Haller, *The Physician and Sexuality in Victorian America* (New York, 1974).
7. William Dean Howells, *A Hazard of New Fortunes* [1890] (Bloomington, Ind., 1976), p. 243; Boorstin, *Democratic Experience*, Part VII; "The Era of Predigestion," *Atlantic* 104 (November 1909); 716–17.
8. Meyer, *Positive Thinkers*, pp. 21–31; Lears, *No Place of Grace*, pp. 47–54.
9. Loren H. B. Knox, "Our Lost Individuality," *Atlantic* 104 (December 1909); 818, 824. On interdependence and its psychic impact, see Thomas L. Hashell, *The Emergence of Professional Social Science* (Urbana, Ill., 1977), chap. 2, and Lears, *No Place of Grace*, pp. 34–37.

10. Henri Laurent, *Personality: How to Build It* (New York, 1916), pp. 97–119; Warren Susman, " 'Personality' and the Making of Twentieth Century Culture," in John Higham and Paul Conkin, eds., *New Directions in American Intellectual History* (Baltimore, 1979), pp. 220–21.

11. David Riesman et al., *The Lonely Crowd: A Study of the Changing American Character*, 3rd. rev. ed. (New Haven, 1969), pp. 21, 25, 127, 149, 157.

12. William James, *Principles of Psychology*, 2 vols. (New York, 1890), 1: 294; George Herbert Mead, *Mind, Self, and Society* (Chicago, 1934); William Dean Howells, *A Boy's Town* (New York, 1890), p. 171.

13. Ethel Dench Puffer, "The Loss of Personality," *Atlantic* 85 (February 1900): 195–204; William James, "The Hidden Self," *Scribner's* 7 (March 1890): 361–73; Nathan Hale, *Freud and the Americans* (New York, 1973), esp. chap. 9; Lears, *No Place of Grace*, pp. 37–41.

14. Hale, *Freud and the Americans*, pp. 236–37; Lears, *No Place of Grace*, pp. 37–41.

15. Nietzsche, quoted in Karl Jaspers, *Nietzsche and Christianity*, trans. E. B. Ashton (Chicago, 1961) p. 14; Lears, *No Place of Grace*, pp. 41–47.

16. "The Growth of Religious Tolerance," *Century* 67 (December 1903): 312–14.

17. Jane Addams, *Twenty Years at Hull House* [1910] (New York, 1960), p. 65; Vida Dutton Scudder, *On Journey* (New York, 1940), pp. 139–72; Claire Sprague, ed., *Van Wyck Brooks: The Early Years* (New York, 1968), pp. 2–3, 37, 43, 55, 56, 59, 127; Randolph Bourne, *Youth and Life* (Boston, 1913); Christopher Lasch, *The New Radicalism in America: The Intellectual as a Social Type, 1889–1963* (New York, 1965).

18. William James, "The Gospel of Relaxation," *Scribner's* 23 (April 1899): 499–507; Joseph S. Zeisel, "The Work Week in American Industry, 1850–1956," in Eric Larrabee and Rolf Meyersohn, eds., *Mass Leisure* (Glencoe, Ill., 1958), p. 146; Lewis A. Erenberg, *Steppin' Out* (Westport, Conn., 1981); John Kasson, *Amusing the Million* (New York, 1978); Simon Nelson Patten, *The New Basis of Civilization* [1907] (Cambridge, Mass., 1968); Walter Lippmann, *A Preface to Politics* [1913] (Ann Arbor, 1962), p. 47. Patten was by no means a simpleminded "prophet of abundance." Daniel Horowitz analyzes the growing sophistication of Patten's thought in "Consumption and Its Discontents," *Journal of American History* 67 (September 1980): 301–317.

19. Silas Weir Mitchell, *Wear and Tear* (Philadelphia, 1887); Hale, *Freud and the Americans*, pp. 60–63; Barbara Sicherman, "The Paradox of Prudence: Mental Health in the Gilded Age," *Journal of American History* 62 (March 1976): 890–912; Frances J. Dyer, "Economize Your Strength: A Reserve Force," *Good Housekeeping* 1 (October 31, 1885): 5; Harvey W. Wiley, M.D. "The League for Longer Life," *Good Housekeeping* 71 (July–August 1920): 71–72.

20. Annie Payson Call, *Power Through Repose* [1891] (Boston, 1913), pp. 60, 64, 87; William James, "The Energies of Men," *Philosophical Review* 16 (January 1907): 1–20 and "The Powers of Men," *American Magazine* 5 (October 1907): 57–65.

21. G. Stanley Hall, *Adolescence* 2 vols. (New York, 1904); Hall, *Jesus, the Christ, in the Light of Psychology* (New York, 1917); Hall, *Morale: The Supreme Standard of Life and Conduct*, (New York, 1920), pp. 16–17.

22. Elwood Worcester, Samuel McComb, and Isador Coriat, *Religion and Medicine* (Boston, 1908), p. 103.

23. Harry Emerson Fosdick, *The Manhood of the Master* (New York, 1913), p. 13; Fosdick, *Adventurous Religion and Other Essays* (New York, 1926), pp. 34–35, 41; Fosdick, *Twelve Tests of Character* (New York, 1923), p. 47. Fosdick has been unaccountably neglected by historians, though there is a thoughtful discussion in Meyer, *Positive Thinkers*, pp. 220–32.

24. Fosdick, *Adventurous Religion*, pp. 10, 18, 26; Fosdick, *Twelve Tests*, p. 3.

25. Fosdick, *Adventurous Religion*, pp. 144–45; Fosdick, *Twelve Tests*, p. 81; Hall, *Morale*, p. 103; Call, *Power Through Repose*, pp. 65, 157.

26. Luther H. Gulick, *The Efficient Life* (New York, 1907), pp. 10, 18, 180, 192–93. Gulick extended these views in *A Philosophy of Play* (New York, 1920), esp. pp. 277–81.

27. Hall, *Morale*, p. 256; Ella Wheeler Wilcox, *Men, Women, and Emotions* (Chicago, 1894), p. 12. Morton White, *Social Thought in America*, 2nd ed. (Boston, 1957) and Robert H. Wiebe, *The Search for Order, 1877–1920* examine the new fascination with process among social thinkers.

28. Hall, *Morale*, p. 208; Gulick, *Philosophy of Play*, pp. 120, 236, 245; Lippmann, *Preface to Politics*, p. 47.

29. Luther H. Gulick, "Exercise and Rest," *North American Review* 192 (October 1910): 536–42 offers one example of this circularity. Two perceptive discussions of the fretfulness behind the pursuit of pleasure are Riesman, *Lonely Crowd*, pp. 141–58; and Martha Wolfenstein, "Fun Morality," in Warren Susman, ed., *Culture and Commitment, 1929–1945* (New York, 1973), pp. 84–92.

30. Worcester et al., *Religion and Medicine*, p. 74. For similar views see Ralph Waldo Trine, *In Tune with the Infinite* (Boston, 1899), a popular mind-cure tract, and Meyer, *Positive Thinkers*, esp. chap. 6.

31. On the corrosiveness of the Enlightenment creed of progress, see Theodor Adorno and Max Horkheimer, *Dialectic of Enlightenment* [1944] trans. J. Cummings (New York, 1972), chap. 1.

32. Hall, *Adolescence* 2:747; Gulick, *Philosophy of Play*, p. 21.

33. See Max Weber, *Economy and Society*, ed. and trans. Guenther Roth and Claus Wittick (Berkeley, 1968), vol. 1, chaps. 1–4; vol. 2, chaps. 7–8; vol. 3, chaps 10, 11, 14.

34. "About Big Newspapers," *Printers' Ink* 2 (September 1890) 294–95. On attention-getting devices, see for example "Advertising Cuts," *Printers' Ink* 3 (December 24, 1890): 698–99; Leon Barrett, "Illustrations in Advertising," *Printers' Ink* 5 (August 5, 1891): 100–101; Charles W. Mears, "Advertising that Appeals to the Senses the Coming Type," *Printers' Ink* 90 (January 14, 1915): 132–35; Frank Presbrey, *The History and Development of Advertising* (New York, 1929), pp. 356–87; James P. Wood, *The Story of Advertising* (New York, 1958), pp. 247–72.

35. Vachel Lindsay, *The Art of the Moving Picture* [1915, 2nd ed. 1922] (New York, 1970), pp. 21–22. Neil Harris, Introduction to *The Land of Contrasts, 1880–1901* (New York, 1970) perceptively discusses the shift toward a visual culture.

36. Wood, *Story of Advertising*, pp. 285–95.

37. Merle Curti, "The Changing Concept of 'Human Nature' in the Literature of American Advertising," *Business History Review* 41 (Winter 1967), esp. 349; David Cohen, *John B. Watson* (London, 1979), pp. 177–87; Walter Dill Scott, *The Psychology of Advertising*, 3rd ed. (Boston, 1921); C. L. Watson, "What Psychology Can Teach Us," *Printers' Ink* 71 (June 16, 1910): 20–21.

38. Scott, *Psychology of Advertising* 34; Scott, *The Theory of Advertising* (Boston, 1903), pp. 47–51.

39. Scott, *Theory*, p. 59; William A. Shryer, *Analytical Advertising* (Detroit, 1912), p. 47; Edward L. Bernays, *Propaganda* (New York, 1928), pp. 50–52, 63.

40. The best general account of these developments is still H. Stuart Hughes, *Consciousness and Society: The Re-Orientation of European Social Thought, 1890–1930* (New York, 1958).

41. Herbert W. Hess, "History and Present Status of the 'Truth-in-Advertising' Movement," *Annals* of the American Academy 101 (May 1922): 211–20; Presbrey, *History*, pp. 531–40; Wood, *Story*, pp. 322–44; Daniel Boorstin, *The Image: A Guide to Pseudo-Events in America* (New York, 1961), chaps. 5, 6; E. P. Corbett, "You

Cannot Fake Sincerity," *Printers' Ink* 3 (April 15, 1920): 97–98 and "How to Acquire Sincerity of Style," *Printers' Ink* 3 (April 22, 1920): 25–26.

42. Rieff, *Triumph of the Therapeutic*, p. 13.

43. Henry Lefebvre, *Everyday Life in the Modern World*, tr. Sacha Rabinovitch (New York, 1971), pp. 110–23. On semiological approaches to advertising, see Mark Poster, "Semiology and Critical Theory: From Marx to Baudrillard," *Boundary 2*, no. 8 (Fall 1979): 275–81. Mary Douglas, in *The World of Goods* (New York, 1979), also argues that patterns of consumption constitute "information systems" but overlooks entirely the ways that advertising can garble information and devalue meaning.

44. Claude Hopkins, *My Life in Advertising* (New York, 1927), pp. 79–82; Grand Rapids Furniture, *Good Housekeeping* 78 (June 1924): 254.

45. "Inappropriate Cuts," *Printers' Ink* 2 (April 30, 1890): 698–99; Drano, *Good Housekeeping* 87 (October 1928): 296.

46. Michael Schudson, "Criticizing the Critics: Toward a Sociology of Mass Marketing," lecture at the University of Missouri, Columbia, November 10, 1980; Ernest Elmo Calkins, *"and hearing not—" Annals of an Ad Man* (New York, 1946), p. 239. For more on advertising's assimilation of modernism, see Jeffrey L. Meikle, *Twentieth Century Limited: Industrial Design in America, 1925–1939* (Philadelphia, 1979).

47. Cook's Flaked Rice, *Good Housekeeping* 30 (December 1900): 369; Laun-dry-ette, *Good Housekeeping* 71 (September 1920): 192; Aetna Life Insurance, *American Magazine* 81 (February 1916): 82; Puffed Rice, *American Magazine* 81 (June 1916): 67; Pro-Phy-Lac-Tic toothbrushes, *Good Housekeeping* 78 (March 1924): 123.

48. Shredded Wheat, *Harper's* 47 (April 25, 1903): 681.

49. Aunt Belle's Comfort Letters, *Good Housekeeping* 71 (July–August 1920): 114.

50. Quaker Oats, *Good Housekeeping* 71 (September 1920): 210.

51. Scott Tissues, *Good Housekeeping* 87 (October 1928): 325, and *Good Housekeeping* 89 (May 1930): 190; Listerine, *Good Housekeeping* 62 (June 1916): 36, and *Good Housekeeping* 87 (July 1928): 229; Pluto Water, *Saturday Evening Post* 201 (July 21, 1928): 137.

52. Church Sani-White Seats, *Good Housekeeping* 78 (May 1924): 188; Brunswick White Seats, *Good Housekeeping* 89 (January 1930): 183.

53. Compare Sozodont, *Harper's Weekly* 36 (January 2, 1892): 21 with Pepsodent, *Good Housekeeping* 71 (July–August 1920): 115.

54. Tarrant's Seltzer, *Harper's* 17 (May 31, 1873): 472; Paine's Celery Compound, *Good Housekeeping* 19 (October 1894): 191; Pabst Malt Extract, *Harper's* 41 (February 20, 1897): 188; White Cross Electric Vibrator, *American Magazine* 75 (May 1913): 127.

55. Home Billiards, *American Magazine* 81 (February 1916): 73; Lucky Strike, *American Magazine* 81 (January 1916): 85.

56. Kotex, *Good Housekeeping* 78 (February 1924): 223; Cantilever Shoes, *Good Housekeeping* 78 (June 1924): 99.

57. Meyer, *Positive Thinkers*, esp. chap. 3; Nathaniel C. Fowler, "Reaching the Men Through the Women," *Printers' Ink* 5 (July 22, 1891), was among the first of numerous such articles in trade journals; "The New Shopping," *Good Housekeeping* 56 (January 1913): 130–31.

58. Ewen, *Captains of Consciousness*, pp. 159–76; Gossard Corsets, *Good Housekeeping* 71 (October 1920): 127. Lary May, *Screening Out the Past: the Birth of Mass Culture and the Motion Picture Industry* (New York, 1980), pp. 125, 146, notes a parallel domestication of female emancipation in popular films.

59. Reo Motor Cars, *American Magazine* 75 (June 1913): 79; Dodge Victory Six, *Saturday Evening Post* 201 (July 28, 1928): 38; Reo Flying Cloud, *Saturday Evening Post* 201 (July 7, 1928): 30.

60. Neil Harris, *Humbug: The Art of P. T. Barnum* (New York, 1973), p. 57; Robin Lydenberg, "The Rhetoric of Advertising," *Michigan Quarterly Review* 17 (1978): 65–75; Williams, "The Magic System," and Williamson, *Decoding Advertisement* are signs that Left historians have begun to abandon their emphasis on consumers' passivity and acknowledge the participation involved in entertainment.

61. May, *Screening Out the Past*, p. 232.

62. May, *Screening Out the Past*, p. 213; Palmolive Soap, *American Magazine* 81 (January 1916): 81. The therapeutic renovation of sensuality had an important impact on marriage, as Elaine May makes clear in *Great Expectations: Marriage and Divorce in Post-Victorian America* (Chicago and London, 1980).

63. May, *Screening Out the Past*, p. 116.

64. Hopkins, *My Life in Advertising*, esp. pp. 8, 31–32, 42.

65. *New York Times*, July 6, 1967, p. 1; Bruce Barton to Mrs. R. T. Morris, July 15, 1926, Barton Papers, University of Wisconsin, Madison; Fred B. Barton, "Bruce Barton as A Brother," unpublished MS, Barton Papers.

66. Exceptions to the general dismissal of Barton are Warren Susman, "Piety, Profits, and Play: The 1920's," in Howart H. Quint and Milton Cantor, eds., *Men, Women, and Issues in American History*, rev. ed. (Homewood, Ill., 1980), pp. 202–27; Meyer, *Positive Thinkers*, pp. 177–80; and Leo P. Ribuffo, "Jesus Christ as Business Statesman: Bruce Barton and the Selling of Corporate Capitalism," *American Quarterly* 33 (Summer 1981); 206–31.

67. Bruce Barton, "Peers of the Pulpit, V. The Rev. Amzi Clarence Dixon, D. D.," *Home Herald* 19 (September 1908): 8–9; Barton, "In the Wake of Billy Sunday," *Home Herald* 20 (June 2, 1909): 3–5; Barton, "Billy Sunday, Baseball Evangelist," *Collier's* 51 (July 26, 1913): 7–8, 30.

68. Bruce Barton, *A Young Man's Jesus* (Boston, 1914), pp. 1–8, 14; "What Do Men Like in Women," *Every Week*, February 21, 1918; "A New Year Starts," *Every Week*, January 10, 1918; "Should We Be Sent to Jail for Eating the Wrong Food?" *Every Week*, February 7, 1918.

69. Barton, "How You Can Do More and Be More," *American Magazine* 96 (November 1923): 14–15; Barton, "Does Anything Come After Death?" *American Magazine* 95 (March 1923): 120, 122; Barton, *On the Up and Up* (Indianapolis, 1929), p. 89; Barton, "The Washing of His Feet," *Good Housekeeping* 87 (August 1928): 50.

70. Barton, "Can You Loaf?" *Review of Reviews*, October 1929, pp. 87–88; Barton, "Ill-gotten Gains," *Collier's* 77 (March 6, 1926): 27. The interview with Ford is "It Would Be Fun to Start Over Again," *American Magazine* 95 (April 1923): 8.

71. Barton, *On the Up and Up*, p. 103; Barton, "What to Do If You Want to Sit at the Boss's Desk," *American Magazine* 93 (February 1922); Barton, "Should an Industry Have a Soul?" transcript of speech to National Electric Light Association, May 1926, Barton Papers.

72. *New York Times*, July 6, 1967, p. 1; Bankers Trust advertisement, February 20, 1928, unpublished typescript in Barton Papers; Bruce Barton to W. E. Fellows, October 31, 1928, copy of telegram in Barton Papers.

73. Barton, *The Man Nobody Knows*, (Indianapolis, 1925), pp. 12, 43, 59, 61, 67, 69, 90, 143, 149, 151.

74. J. L. Lasky to Bruce Barton, July 16, 1926; Bruce Barton to W. E. Barton, July 17, 1926. Both letters in Barton Papers.

75. Barton, "Modern Distribution," *Chain Store Age*, November 1929, pp. 63–64, 76–78; Barton, "Our First Reader," *American Magazine*, August 1930, p. 156; Barton, "Back to the Land," *Home Herald* 19 (February 19, 1908): 11; "Being a Real Producer," *Every Week*, January 31, 1918. On Barton's insomnia, see Ribuffo, "Jesus Christ," pp. 223, 233.

76. Barton, *On the Up and Up*, pp. 106–7; Barton, "Courage to Dive Off the Dock," *American Magazine* 94 (August 1922): 24.
77. Barton, *On the Up and Up*, pp. 54–55.
78. Barton, "My Father's Business," *Outlook* 107 (June 27, 1914): 494, 497.
79. W. E. Barton, "Jesus in the Twentieth Century," December 25, 1898, unpublished typescript of sermon in Barton Papers; WEB, unpublished autobiography in Barton Papers, pp. 359–61, 366; WEB to BB, June 28, 1921, Barton Papers.
80. Barton, *A Young Man's Jesus*, pp. 1–2; Barton, *Man Nobody Knows*, unpaginated introduction. Ribuffo, "Jesus Christ," presents an alternative speculation: that BB's memory of Sunday school was "synthetic," a deception designed to boost sales.
81. Barton, "Should an Industry Have a Soul?"; Barton, *What Can a Man Believe?* (Indianapolis, 1927), pp. 231–43.
82. Barton, *Man Nobody Knows*, pp. 179, 180, 153.
83. For example: Charles E. Adams to BB, April 14, 1925; A. M. Stouffer to BB, October 20, 1921; J. R. Angell to BB, September 29, 1925; Harold R. Thompson to BB, April 29, 1926.
84. Helen Woodward, "Republican in Sheep's Clothing," *The Nation* 147 (November 5, 1938): 475; memorandum, BB to staff, B.B.D. & O., August 24, 1948, Barton Papers.
85. Williams, "Magic System," pp. 192–93.

II
THE RHETORIC OF CONSUMPTION:
Mass-Market Magazines and the Demise of the Gentle Reader, 1880–1920

Note: The epigraphs are quoted from Finley Peter Dunne, "Mr Dooley on the Magazines," *American Magazine*, 68 (October 1909): 539–42, and John Milton Cooper, *Walter Hines Page* (Chapel Hill, 1977), p. 121.

Abbreviations
LHJ: *Ladies' Home Journal*
McC: *McClure's*
SEP: *Saturday Evening Post*
WW: *The World's Work*

1. Burton Bledstein, *The Culture of Professionalism* (New York: 1976), p. 77.
2. Samuel McChord Crothers, "The Gentle Reader," *Atlantic* 86 (November 1900): 654–63; Gerald Stanley Lee, *The Lost Art of Reading* (New York, 1902), p. 18; Bliss Perry, "On Reading the Atlantic Cheerfully," *Atlantic* 89 (January 1902): 1–4; Alden quoted from "Editor's Study," *Harper's* 112 (April 1906): 801. For other commentary on the demise of the gentle reader, see C. M. Francis, "Fighting Magazines," *The Bookman* 31 (July 1910): 474–77; Frank A. Munsey, *The Founding of the Munsey Publishing House* (New York, 1907), p. 40; Gertrude Atherton, "Literary Merchandise," *New Republic*, July 3, 1915, pp. 223–24; and Algernon Tassin, *The Magazine in America* (New York, 1916), pp. 350–51.
3. Wolfgang Iser, *The Implied Reader* (Baltimore, 1974), pp. 29–56, 101–20, (Sterne quoted on p. 31); John Preston, *The Created Self* (London, 1970), esp. pp. 1–7. On the French context, see Roland Barthes, *Writing Degree Zero*, trans. Annette Lavers and Colin Smith (New York, 1968), esp. pp. 2–6, 33–35. Walter Benjamin also notes that film realism encourages "direct, intimate fusion of visual and emotional enjoyment with the orientation of the expert." "The Work of Art in the Age of

Mechanical Reproduction," in *Illuminations*, trans. Harry Zohn (New York, 1968), p. 234.

4. For good summaries of the Gilded Age editorial philosophy, see "Editor's Study," *Harper's* 105 (September 1902): 646–48, and Henry Mills Alden, *Magazine Writing and the New Literature* (New York, 1908).

5. On "naturalizing" see Roland Barthes, *Mythologies*, trans. Annette Lavers (New York, 1979), pp. 129–31 ff.

6. The best recent account is Richard Ohmann, "Where Did Mass Culture Come From? The Case of the Magazines," *Berkshire Review* 16 (1981): 85–101.

7. Aside from their pathbreaking role, I have chosen these magazines because they represent a diversity of approaches: a newsmagazine; a muckraking journal; a businessman's weekly; a domestic monthly. Political views also varied; some ran ads, some did not; some were based in New York, others in Philadelphia.

8. My use of "realism" follows the lead of Iser, Barthes, and William Scott's *Documentary Expression in Thirties America* (New York, 1973), in which realism is defined as a narrative mode by which an author uses the illusion of veracity (persuasive narration, detail, the feeling of immediacy) to direct the reader's interaction with a text —in effect, to manage the "reader's" responses.

9. See Richard Wightman Fox, "Breathless: The Cultural Consternation of Daniel Bell," *American Quarterly* 24 (Spring 1982): 70–77.

10. Market research actually had its origins in Curtis magazines. See Wroe Anderson, "Charles Coolidge Parlin," *Journal of Marketing* 21 (July 1956): 1–2.

11. Salme Harju Steinberg, *Reformer in the Marketplace* (Baton Rouge, 1974), pp. 3–7; Robert and Helen Lynd, *Middletown* (New York, 1929), pp. 239–40.

12. Edward Bok, *The Americanization of Edward Bok* (New York, 1920); Steinberg, *Reformer*; S. S. McClure, *My Autobiography* (New York, 1914); Peter Lyon, *Success Story* (Deland, Fla., 1967); Cooper, *Walter Hines Page*; and John Tebbel, *George Horace Lorimer and the Saturday Evening Post* (Garden City, N.Y., 1948).

13. On this older generation, see John Tomsich, *A Genteel Endeavor* (Stanford, 1971).

14. Herbert F. Smith, *Richard Watson Gilder* (New York, 1970), p. 21; L. Frank Tooker, *The Joys and Tribulations of an Editor* (New York, 1923), pp. 54, 62, 82–83, 89–90, 124; Bliss Perry, *Park Street Papers* (Boston, 1908), pp. 160–61; M. A. DeWolfe Howe, *The Atlantic Monthly and Its Makers* (Boston, 1919), p. 91; and Robert Underwood Johnson, *Remembered Yesterdays* (Boston, 1923), p. 148.

15. Johnson, *Remembered Yesterdays*, p. 149; "Magazines—Their Scope and Influence," *Independent*, Oct. 1, 1908, pp. 796–98; McClure, *Autobiography*, p. 182.

16. For the influence of newspapers on magazine prose, see Arthur Reed Kimball, "The Invasion of Journalism," *Atlantic* 86 (July 1900): 119–24, and F. C. Bray, "Some Recent Phases of Journalism," *Chautauquan* 66 (March 1912): 98–104.

17. See Issac Marcosson, *Adventures in Interviewing* (New York, 1919), pp. 58, 38, 41.

18. Edward Bok, *The Young Man and the Church* (Philadelphia, 1896), pp. 10, 11, 20, 16; McClure, *Autobiography*, p. 130 ff; Tebbel, *Lorimer*, p. 7 ff.

19. "Scientific Management in Reading," *The Independent*, January 9, 1913, pp. 75–77.

20. Mark Sullivan, *The Education of an American* (New York, 1938), pp. 198–99; Charles Hanson Towne, *Adventures in Editing* (New York, 1926), pp. 25–27, 37, 40, 57, 83; Lorimer quoted in Tebbel, p. 246. The best survey of these trends is George Jean Nathan, "The Magazine in the Making," *The Bookman* 34 (December 1911): 414–16.

21. See "Tyranny of Timeliness," *Atlantic* 98 (August 1906): 285–87; "A Word About Ourselves," *The Outlook*, December 21, 1912, pp. 841–42; H. L. Nelson, "American Periodicals, 1880–1900," *The Dial*, May 1, 1900, pp. 349–52; "Wanted —A Retrospective Review," *Atlantic* 86 (September 1900): 428–30; and "Deserters from Fiction," *The Nation*, June 2, 1910, p. 552.

22. See W. D. Howells, "The Editor and the Young Contributor," in *Literature and Life* (New York, 1902), pp. 63–77.

23. McClure, *Autobiography*, p. 196. See also Lyon, *Success Story*, p. 70; Tebbel, *Lorimer*, pp. 21, 215, 216, 217; Marcosson, *Interviewing*, pp. 41, 58; Cooper, *Page*, pp. 122–23; John Drewry, *Some Magazines and Magazine Makers* (Boston, 1924), pp. 54–55.

24. Bok, *Americanization*, p. 296; Page, "An Intimate View of Publishing," *WW* 4 (October 1902): 2562; Page to Scudder, letter of September 9, 1897, Walter Hines Page Papers, Houghton Library, Harvard University; Munsey quoted in Peterson, *Magazines*, p. 15.

25. Compare my discussion with David Potter, *People of Plenty* (Chicago, 1954), p. 182 ff.

26. See Barton's and Carnegie's use of "sincerity" in Moses Rischin, ed. *The American Gospel of Success* (Chicago, 1956), pp. 415–18, and in *Culture and Commitment*, ed. Warren Susman (New York, 1973), pp. 60–67.

27. Bok, *Americanization*, pp. 162–63, 153.

28. "The Literature of Business," *The Nation*, November 15, 1905, pp. 409–10.

29. Tassin, *Magazine*, pp. 355–57. See also Barthes, *Mythologies*, p. 124.

30. See Robert Stinson, "McClure's Road to *McClure's*: How Revolutionary Were 1890s Magazines?" *Journalism Quarterly* 47 (Summer 1970): 256–62.

31. See Bok, *Americanization*, pp. 179, 292–93. Compare Lorimer as quoted in *Current Literature* 40 (January 1906): 48.

32. "The Uplift of a Whole Nation," *WW* 8 (July 1904): 4944, 4947.

33. See, for example, the issue on the Pan American Exposition in Buffalo: *WW* 2 (August 1901).

34. Page, "The Cultivated Man in an Industrial Era," *WW* 8 (July 1904): 4980–85; "A Year of the Magazine," *WW* 2 (October 1901); 1257; "McClure's Magazine—Reminiscences and Forecasts," *McC* 9 (October 1897): 101; Lyon, *Success Story*, p. 95; "The Railroads on Trial," *McC* 25 (October 1905): 673–74.

35. See McClure, *Autobiography*, p. 225; Neil Harris, *Humbug* (New York, 1973), p. 57. "Leaping Tuna," *McC* 16 (February 1901): 369–74; "The Memoirs of Carl Schurz," *McC* 25 (October 1905): 670.

36. George Horace Lorimer, "The Unpopular Editor of the Popular Magazine," *The Bookman* 60 (December 1924): 396–97; Curtis Publishing Co., *Selling Forces* (Philadelphia, 1913), pp. 249–50; "Money and Health," *SEP*, Jan. 30, 1904, p. 14; John B. Kennedy, "Nothing Succeeds like Common Sense," *Collier's*, November 27, 1926, p. 47; Marcosson, *Interviewing*, pp. 59–60.

37. "The American Business Method," *SEP*, February 20, 1904, p. 12; Tebbel, *Lorimer*, p. 113.

38. *Selling Forces*, p. 254.

39. Hale, "Editor's Table," *Godey's Ladies' Book* 42 (January 1851): 65–66; Bok as quoted in Steinberg, *Reformer*, p. 75.

40. Curtis, "We Ask a Favor," *LHJ* 1 (January 1884): 4; Edward Bok, *A Man from Maine* (New York, 1934), pp. 108–10.

41. Curtis in *LHJ* 2 (December 1894): 4; *LHJ* 2 (February 1885): 4; *LHJ* 2 (March 1885): 4; *LHJ* 3 (September 1886): 6; and *LHJ* 3 (April 1886): 6. Bok in *LHJ* 8 (November 1890): 12, and *LHJ* 10 (July 1892): 12; *LHJ* 10 (May 1892): 12; "Frittering Away Our Time," *LHJ* 12 (April 1895): 14; *LHJ* 10 (February 1893): 12. Octave Thanet, "That Man: Your Husband," *LHJ* 10 (February 1893): 8; Steinberg, *Reformer*, p. 72.

42. See Bok, *Americanization*, pp. 179, 292–93. Compare Ohmann, "Mass Culture," p. 100.

43. Notes to speech, "Magazine Development," in Page Papers, Harvard.

44. Page, "Magazine Development."

45. See Marcosson, *Interviewing*, p. 41.
46. Cooper, *Page*, p. 179; "Shall We Promise the Filipinos Independence?" *WW* 4 (July 1901): 2253–54; Raymond Stevens, "The Business 'Engineer,' " *WW* 6 (May 1903): 3445–49.
47. On the resistance of Americans to interviewing, see my "The Era of the Reporter Reconsidered: The Case of Lincoln Steffens," *Journal of Popular Culture* 15 (Fall 1981): 41–49. On "inside dope," see David Riesman, *The Lonely Crowd* (New Haven, 1969), p. 180 ff.
48. Editorial announcement, "Studying the Criminal," *McC* 16 (March 1901): 479–80.
49. R. S. Baker, "The Kaiser as Seen in Germany," *McC* 16 (January 1901): 222–28.
50. White, "Croker," *McC* 16 (February 1901): 317–26; editorial announcement prior to Francis H. Nichols, "Children of the Coal Shadow," *McC* 20 (February 1903): 435; announcement before White, "Bryan," *McC* 15 (July 1900): 232–37.
51. "Gossip," *SEP*, August 25, 1906, p. 14.
52. *Selling Forces*, p. 234; see also Steinberg, *Reformer*, pp. 19–20, 52, 56; Bok, *Americanization*, pp. 164–79; Bok, "A Bond of Common Sympathy," *LHJ* 8 (April 1890): 8.
53. Mrs. Curtis in *LHJ* 4 (June 1886): 6. John A Thayer, *Astir* (Boston, 1910), p. 88 ff. This practice clearly anticipated the effort of twentieth-century political market analysts: Here Curtis & Co., in effect, "sold" readers to advertisers.
54. On ad-stripping, see Bok, *Americanization*, p. 234; cf. Steinberg, *Reformer*, p. 62.
55. "Confidence in Our Columns," *LHJ* 4 (April 1886): 6. On Bok's standing as a reformer, see Steinberg.
56. John F. Kasson, *Amusing the Millions* (New York, 1978), pp. 53, 82.
57. For this aspect of advertising psychology, see John Berger, *Ways of Seeing* (London, 1972), pp. 132–33.
58. Compare Mrs. Curtis in *LHJ* 4 (October 1886): 6, and Bok, "Woman's Mission of the Future," *LHJ* 7 (March 1890): 8; and *LHJ* 11 (May 1894): 12.
59. See Warren Susman, " 'Personality' and the Making of Twentieth Century Culture," in *New Directions in American Intellectual History*, ed. John Higham and Paul Conkin (Baltimore, 1979), pp. 212–26. Quotation from George Horace Lorimer, *Letters from a Self Made Merchant to His Son* (New York, 1902), pp. 173, 178.
60. Bok, *Twice Thirty* (New York, 1927), pp. 382–383.
61. On this tendency of consumer culture to fragment needs, see William Leiss, *The Limits to Satisfaction* (Toronto, 1976), p. 49 ff.
62. "The Melancholy of Woman's Pages," *Atlantic* 97 (April 1906): 574–75.

III
THE CONSUMING VISION OF HENRY JAMES

Note: I would like to acknowledge the suggestions and criticisms given to me on the initial drafts of this essay by my co-authors and by my editor at Pantheon, Philip Pochoda, as well as by Betsy Blackmar, Deborah Kaplan, David Marshall, Roy Rosenzweig, and Alan Trachtenberg.

1. T. S. Ashton, "The Standard of Life of the Workers in England, 1790–1830," in *Capitalism and the Historians*, F. A. Hayek, ed., (Chicago, 1954), pp. 127–59; E. J. Hobsbawm, "The British Standard of Living, 1790–1850," *Economic History Review* 10 (August 1957): 46–68; A. J. P. Taylor, "Progress and Poverty in Britain, 1780–1850," *History* 55 (February 1960): 16–31.
2. See Philip Abrams, "History, Sociology, Historical Sociology," *Past and Present* 87 (May 1980): 3–16; Clifford Geertz, "Thick Description: Toward an Interpretative Theory of Culture," in *The Interpretation of Cultures* (New York, 1973), pp. 3–30.

E. P. Thompson gives an admirably detailed account of the cultural background of industrialization in *The Making of the English Working Class* (New York, 1963), chap. 6 and passim.

3. John A. Howard, *Marketing Theory* (Boston, 1965), p. 74; two notable exceptions to this view are Daniel Boorstin and Stuart Ewen, both discussed elsewhere in this volume; but even David Potter's otherwise prescient *People of Plenty* (Chicago, 1954) collapses consumer culture into a question of an "abundance" mentality.

4. See, for example, Bernard Bailyn, David Brion Davis, David Herbert Donald, John C. Thomas, Robert H. Wiebe, Gordon S. Wood, *The Great Republic* (Lexington, Mass., 1977), pp. 1126–28, 1200–1202; Melvyn Dubofsky, Athan Theoharis, Daniel M. Smith, *The United States in the Twentieth Century* (Englewood Cliffs, N.J., 1978), pp. 172–74, 426–28; John A. Howard and Lyman E. Ostlund, eds. *Buyer Behavior* (New York, 1973).

5. See George Katona, *The Powerful Consumer* (New York, 1960) and *The Mass Consumption Society* (New York, 1964).

6. See, for example, Kelvin Lancaster, *Consumer Demand: A New Approach* (New York and London, 1971); Duncan Ironmonger, *New Commodities and Consumer Behavior* (Cambridge, 1972).

7. Sandra Salmans, "Introducing a New Product," *New York Times*, July 14, 1981; Lancaster, *Consumer Demand*, pp. 6–11; Ironmonger, *New Commodities*, p. 9. For a closely scrutinized example of this phenomenon, see Michael Arlen's study of A.T.&T.'s campaign to promote long-distance calls in *Thirty Seconds* (New York, 1979).

8. Lancaster, *Consumer Demand*, p. 114.

9. Tony Schwartz, *The Responsive Chord* (Garden City, N.Y., 1974), p. 65; William Leiss, *The Limits to Satisfaction* (Toronto and Buffalo, 1976), pp. 88–89, 93. The following analysis is deeply indebted to Leiss's work. See also Leiss, "Needs, Exchanges and the Fetishism of Objects," *Canadian Journal of Political and Social Theory* 2 (Fall 1978): 27–48 and Leiss and Stephen Kline, "Advertising, Needs, and "Commodity Fetishism,' " ibid. 2 (Winter 1978): 5–27.

10. Leiss, *Limits to Satisfaction*, p. 92; Karl Marx and Friedrich Engels, "The Communist Manifesto," in *Essential Works of Marxism*, Arthur P. Mendel, ed. (New York, 1961), p. 16.

11. For an overview of these issues, see Jean-Christophe Agnew, "The Threshold of Exchange: Speculations on the Market," *Radical History Review* 21 (Fall 1979): 99–118.

12. E. P. Thompson, "The Moral Economy of the English Crowd in the Eighteenth Century," *Past and Present* 50 (February 1971): 85, 93.

13. Karl Polanyi, "The Economy as Instituted Process," in *Trade and Market in the Early Empires*, Karl Polanyi, Conrad M. Arensberg, Harry W. Pearson, eds. (New York, 1957), pp. 243–70; Polanyi, "Aristotle Discovers the Economy," ibid., p. 68 ff; Henry James, *The Art of the Novel*, R. P. Blackmur, ed. (New York, 1934), p. 33. On the association of the marketplace with symbolic disruptions and reversals, see Mikhail Bakhtin, *Rabelais and His World*, Helene Iswolsky, tr. (Cambridge, Mass., 1968), pp. 145–277; Barbara Babcock-Abrahams, "The Novel and the Carnival World," *MLN* 89 (December 1974): 911–37.

14. *New York Times*, April 2, 1982; Sandra Salmans, "Selling Via the Movies," ibid., August 20, 1981.

15. Schwartz, *Responsive Chord*, pp. 76–77; on the questions of aesthetic economy and psychological plausibility, see again, Arlen, *Thirty Seconds*.

16. Jean Baudrillard, *For a Critique of the Political Economy of the Sign*, trans. Charles Levin (St. Louis, 1981), p. 92, and *Le Système des objets: la consommation des signes* (Paris, 1968), pp. 221–39.

222

17. Agnew, "Threshold of Exchange," pp. 100–101; Vivian Garrison and Conrad M. Arensberg, "The Evil Eye: Envy or Risk of Seizure? Paranoia or Patronal Dependency?" in *The Evil Eye*, Clarence Maloney, ed. (New York, 1976), pp. 286–328; Sheila Cominsky, "The Evil Eye in a Quiche Community," in ibid., pp. 163–74.

18. Nathan Rosenberg, "Adam Smith, Consumer Tastes, and Economic Growth," *Journal of Political Economy* 76 (May–June 1968): 361–74; Judith N. Shklar, "Rousseau's Two Models: Sparta and the Age of Gold," *Political Science Quarterly* 81 (March 1966): 25–61; Karl Marx, "Private Property and Communism" (1844), in *Writings of the Young Marx on Philosophy and Society*, Loyd D. Easton and Kurt H. Guddat, eds. (Garden City, N.Y., 1967), p. 308; but see also Marx's 1857 discussion of the "civilizing influence of capital" in developing new use values and new needs, in *Grundrisse*, trans. Martin Nicolaus (New York, 1973), pp. 409–10; Raymond Williams, *The Country and the City* (New York, 1973), p. 249.

19. On "defamiliarization," see R. H. Stacy, *Defamiliarization in Language and Literature* (Syracuse, 1977) and Frederick Jameson, *The Prison-House of Language* (Princeton, 1972), pp. 50–59, 75–79.

20. R. W. Perry, *The Thought and Character of William James* (Boston, 1935), 1: 203.

21. Henry James, *The American Scene* (Bloomington, Ind., 1968), pp. 66, 67.

22. Ibid., pp. 9, 10, 197.

23. Ibid., pp. 406, 102, 408, 438, 105.

24. Ibid., pp. 106–7.

25. See, for example, Max Horkheimer and Theodor W. Adorno, "The Culture Industry: Enlightenment as Mass Deception," in *Dialectic of Enlightenment*, John Cumming, tr. (New York, 1972), pp. 120–67.

26. James, *American Scene*, pp. 136, 137.

27. Ibid., p. 136.

28. Henry James, *Autobiography*, Frederick W. Dupee, ed. (New York 1956), pp. 38, 39–42.

29. Ibid., pp. 89–90.

30. Ibid., pp. 94–95.

31. Neil Harris, *Humbug: The Art of P. T. Barnum* (Boston, 1973), pp. 77–79.

32. James, *Autobiography*, pp. 94–95.

33. Ibid., pp. 253–54, 246, 8, 481.

34. Ibid., pp. 133–44, 122–23, 256, 337–38, 273, 280.

35. Ibid., pp. 337–38; Letter, Henry James to his family, November 1, 1875, in *Henry James Letters*, Leon Edel, ed., vol. 1, p. 484; James quoted in Leon Edel, *Henry James, The Conquest of London: 1870–1881* (New York, 1962), p. 279; James quoted in Leon Edel, *Henry James, The Master: 1901–1916* (New York, 1972), p. 504.

36. See Daniel J. Schneider, "The Divided Self in the Fiction of Henry James," *PMLA* 90 (May 1975): 449; *The Crystal Cage: Adventures of the Imagination in the Fiction of Henry James* (Lawrence, Kan., 1978), chaps. 4, 5.

37. James, *Autobiography*, pp. 460, 443.

38. For discussions of the emergence of a "new middle class" and of the role of the mass media, see Robert H. Wiebe, *The Search for Order, 1877–1920* (New York, 1967), chap. 5; Burton J. Bledstein, *The Culture of Professionalism* (New York, 1976), chaps. 2, 3; Magali Sarfatti Larson, *The Rise of Professionalism* (Berkeley, 1977); Pat Walker, ed., *Between Labor and Capital: The Professional-Managerial Class* (Boston, 1979); Raymond Williams, "Means of Communication as Means of Production," in *Problems in Materialism and Culture* (London, 1980), pp. 50–63.

39. James, *Autobiography*, p. 268.

40. Ibid., p. 455; James gave form to this alter ego in his short story "The Jolly Corner" of 1908.

41. James, *Art of Novel*, pp. 32–33.
42. Raymond Williams, *Keywords: A Vocabulary of Culture and Society* (New York, 1976), p. 197.
43. Henry James, *The Tragic Muse* (Harmondsworth, 1978), p. 82; all references to James's novels, with the exception of *The Sacred Fount*, are to Penguin softbound editions; these are readily available reprints of the original, unrevised editions of James's work.
44. Henry James, *The Portrait of a Lady* (Harmondsworth, 1963), pp. 191–92, 201–2.
45. On the Manichean dimension of James's novels, see Dorothea Krook, *The Ordeal of Consciousness in Henry James* (Cambridge, 1967) and Peter Brooks, *The Melodramatic Imagination* (New Haven, 1976), chap. 6.
46. James, *Portrait*, pp. 247, 431, 350, 392.
47. Henry James, *The Princess Casamassima* (Harmondsworth, 1977), p. 134; for an alternative view of James's consuming vision, see Mark Seltzer, "*The Princess Casamassima*: Realism and the Fantasy of Surveillance" in *American Realism: New Essays*, Eric J. Sundquist, ed. (Baltimore and London, 1982), pp. 95–118.
48. Schneider, *Crystal Cage*, p. 35.
49. The reciprocities among James's characters are systematically and admiringly traced in Donald L. Mull's *Henry James's 'Sublime Economy': Money as Symbolic Center in the Fiction* (Middletown, Conn., 1973).
50. Henry James, *The Aspern Papers and Other Stories* (New York, 1976), pp. 12, 79, 25, 39, 106.
51. Henry James, *The Sacred Fount* (New York, 1953), pp. 1, 149.
52. Ibid., pp. 136, 80, 29.
53. Ibid., pp. 177, 214, 199, 200.
54. Ibid., pp. 182–83, 156, 23, 313, 297.
55. James quoted in Leon Edel, "Introductory Essay" in ibid., p. xxx.
56. Henry James, *The Golden Bowl* (Harmondsworth, 1966), pp. 86, 47–48.
57. Ibid., pp. 35–36, 43.
58. Ibid., pp. 245–46.
59. Ibid., pp. 58–59.
60. Ibid., pp. 484, 153–54.
61. Laurence B. Holland, *The Expense of Vision: Essays on the Craft of Henry James* (Princeton, 1964), p. 391.
62. James, *Golden Bowl*, pp. 223, 160, 169, 173.
63. Ibid., pp. 436, 353, 439, 458.
64. Ibid., p. 541.
65. James, preface to *The Golden Bowl*, in *Art of Novel*, p. 329.
66. Seymour Chatman, *The Later Style of Henry James* (Oxford, 1972), p. 30.
67. Ibid., p. 22; Henry James, preface to *What Maisie Knew*, in *Art of Novel*, p. 146.
68. James, *Golden Bowl*, p. 459; Ruth Bernard Yeazell, *Language and Knowledge in the Late Novels of Henry James* (Chicago and London, 1976), p. 71.
69. Raymond Williams, *Television: Technology and Cultural Form* (New York, 1974), pp. 70–71.
70. James, preface to *What Maisie Knew*, in *Art of Novel*, p. 155.
71. Though James's view of the commutability of forms is scarcely as radical or as complete as that of many current novelists and their 'deconstructionist' critics, he does stand in a kindred relation with them, as Gerald Graff has observed; see *Literature Against Itself: Literary Ideas in Modern Society* (Chicago and London, 1979), pp. 53–54.
72. Erving Goffman, *Gender Advertisements* (New York, 1979), p. 84; Mary Douglas and Baron Isherwood, *The World of Goods* (New York, 1979), p. 62.

73. James, *Golden Bowl*, p. 547; I am indebted to Elizabeth Roderick for this reading of the scene.

IV
EPITAPH FOR MIDDLETOWN:
Robert S. Lynd and the Analysis of Consumer Culture

Note: This essay could not have been written without the aid of the late Helen Lynd and her son Staughton, to whom I express my gratitude. Special thanks also to Robert Westbrook, whose work on John Dewey and whose oral suggestions helped me formulate my ideas on Robert Lynd, and to Warren Susman, Jackson Lears, and Christopher Wilson for unusually fine readings of an earlier draft.

1. Stuart Ewen, *Captains of Consciousness* (New York, 1976). On the relationship between "class" and "professionalization," see Christopher Lasch, *Haven in a Heartless World* (New York, 1977), esp. chap. 1, and the essays in Pat Walker, ed., *Between Labor and Capital* (Boston, 1979).
2. Robert Lynd's typewritten memorandum, "Miscellaneous Items about Robert Lynd," March 9, 1954, Robert and Helen Lynd Papers, Library of Congress; Lynd's handwritten notes on Rev. S. W. Lynd, *Memoir of the Rev. William Staughton, D.D.* (Boston, 1834), Lynd Papers; Helen Merrell Lynd, *Possibilities* (Youngstown, Ohio, 1980), pp. 30, 32. Lynd's claim in the preface to *Middletown in Transition* (New York, 1937), p. xiii, that he was "reared during his first eighteen years" in New Albany is not literally true.
3. Helen Lynd, *Possibilities*, pp. 32–33; Lynd, "Crude-Oil Religion," *Harper's* 145 (September 1922): 427.
4. [Lynd], "—But Why Preach?," *Harper's* 143 (June 1921): 82–83.
5. Lynd, "Crude-Oil Religion," p. 425; "—But Why Preach?," pp. 83–84. His italics.
6. Lynd's official transcript, Union Theological Seminary, Registrar's Office. For more details on his experience at Union, see his handwritten memorandum, "Addenda, March, 1963," Lynd Papers.
7. Lynd, "Addenda, March, 1963."
8. Lynd to Edward S. Martin, May 1921, selections published in Martin, "Personal and Otherwise," *Harper's* 143 (August 1921): supp.[n.p.].
9. Lynd, "Crude-Oil Religion," pp. 427, 428–31, 434.
10. Lynd, "Done in Oil," *The Survey* 49 (November 1, 1922): 137–46, 175; John D. Rockefeller, Jr., "A Promise of Better Days," pp. 147–48; "16 Million Listen In," *Survey* 49 (December 1, 1922): 341. The widely circulated *Literary Digest* reprinted the Lynd-Rockefeller exchange in its November 11, 1922, number. "Crude-Oil Religion," anticipating *Middletown*, had used a fictional name, "Wolf Basin," to identify Elk Basin; "Done in Oil," in keeping with its muckraking "realism," used the true name.
11. Lynd, "Done in Oil," pp. 141, 138, 145–46, 140. Staughton Lynd notes in passing this stark contrast between the two articles in his "Robert S. Lynd: The Elk Basin Experience," *Journal of the History of Sociology* 2 (Fall–Winter 1979–1980): 19 [special issue on Robert S. Lynd].
12. Lynd, "Addenda, March, 1963"; Lynd's rebuttal to Rockefeller, *Survey* 49 (November 1, 1922): 148; Paul Kellogg's rebuttal, pp. 167–69. Raymond Fosdick makes general reference to the exchange in his *John D. Rockefeller, Jr., A Portrait* (New York, 1956), pp. 180–81.

225

13. Galen M. Fisher, *The Institute of Social and Religious Research* (New York, 1934) [pamphlet issued by the institute], copy in the John R. Mott Papers, Yale Divinity School; Fosdick, *John D. Rockefeller, Jr., A Portrait*, pp. 207–13. Edmund Brunner discusses the early work of the CSRS in "Sociological Significance of Recent Religious Surveys," *American Journal of Sociology* [hereafter *AJS*] 29 (November 1923): 325–37.

14. Committee on Social and Religious Surveys, "A Forecast for the Future, December 20, 1921," typewritten memorandum, carbon copy in John R. Mott Papers.

15. Galen M. Fisher, "History of the Small City Study," unpublished typescript, March 20, 1924, pp. 1–14, Private Archives of the Messieurs Rockefeller, Record Group 2, Religious Interests, Box 44 (hereafter cited as Rockefeller Papers), Rockefeller Center, New York City.

16. Lynd, "Crude-Oil Religion," pp. 434, 425; Lynd's handwritten memorandum, "Creed —R.S.L., 1922," Lynd Papers.

17. Lynd, "A Critique of Preaching from the Standpoint of Modern Educational Method," unpublished manuscript, pp. 1, 3, 9, Lynd Papers.

18. Lynd, "A Critique of Preaching," pp. 7–8.

19. Robert Lynd and Helen Lynd, *Middletown* (New York, 1929), p. xi. The ISRR files in the Rockefeller Papers contain correspondence and minutes on all aspects of the institute's work, including the Small City Study. The following account draws on a complete perusal of the files; it would be impractical to cite every item that has contributed to it.

20. On the history and types of social surveys, see Niles Carpenter, "Social Surveys," in E. R. A. Seligman, ed., *Encyclopedia of the Social Sciences* (New York, 1934), 14: 162–65, and Harriet M. Bartlett, "The Social Survey and the Charity Organization Movement," *AJS* 34 (September 1928): 330–41.

21. Fisher, "History of the Small City Study," pp. 15–17.

22. Lynd to Galen Fisher, April 7, 1924, carbon copy in Lynd Papers.

23. Fisher, "History of the Small City Study," pp. 17–19; Fisher to Raymond Fosdick, March 19, 1924, Rockefeller Papers; author's interview with Helen Lynd, February 5, 1980 [on her joining Robert in January 1924]; Lynd to Fisher, April 7, 1924; *14th Census of the United States*, 1920, vol. 3, *Population* (Washington, D.C., 1922), p. 297.

24. Lynd and Lynd, *Middletown*, p. 8; Helen Lynd, *Possibilities*, pp. 34–37; Faith Williams to Robert Lynd, May 20, 1926, Lynd Papers [on Max Mathews' stealing].

25. Minutes of staff conference, March 19, 1926; Lynd to Fosdick, June 16, 1926; Wissler to Lynd, June 7, 1926, Lynd Papers; Wissler to Fisher, July 7, 1926, carbon copy in Lynd Papers; Fisher to Fosdick, June 23, 1926, Rockefeller Papers. On the movement to bring "culture" to sociology, see Melville J. Herskovits and Malcolm M. Willey, "The Cultural Approach to Sociology," *AJS* 29 (September 1923): 188–99, Lawrence K. Frank, "Social Problems," *AJS* 30 (January 1925): 462–73, Clark Wissler, "The Culture-Area Concept in Social Anthropology," *AJS* 32 (May 1927): 881–91, and Clarence Marsh Case, "The Culture Concept in Social Science," *Journal of Applied Sociology* 8 (January–February 1924): 146–55.

26. Wesley Mitchell to Lynd, September 2, 1927; Fisher to Lynd, March 7, 1928, Lynd Papers; Helen Lynd, *Possibilities*, p. 40.

27. Lynd and Lynd, *Middletown*, p. 206. On the rise of functionalism in American sociology, see Robert Friedrichs, *A Sociology of Sociology* (New York, 1970), pp. 246–48.

28. Lynd and Lynd, *Middletown*, pp. 80–81, 434.

29. On the Chicago School, T. V. Smith and Leonard D. White, eds., *Chicago: An Experiment in Social Science Research* (Chicago, 1929), and Fred H. Matthews,

Quest for an American Sociology: Robert E. Park and the Chicago School (Montreal, 1977), esp. ch. 5.

30. Lynd and Lynd, *Middletown*, pp. 283, 502; Helen Lynd, *Possibilities*, p. 36.
31. Lynd and Lynd, *Middletown*, pp. 421–22, 343.
32. Ibid., pp. 87, 81–82, 45, 82 n. 18, 158.
33. Ibid., pp. 88–89.
34. Ibid., pp. 222, 196, 176.
35. H. L. Mencken, "A Treatise on the Americano," Baltimore *Evening Sun*, January 14, 1929, clipping in Lynd Papers; Prof. Henry M. Busch to Robert Lynd, March 15, 1929, Lynd Papers; John Dewey, "The House Divided Against Itself," *New Republic*, April 24, 1929, pp. 270–71. Mencken wrote a longer and even more viciously condescending attack on the "unbelievable stupidities" of Middletowners in "A City in Moronia," *American Mercury* 16 (March 1929): 379–81.
36. Robert Lynd to Alfred Harcourt, February 22, 1929; Lynd to Fosdick, June 16, 1926, carbon copies in Lynd Papers. On the Michigan and Columbia offers, Robert Lynd to Dallas W. Smythe, June 9, 1965, carbon copy in Lynd Papers. On cutting Helen's contribution out of the dissertation version, Helen Lynd, *Possibilities*, p. 38. I have been unable to locate a copy of the "dissertation" version of *Middletown* at Columbia University.
37. Wesley Mitchell, "The Backward Art of Spending Money," *American Economic Review* 2 (June 1912): 281; Lynd and Lynd, *Middletown*, p. 151.
38. Ibid., pp. 499, 48, 115 n. 9.
39. On John Dewey's democratic theory in the context of Anglo-American social thought, see Robert B. Westbrook, "John Dewey and American Democracy," unpublished Ph.D. dissertation, Department of History, Stanford University, 1980, a work that has greatly influenced my understanding of Robert Lynd.
40. "Lynd, Author of Middletown, Back in City After 10 Years," Muncie *Evening Press*, June 12, 1935, clipping in Lynd Papers. See also Lynd's notes for his address to Muncie's Rotary Club, and the *Evening Press* report on it (June 28, 1935), both in Lynd Papers. In this talk Lynd noted that someone in Muncie had charged he had reaped personal profit from turning Muncie into a laboratory. He denied any financial gain but granted that the book led directly to his professorship. "Any recognition" he had received, he told the Rotarians, was "just [the] fortunes of war."
41. Robert Lynd and Helen Lynd, *Middletown in Transition*, pp. xii, xv–xvi. George Dale, radical mayor of Muncie in the early thirties, was one of those who charged during the return visit (in the Muncie *Post-Democrat*, which he edited), that *Middletown* had "failed to find the heart of Muncie." Robert Lynd, notes for address to Rotary Club.
42. A convenient summary of the psychological surveys of American draftees is Robert H. Gault, "Recent Developments in Psychology Contributory to Social Explanation," in Charles A. Ellwood et al., eds., *Recent Developments in the Social Sciences* (New York, 1927), pp. 111–15. On Walter Lippmann as propagandist, see Ronald Steel, *Walter Lippmann and the American Century* (New York, 1980).
43. Robert Lynd, "The People as Consumers," in *Recent Social Trends in the United States: Report of the President's Research Committee on Social Trends* (New York, 1932), 2: 872, 868, 877, 866, 885. For further detail on Lynd's dealings with Ogburn, which call to mind his earlier dealings with Fisher and Fosdick, see Mark C. Smith, "Robert Lynd and Consumerism in the 1930s," *Journal of the History of Sociology* 2 (Fall–Winter, 1979–1980): 99–119. On the Research Committee itself, see Barry Karl's excellent analysis in "Presidential Planning and Social Science Research: Mr. Hoover's Experts," *Perspectives in American History* 3 (1969): 347–409.

44. Robert Lynd, "Introduction," *Annals of the American Academy of Political and Social Science* 173 (May 1934) [special issue on "The Ultimate Consumer"]: xi; Lynd, "Family Members as Consumers," *Annals* 160 (March 1932) [special issue on "The Modern American Family"]: 92. See also, in addition to "The People as Consumers," the following articles by Lynd: "Why the Consumer Wants Quality Standards," *Advertising and Selling* 22 (January 4, 1934): 15–16, 46–49; "The Consumer's Advisory Board in the N.R.A.," *Publishers' Weekly* 125 (April 28, 1934): 1607–8; "The Consumer Becomes a Problem," *Annals* 173 (May 1934): 1–6; "Democracy's Third Estate: The Consumer," *Political Science Quarterly* 51 (December 1936): 481–515.

45. Robert MacIver memorandum, November 10, 1930, quoted in Lynd obituary in *Political Science Quarterly* 86 (Summer 1971): 556; *The Reminiscences of Paul Lazarsfeld*, Columbia University, Oral History Research Office, 1973, pp. 35, 324. On the projected Manhattan study, see Lynd's prospectus "A Study of the Impact of the Depression on Family Organization and Function" (5 pp.), n.d., and his "Memorandum on the Study of Changing Family Patterns in the Depression" (6 pp.), March 14, 1933, both in Lynd Papers. On the Montclair study, *Reminiscences of Paul Lazarsfeld*, pp. 20, 321, and sample survey schedules in Lynd Papers. As late as 1945 Lynd was still making an effort to get the Montclair study off the ground. Eva Hofberg [research assistant] to Robert Lynd, Memorandum No. 1, May 28, 1945, Lynd Papers.

46. "The New Deal and the Consumer," transcript of N.B.C. radio debate, n.d., p. 8, copy in Robert S. Lynd Collection, Columbia University Library, manuscript room. This collection contains several folders of material on the C.A.B. For Robert Lynd's retrospective view of the C.A.B., see his foreword to Persia Campbell, *Consumer Representation in the New Deal* (New York, 1940), pp. 9–13.

47. Lynd, "Democracy's Third Estate: The Consumer," pp. 487–88.

48. Lynd reported that "the Middletown study of 1935–36 interrupted [his] detailed analysis" of family problems during the Depression. *Middletown in Transition*, p. 179, n. 59. On Harcourt's suggestion of a third study, author's interview with Helen Lynd, February 5, 1980.

49. Lynd and Lynd, *Middletown in Transition*, pp. 110 n. 16, 77, 86, 79, 97, 92. On Robert's admission regarding the Balls, author's interview with Helen Lynd.

50. Lynd and Lynd, *Middletown in Transition*, pp. 367, 449, 490, 471, 475, 387, 509–10.

51. Ibid., pp. 136, 369, 125. Lynds' italics.

52. Ibid., p. 46. Among the critiques of the second volume are: Theodore Caplow, "Middletown Fifty Years After," *Contemporary Sociology* 9 (January 1980): 46–50; Nelson W. Polsby, "Power in Middletown: Fact and Value in Community Research," *Canadian Journal of Economic and Political Science* 26 (November 1960): 592–603; Carrolyle M. Frank, "Who Governed Middletown? Community Power in Muncie, Indiana, in the 1930s," *Indiana Magazine of History* 75 (December 1979): 321–42 [special issue on *Middletown* and the Lynds].

53. Robert Lynd, review of Thurman Arnold, *The Folklore of Capitalism*, *Science and Society* 2 (Summer 1938): 401, 400.

54. "Dr. Lynd Completes Series of Lectures on Social Sciences," *The Daily Princetonian*, March 25, 1938, clipping in Lynd Papers; Lynd and Lynd, *Middletown in Transition*, pp. 509–510.

55. Robert Lynd, "Trip of Robert and Helen Lynd to Soviet Union in '38," typewritten memorandum, March 9, 1954, Lynd Papers.

56. Robert Lynd, *Knowledge for What?* (Princeton, 1939), p. 166. Among the most important reviews, each of which overlooked the "outrageous hypotheses," were: Max Lerner, "The Revolt Against Quietism," *New Republic*, July 5, 1939, pp. 257–58; Alexander Goldenweiser, *American Anthropologist* 42 (1940): 164–66; George A.

Lundberg, *American Journal of Sociology* 45 (September 1939): 270–74; Robert MacIver, "Enduring Systems of Thought," *Survey Graphic* 28 (August 1939): 496–97 [with a rejoinder by Lynd, "Intelligence Must Fight," pp. 498–99]. (MacIver mentions the exchange in his autobiography *As a Tale that is Told* (Chicago, 1968), pp. 137–38.) One of the few who was outraged by the hypotheses was Crane Brinton, "What's the Matter with Sociology?," *Saturday Review*, May 6, 1939, pp. 3–4, 14. David Riesman was another who expressed his misgivings about Lynd's "Rousseauistic touch"—his "implication that human cravings are fundamentally decent and that a system of control will not necessarily be abused." David Riesman to Robert Lynd, October 28, 1939, Lynd Papers.

57. Robert Lynd, *Knowledge for What?*, pp. 228–31.

58. Lynd, *Knowledge for What?*, pp. 212 n. 4, 86–87, 106 n. 50, 231, 235.

59. On Lynd's feeling of intimidation and inadequacy, see his correspondence with Paul Lazarsfeld and Robert K. Merton, 1940s and 1950s, Lynd Papers, and *Reminiscences of Paul Lazarsfeld*.

60. Robert Lynd to Harry F. Ward, January 25, 1940, Ward Papers, Union Theological Seminary; Robert Lynd, "Miscellaneous Items about Robert S. Lynd," March 9, 1954, Lynd Papers.

V

POLITICS AS CONSUMPTION:
Managing the Modern American Election

Note: I would like to thank my fellow contributors to this volume for their valuable counsel, particularly Jean-Christophe Agnew, who has, as always, made generous loans from his wealth of insight into the culture of market society. Thanks also to Michael McGerr, who permitted me to draw on his masterful knowledge of nineteenth-century American politics, and to Shamra Westbrook for thoughtful criticism and much else besides.

1. Edward Bernays, *Propaganda* (New York, 1928), pp. 94–96.

2. Abigail McCarthy, "Why We Stay Home: Authenticity and the Vote," *Commonweal*, January 16, 1981, p. 8.

3. Raymond Williams, *Television: Technology and Cultural Form* (New York, 1974), pp. 70–71; Georg Lukács, *History and Class Consciousness* (Cambridge, Mass., 1971), p. 84.

4. Christopher Lasch, "Democracy and the 'Crisis of Confidence,'" *Democracy* 1 (January 1981): 29–30.

5. Walter Dean Burnham, "The Changing Shape of the American Political Universe," *American Political Science Review* 59 (1965): 10, 22, and "The United States: The Politics of Heterogeneity" in Richard Rose, ed., *Electoral Behavior: A Comparative Handbook* (New York, 1974), p. 677; Robert D. Marcus, *Grand Old Party: Political Structure in the Gilded Age* (New York, 1971), pp. 5–15.

6. Richard Jensen, "Armies, Admen, and Crusaders: Types of Presidential Election Campaigns," *History Teacher* 2 (1969): 34–37; Michael E. McGerr, "Political Spectacle and Partisanship in New Haven, 1860–1900," paper delivered at the Annual Meeting of the Organization of American Historians, 1982; Marcus, *Grand Old Party*, pp. 13, 138–45.

7. Burnham, "Party Systems and the Political Process," in William H. Chambers and Walter D. Burnham, eds., *The American Party Systems*, 2nd ed., (New York, 1975), p. 300; E. E. Schattschneider, *The Semisovereign People* (New York, 1960), p. 85;

J. Morgan Kousser, *The Shaping of Southern Politics: Suffrage Restriction and the Establishment of the One-Party South, 1880–1910* (New Haven, 1974).

8. Burnham, *Critical Elections and the Mainsprings of American Politics* (New York, 1970), pp. 74–76; V. O. Key, Jr., "The Direct Primary and the Party Structure," *American Political Science Review* 48 (1954): 1–26; Samuel P. Hays, "The Politics of Reform in Municipal Government in the Progressive Era," *Pacific Northwest Quarterly* 55 (1964): 152–69; Richard L. McCormick, "The Discovery that Business Corrupts Politics: A Reappraisal of the Origins of Progressivism, *American Historical Review* 86 (1981): 247–74, and *From Realignment to Reform: Political Change in New York State, 1893–1910* (Ithaca, N.Y., 1981); Stephen Skowronek, *Building a New American State* (New York, 1982).

9. Samuel Hays, "Political Parties and the Community-Society Continuum" in Chambers and Burnham, eds., *American Party Systems*, pp. 152–81; Theodore Lowi, "Party, Policy, and Constitution in America" in ibid., p. 276; Richard L. McCormick, "The Party Period and Public Policy: An Exploratory Hypothesis," *Journal of American History* 66 (1979): 279–98. On the decay of the entertainment functions of partisan culture see Lary May, *Screening Out the Past: The Birth of Mass Culture and the Motion Picture Industry* (New York, 1980), and on the emergence of "objectivity" in mass journalism see Michael Schudson, *Discovering the News* (New York, 1978).

10. Kristi Andersen, *The Creation of a Democratic Majority, 1928–1936* (Chicago, 1979); Burnham, "Party Systems and the Political Process," pp. 302–4; Schattschneider, *Semisovereign People*, pp. 85–96; Burnham, "Changing Shape," pp. 10–12; Norman H. Nie et al., *The Changing American Voter* (Cambridge, Mass., 1976), p. 84.

11. Nie et al., *Changing American Voter*, pp. 47–73; Everett C. Ladd, "The Brittle Mandate: Electoral Dealignment and the 1980 Presidential Election," *Political Science Quarterly* 96 (1981): 4.

12. Ladd, "Brittle Mandate," pp. 3, 11–20; Nie et al., *Changing American Voter*, pp. 346–52; James D. Wright, *The Dissent of the Governed: Alienation and Democracy in America* (New York, 1976), pp. 168–200; Richard A. Brody, "The Puzzle of Political Participation in America" in Anthony King, ed., *The New American Political System* (Washington, D.C., 1978), pp. 303–6.

13. Gerald M. Pomper, "The Decline of the Party in American Elections," *Political Science Quarterly* 92 (1977): 25–27; Robert Agranoff, "The New Style of Campaigning" in Agranoff, ed., *The New Style in Election Campaigns* (Boston, 1976), pp. 10–19; Thomas E. Patterson, *The Mass Media Election* (New York, 1980), p. 4.

14. Burnham, "Changing Shape," p. 24.

15. Lawrence Goodwyn, *Democratic Promise* (New York, 1976), p. iii.

16. Jensen, "Armies, Admen, and Crusaders," p. 43; McGerr, "Political Spectacle."

17. See David Lawrence's appeal to his troops in 1936, quoted in Bruce Stave, *The New Deal and the Last Hurrah* (Pittsburgh, 1970), p. 9.

18. Jensen, *The Winning of the Midwest* (Chicago, 1971), pp. 164–77 and "Armies, Admen, and Crusaders," pp. 39–42.

19. Stanley Kelly, Jr., *Professional Public Relations and Political Power* (Baltimore, 1956), pp. 13–14, 30–35; Alan R. Raucher, *Public Relations and Business, 1900–1929* (Baltimore, 1968), pp. 15–19; Charles Michelson, *The Ghost Talks* (New York, 1944); Ralph D. Casey, "Republican Propaganda in the 1936 Campaign," *Public Opinion Quarterly* 1 (1937): 27–45; C. A. H. Thompson, "Research and the Republican Party," ibid. 3 (1939): 306–13; Pendleton Herring, *The Politics of Democracy* (New York, 1940), p. 259.

20. V. O. Key, Jr. and Winston W. Crouch, *The Initiative and Referendum in California* (Berkeley, 1939); Dean E. McHenry, "The Pattern of California Politics," *Western*

Political Quarterly 1 (1948): 44–53; Clem Whittaker, "The Public Relations of Election Campaigns," *Public Relations Journal* 2 (July 1946): 7–10.

21. Whittaker, "Public Relations of Election Campaigns," pp. 8–9; Kelley, *Professional Public Relations*, pp. 39–66; Carey McWilliams, "Government by Whittaker and Baxter," *Nation* 172 (April 14, April 21, and May 5, 1951); Robert J. Pitchell, "The Influence of Professional Campaign Management Firms in Partisan Elections in California," *Western Political Quarterly* 11 (1958): 278–300.

22. Vance Packard, *The Hidden Persuaders* (New York, 1957), pp. 160–61, 166; Kelley, *Professional Public Relations*, p. 2.

23. Kelley, *Professional Public Relations*, p. 161; "Admen Analyze the Campaign Strategy," *Tide*, November 7, 1952, p. 15.

24. Kelley, *Professional Public Relations*, p. 159.

25. Kelley, *Professional Public Relations*, p. 90n; Packard, *Hidden Persuaders*, pp. 170–72; Melvyn H. Bloom, *Public Relations and Presidential Campaigns* (New York, 1973), p. 71.

26. James Perry, *The New Politics* (New York, 1968), pp. 107–38.

27. Walter Troy Spencer, "The Agency Knack of Political Packaging," in Agranoff, *New Style*, p. 96.

28. David L. Rosenbloom, *The Election Men* (New York, 1973), pp. 50–53; Agranoff, "New Style of Campaigning," p. 25.

29. Larry J. Sabato, *The Rise of Political Consultants* (New York, 1981), pp. 24–34.

30. Ibid., p. 20; Sidney Blumenthal, *The Permanent Campaign* (Boston, 1980), p. 81.

31. William Livant, "The Audience Commodity: On the 'Blindspot' Debate," *Canadian Journal of Political and Social Theory* 3 (1979): 92. Livant's article is a comment on Dallas Smythe's important essay on the audience commodity, "Communications: Blindspot of Western Marxism," ibid. 1 (1977): 1–27.

32. Smythe, "Communications," pp. 2–6. Christopher Wilson's essay in this volume is an important contribution to the history of the audience commodity.

33. Alasdair MacIntyre, *After Virtue* (Notre Dame, Ind., 1981), p. 82.

34. Ibid., p. 102.

35. On technocratic progressivism see Richard Fox's essay on Lynd in this book and my "Tribune of the Technostructure: The Popular Economics of Stuart Chase," *American Quarterly* 32 (1980): 387–408. On Dewey's efforts to envision a democratic social engineering see my "John Dewey and American Democracy" (Ph.D. diss., Stanford, 1980), pp. 180–211.

36. Todd Gitlin, "Mass Media Sociology: The Dominant Paradigm," *Theory and Society* 6 (1978): 226.

37. Useful surveys of research on attitudes are Gordon W. Allport, "Attitudes" in C. A. Murchison, ed., *Handbook of Social Psychology* (Worcester, Mass., 1935), pp. 798–814; Milton Rokeach, "Attitudes: Change" in *International Encyclopedia of the Social Sciences* (New York, 1968), 1: 449–67; and Forrest P. Chisman, *Attitude Psychology and the Study of Public Opinion* (University Park, Pa., 1976), pp. 23–58.

38. Donald Fleming, "Attitude: The History of a Concept," *Perspectives in American History* 1 (1967): 359.

39. Ibid., 329, 339–47, 360–61. See also L. L. Thurstone, "Attitudes Can Be Measured," *American Journal of Sociology* 23 (1928): 539–44.

40. See George Gallup, *The Pulse of Democracy* (New York, 1940); Allen H. Barton, "Paul Lazarsfeld and Applied Social Research," *Social Science History* 3 (1979): 4–44; and *Institute for Social Research, 1946–1956* (Ann Arbor, Mich., n.d.).

41. Seymour M. Lipset et al., "The Psychology of Voting" in Gardner Lindsey, ed., *Handbook of Social Psychology* (Cambridge, Mass., 1954), 2: 1124–25. See also

Bernard Berelson, Paul F. Lazarsfeld, and William N. McPhee, *Voting* (Chicago, 1954), chap. 13. An excellent critique of this assumption is Walter Berns, "Voting Studies" in Herbert J. Storing, ed., *Essays on the Scientific Study of Politics* (New York, 1962.)

42. On Lazarsfeld's career and his relationship with corporate clients see Lazarsfeld, "An Episode in the History of Social Research: A Memoir" in Donald Fleming and Bernard Bailyn, eds., *The Intellectual Migration: Europe and America, 1930–1960* (Cambridge, Mass., 1969), pp. 338–70; Mark Abrams, "Social Research and Market Research: The Case of Paul Lazarsfeld," *Journal of the Market Research Society* 19 (1977): 12–17; David Morrison, "The Beginnings of Modern Mass Communications Research," *Archives européennes de sociologie* 19 (1978): 347–59. The best critical examination of Lazarsfeld's career is Gitlin, "Media Sociology."

43. Arthur Kornhauser and Paul F. Lazarsfeld, "The Analysis of Consumer Actions" in Lazarsfeld and Morris S. Rosenberg, eds., *The Language of Social Research* (New York, 1955), pp. 393, 395. This essay was originally published in *Institute of Management* (1935), a publication of the American Management Association. See also "The Psychological Aspect of Market Research," *Harvard Business Review* 13 (1934): 54–71, and "The Art of Asking Why," *National Marketing Review* 1 (1935): 32–43.

44. John C. Maloney, "Advertising and an Emerging Science of Mass Persuasion," *Journalism Quarterly* 41 (1964): 520. On the failure of social science to deliver a theory for effective consumer management see Charles Y. Glock and Francesco M. Nicosia, "The Consumer" in Paul F. Lazarsfeld et al., *The Uses of Sociology* (New York, 1967), pp. 359–90.

45. Paul F. Lazarsfeld, Bernard Berelson, and Hazel Gaudet, *The People's Choice*, 2nd ed. (New York, 1948); Peter Rossi, "Four Landmarks in Voting Research" in Eugene Burdick and Arthur J. Brodbeck, eds., *American Voting Behavior* (Glencoe, Ill., 1959), pp. 15–16.

46. Committee on Political Parties of the American Political Science Association, *Toward a More Responsible Two-Party System* (New York, 1950), p. 31; Packard, *Hidden Persuaders*, p. 161.

47. On the "law of minimal effects" see Joseph T. Klapper, *The Effects of Mass Communication* (New York, 1960); Maxwell E. McCombs, "Mass Communication in Political Campaigns: Information, Gratification, and Persuasion" in F. Gerald Kline and Philip J. Tichner, eds., *Current Perspectives in Mass Communications Research* (Beverly Hills, Calif., 1972), pp. 169–94; L. John Martin, "Recent Theory on Mass Media Potential in Political Campaigns," *Annals* 427 (1976): 125–33; and Dan Nimmo, *The Political Persuaders* (Englewood Cliffs, N.J., 1970), pp. 163–93.

48. Thomas E. Patterson and Robert D. McClure, *The Unseeing Eye* (New York, 1976), p. 154.

49. Sabato, *Rise of Political Consultants*, p. 17.

50. "Voter Perspectives" advertisement in David Rosenbloom, ed., *The Political Marketplace* (New York, 1972), p. 863.

51. Sabato, *Rise of Political Consultants*, p. 75; Richard J. Meislin, "Niagara Voters Given a Choice by Computer," *New York Times*, October 30, 1980.

52. Sabato, *Rise of Political Consultants*, pp. 75–77; Michael Rowan, "Candidates Aren't Packaged—You Are!" *Politeia* 1 (Autumn 1971): 7; Stephen Kline and William Leiss, "Advertising, Needs, and 'Commodity Fetishism,'" *Canadian Journal of Political and Social Theory* 2 (1978): 18.

53. Joseph Napolitan, *The Election Game and How to Win It* (Garden City, N.Y., 1972), p. 7.

54. Jay Weitzner, "Handling the Candidate on Television" in Ray Hiebert et al., *The Political Image Merchants* (Washington, D.C. 1971), pp. 104–5.

55. Kline and Leiss, "Advertising," p. 18.
56. Sabato, *Rise of Political Consultants*, p. 145; Joe McGinniss, *Selling of the President* (New York, 1969); Nimmo, *Political Persuaders*, pp. 46–47.
57. Sabato, *Rise of Political Consultants*, p. 163.
58. Benjamin I. Page, *Choices and Echoes in Presidential Elections: Rational Man and Electoral Democracy* (Chicago, 1978), pp. 152–53; Garry Wills, *Confessions of a Conservative* (New York, 1979), p. 88.
59. Sabato, *Rise of Political Consultants*, p. 146; Kline and Leiss, "Advertising," pp. 19–20.
60. Sabato, *Rise of Political Consultants*, p. 123; Arnold Fochs, ed., *Advertising that Won Elections* (Duluth, Minn., 1974), p. 32.
61. Roland Barthes, *Mythologies* (New York, 1972), pp. 92–93.
62. Sabato, *Rise of Political Consultants*, p. 173.
63. On "pseudo-events" see Daniel Boorstin, *The Image* (New York, 1961).
64. Ray Price, "Memorandum" in McGinniss, *Selling of the President*, p. 192.
65. John D'Arc Lorenz, "Probing for Political Attitudes" in Hiebert, *Political Image Merchants*, p. 129.
66. Staffan Linder, *The Harried Leisure Class* (New York, 1970), pp. 59, 70–71; William Leiss, *The Limits to Satisfaction* (Toronto, 1976), p. 15.
67. See Samuel Popkin, John W. Gorman, Charles Phillips, and Jeffery A. Smith, "What Have You Done for Me Lately?: Toward an Investment Theory of Voting," *American Political Science Review* 70 (1976): 779–805.
68. Robert Merton, *Mass Persuasion* (New York, 1946), pp. 142–43.
69. *New York Times*, November 4, 1980; "Talk of the Town," *New Yorker*, October 6, 1980, 48; Wright, *Dissent of the Governed*.
70. Alexis de Tocqueville, *Democracy in America* (Garden City, N.Y., 1969), p. 511. On Van Buren and the role of parties in a republican democracy see Wilson Carey McWilliams, "Parties as Civil Associations" in Gerald M. Pomper, ed., *Party Renewal in America* (New York, 1980), pp. 51–68, and Josiah L. Auspitz, "A 'Republican' View of Both Parties," *The Public Interest* 67 (1982): 94–117.

VI
SELLING THE MOON:
The U.S. Manned Space Program and the Triumph of Commodity Scientism

1. Columbia Broadcasting System, *Apollo 11: Eagle Landing, July 20, 1969 (Part I)*, videotape, Museum of Broadcasting, New York; Guy Debord, *La Société du spectacle* (Paris, 1968). I am particularly indebted to the Museum of Broadcasting, the NASA History Office (Washington, D.C.), and Prof. Alex Roland (History Department, Duke University) for their assistance in my research.
2. All professions listed under both categories fall within the purview of what some scholars have called the "Professional-Managerial Class" (see Barbara and John Ehrenreich, "The Professional-Managerial Class," in Pat Walker, ed., *Between Labor and Capital* [Boston, 1979], pp. 5–45). Yet support for the manned space program split the PMC into those who perceived their interests to be aligned with the military-industrial complex and those who did not. This division suggests an important postwar dynamic obscured by the notion of a unified PMC.
3. John Noble Wilford, *We Reach the Moon* (New York, 1969), p. 14.
4. Herbert Marcuse, *One-Dimensional Man* (Boston, 1964), p. 32.
5. Lewis Mumford, quoted in "Prize—or Lunacy?" *Newsweek*, July 7, 1969, pp. 60–61.

6. William Goetzmann, *Exploration and Empire: The Explorer and the Scientist in the Winning of the American West* (New York, 1966), pp. xii–xiv, passim; A. Hunter Dupree, *Science in the Federal Government: A History of Policies and Activities to 1940* (Cambridge, 1957), pp. 91–114, 195–214.

7. William Dean Howells, "A Sennight of the Centennial," *Atlantic* 38 (July 1876): 96; cited in John F. Kasson, *Civilizing the Machine: Technology and Republican Values in America, 1776–1900* (New York, 1977), p. 165.

8. *Going to the Fair: A Preview of the New York World's Fair 1939* (New York, 1939), p. 10.

9. Warren Susman, "The People's Fair: Cultural Contradictions of a Consumer Society," in *Dawn of a New Day: The New York World's Fair, 1939/40* (New York, Queens Museum exhibition catalog, 1980), p. 27.

10. Raymond Loewy, cited in Jeffrey L. Meikle, *Twentieth Century Limited: Industrial Design in America, 1925–1939* (Philadelphia, 1979), p. 197.

11. Raymond Williams, "Advertising: The Magic System," in *Problems in Materialism and Culture: Selected Essays* (New York, 1981), p. 185.

12. Erving Goffman, *Gender Advertisements* (New York, 1976), p. 27.

13. John William Ward, "The Meaning of Lindbergh's Flight," *American Quarterly* 10 (Spring 1958): 3–16. See Norbert Wiener's formulation of *Cybernetics* (Cambridge, Massachusetts, 1948) (from the Greek "kubernetes": steersman, helmsman) as a way of examining the relation of man, machines, and control in the postwar world.

14. Sara Evans, *Personal Politics: The Roots of Women's Liberation in the Civil Rights Movement and the New Left* (New York, 1980), pp. 12n–13n. For a detailed consideration of gender display in advertising, see Goffman, *Gender Advertisements*.

15. Robert Glatzer, *The New Advertising: The Great Campaigns from Avis to Volkswagen* (New York, 1970), pp. 123, 124, 131–32, 134; Vance Packard, *The Hidden Persuaders* (New York, 1957), p. 96.

16. Martin Mayer, *Madison Avenue, USA* (New York, 1958), p. 117; Jane Stern and Michael Stern, *Auto Ads* (New York, 1978), pp. 88–89.

17. *Life*, November 24, 1958, p. 103.

18. *Time*, October 6, 1958, p. 5.

19. John Morton Blum, "The Selling of the War," chapter 1 of *V Was for Victory* (New York, 1976).

20. Winston Churchill, quoted in Godfrey Hodgson, *America in Our Time: From World War II to Nixon—What Happened and Why* (New York, 1976), p. 18.

21. Martin J. Sherwin, *A World Destroyed: The Atomic Bomb and the Grand Alliance* (New York, 1977), p. 228 (emphasis mine).

22. Ibid., pp. 202, 212 (emphasis his).

23. David Riesman, with Nathan Glazer and Reuel Denney, *The Lonely Crowd: A Study of the Changing American Character* (New Haven, 1950).

24. William Leiss, *The Limits to Satisfaction: An Essay on the Problem of Needs and Commodities* (Toronto, 1976), p. 10; Christopher Lasch, *The Culture of Narcissism* (New York, 1979), p. 72.

25. James Fallows, *National Defense* (New York, 1981), pp. 57, 62–69, 75. On the "doctrine of credibility" in the Nixon White House, and its link with nuclear deterrence, see Jonathan Schell, *The Time of Illusion: An Historical and Reflective Account of the Nixon Era* (New York, 1976), pp. 9–10, 133, passim.

26. Richard J. Barnet, *Real Security: Restoring American Power in a Dangerous Decade* (New York, 1981), p. 39.

27. James Grimwood, *This New Ocean* (Washington, 1964), p. 28.

28. Ken Hechler, *Toward the Endless Frontier: History of the Committee on Science and Technology, 1959–1979* (Washington, 1980), p. 5.

29. Lyndon Johnson, quoted in "Orderly Formula," *Time*, October 28, 1957, p. 17.

30. On the "technological astrology" surrounding U.S. response to Sputnik, see Tom Wolfe, *The Right Stuff* (New York, 1979), p. 71.

31. Quoted in John W. Jeffries, "The 'Quest for National Purpose' of 1960," *American Quarterly* 30 (Fall 1978): 454, 455; Rockefeller Brothers Fund, *Prospect for America: The Rockefeller Panel Reports* (New York, 1961), p. 387; Jeffries, pp. 457, 459.

32. President's Science Advisory Committee, "Introduction to Outer Space," *Congressional Quarterly Weekly Review* 16 (January–June 1958): 421.

33. "Introduction to Outer Space," pp. 421–23 (emphasis mine).

34. Roger Caillois, *Man, Play, and Games* (New York, 1961), pp. 11–35.

35. "The number of scientists and engineers on NASA contract work nearly doubled from 1963 to 1964—from 34,000 to 62,000," Senator J. W. Fulbright reminded the Senate in 1964. This meant that "from 60 to 70 percent of the nation's 90,000 engineers are tied directly or indirectly to defense and space work" (Fulbright, "Remarks before the Senate," June 24, 1964, *Congressional Record*, 88th Congress, 2nd Session, pp. 14367–69).

36. Quoted in "Orderly Formula," p. 17.

37. *Hearings before the Select Committee on Astronautics and Space Exploration, House of Representatives, on H.R. 11881, 85th Congress, 2nd Session, April–May 1958* (Washington, 1958). p. 2.

38. Ibid., pp. 39, 38.

39. Ibid., pp. 775–77.

40. *The National Space Program: Report of the Select Committee on Astronautics and Space Exploration* (Washington, 1958), p. 3.

41. Hechler, *Toward the Endless Frontier*, p. 11; National Space Program, p. 4. For Dryden's elaboration on this remark during the April 27, 1958, broadcast of CBS television's *Face the Nation*, see *National Space Program*, pp. 950–51.

42. Cited in John M. Logsdon, *The Decision to Go to the Moon: Project Apollo and the National Interest* (Cambridge, 1970), pp. 25–26.

43. Wilford, *We Reach the Moon*, pp. 8, 10–11.

44. "The Sixties: The Decade of Man in Space," *Newsweek*, December 14, 1959, p. 34.

45. Edwin Diamond, "The Dawn," *Newsweek*, July 11, 1960, p. 55; Carl Dreher, "Hell-bent for the Moon," *The Nation*, September 16, 1961, pp. 151–52.

46. M. Scott Carpenter et al., *We Seven* (New York, 1962), pp. 62, 58. Contents originally appeared as articles in *Life*.

47. "Here Are the U.S. Spacemen—Married, Mature, Fathers," *U.S. News and World Report*, April 20, 1959, pp. 112–13; "How Seven Were Chosen," *Newsweek*, April 20, 1959, p. 64.

48. "Freedom's Flight," *Time*, May 12, 1961, p. 56; Loudon Wainwright, "The Chosen Three for the First Space Ride," *Life*, March 3, 1961, p. 30; Carpenter et al., *We Seven*, pp. 174, 182.

49. "Freedom's Flight," p. 58; "Shepard and the U.S.A. Feel 'AOK,' " *Life*, May 12, 1961, p. 18; Felix Morley, "Saving the Nation Means Saving Traditions," *Nation's Business* 49 (June 1961): 28.

50. Wolfe, *The Right Stuff*, pp. 74–78, 83–84.

51. "The New Ocean," *Time*, March 2, 1962, p. 16; Carpenter et al., *We Seven*, p. 29; Wainwright, "The Chosen Three," p. 26.

52. "The New Ocean," p. 18; Raymond Moley, "What's Back of a Hero?" *Newsweek*, April 9, 1962, p. 116; "The New Ocean," pp. 14–15; L. C. McHugh, "Glenn and the New Breed," *America*, March 17, 1962, p. 791.

53. Robert Hotz, "Man in Space," *Aviation Week*, March 5, 1962, p. 13; "Cooperation in Space," *New Republic*, March 5, 1962, p. 3; "The New Ocean," p. 11.

54. Don Kirkman, "Moon Astros Were All Test Pilots," Washington *Daily News*, July 7, 1969; "Apollo 11's Team: The Three Who Will Carry the Flag," *U.S. News and*

World Report, July 21, 1969, p. 33; Gene Farmer, "Buzz Aldrin Has 'The Best Scientific Mind We Have Sent into Space,' " *Life*, July 4, 1969, p. 22; "NASA Biographical Data," *NASA News*, June 2, 1969.

55. "Today's Astronauts: New Breed of Cosmic Explorer," *U.S. News and World Report*, July 21, 1969, p. 34.
56. "The Saturn and the Santa Maria," editorial, Chicago *Tribune*, July 18, 1969.
57. Anthony Sampson, *The Arms Bazaar: From Lebanon to Lockheed* (New York, 1978), pp. 235, 4.
58. National Aeronautics and Space Administration, *Press Kit: Apollo Lunar Landing Mission*, (Washington, 1969), pp. 93, 30, 33, 42, 48, 53, 57, 64, 65. See also Michael Collins, *Carrying the Fire: An Astronaut's Journey*, (New York, 1975), p. 425.
59. "Apollo 11 Crew Pre-Mission Press Conference, 7/5/69, 2:00 p.m.," *Apollo 11: Press Briefings and Conferences*, vol. 1, bound transcripts, NASA Historical Office, Washington, D.C.
60. Loudon Wainwright, "Apollo's Great Leap for the Moon," *Life*, July 25, 1969, p. 18D.
61. *Time*, October 6, 1958, pp. 48–49; *Newsweek*, August 4, 1969, p. E1.
62. "Has U.S. Settled for No. 2 in Space?" *U.S. News and World Report*, October 14, 1968, pp. 74–75.
63. "A U.S. Flag on the Moon," *U.S. News and World Report*, July 21, 1969, p. 29; "How U.S. Beat the Russians to the Moon," *U.S. News and World Report*, July 14, 1969, p. 32; "Apollo's Moon Mission: Here Are the Results," *U.S. News and World Report*, August 4, 1969, pp. 24–27; "How Useful Is the Moon? A Practical Answer," *U.S. News and World Report*, July 28, 1969, pp. 24–25 (emphasis mine).
64. "Flat-Earth Liberals," *National Review*, July 29, 1969, pp. 737–38; William F. Buckley, "Moon Thoughts," *National Review*, August 12, 1969, p. 819; Carey McWilliams, "What Price Moondust?" *The Nation*, July 28, 1969, pp. 66–67.
65. "The Moon and Middle America," *Time*, August 1, 1969, p. 11; Peter Collier, "Apollo 11: The Time Machine," *Ramparts* 8 (October 1969): 56–58.
66. Isaac Asimov, "The Moon Could Answer the Riddle of Life," *New York Times Magazine*, July 13, 1969, pp. 24–27.
67. Louis J. Halle, "Why I'm for Space Exploration," *The New Republic*, April 6, 1968, pp. 12–14.
68. "Giant Leap for Mankind?" *Ebony* 24 (Sptember 1969): 58; Kurt Vonnegut, "Excelsior! We're Going to the Moon! Excelsior," *New York Times Magazine*, July 13, 1969, pp. 9–11 (emphasis his).
69. Anthony Lewis, "Heroic Materialism Is Not Enough," *New York Times*, July 20, 1969, p. E-12.
70. Reprinted in Robert Atwan, Donald McQuade, and John L. Wright, *Edsels, Luckies, and Frigidaires: The American Way of Advertising* (New York, 1979), p. 323.
71. *New York Times*, January 28, 1979, p. 42.
72. Plato, *Republic*, book VII, in Edith Hamilton and Huntington Cairns, eds., *The Collected Dialogues of Plato* (Princeton, 1963), pp. 747–48.

ABOUT
THE AUTHORS

Jean-Christophe Agnew holds a Ph.D. from Harvard University and has taught at Harvard, Boston College, and the College of the Holy Cross in Worcester, Massachusetts. He is currently an assistant professor of American studies and history at Yale, and a member of the editorial collective of the *Radical History Review*.

Richard Wightman Fox was educated at Stanford University. He served as assistant professor of history and American studies at Yale University and is currently associate professor of history and humanities at Reed College. He is the author of *So Far Disordered in Mind: Insanity in California, 1870–1930* (University of California Press, 1978) and has contributed articles to numerous periodicals.

T. J. Jackson Lears received his Ph.D. in American studies from Yale University. He has taught at Yale and at the University of Missouri. His first book, *No Place of Grace: Antimodernism and the Transformation of American Culture, 1880–1920* (Pantheon, 1981) was nominated for a National Book Critics Circle Award. Presently a Fellow at the Woodrow Wilson International Center for Scholars, he is at work on a history of American advertising.

Michael L. Smith holds a Ph.D. in American studies from Yale University. He has taught history and American studies at Yale and is currently an assistant professor of history at Williams College. His publications have appeared in *The Nation* and the *Chronicle of Higher Education*.

Robert Westbrook received his Ph.D. from Stanford University and is currently assistant professor of American studies and history at Yale University. He has contributed articles on modern American cultural history to several journals and magazines and is completing a study of the social theory and political activism of John Dewey.

Christopher P. Wilson obtained his doctorate in American studies from Yale and is currently assistant professor of English and director of American studies at Boston College. He has written on Progressive-era literature and culture for *American Literature* and the *Journal of Popular Culture*. At present he is at work on a history of literary professionalism in the Progressive era.